Confessions
of an Art Dealer

An Autobiography

by John Howard (Jack) Swanson

To
Frank &
Irene
" "Best Wishes"
Jack Swanson

Vitality Publications
San Francisco

Confessions of an Art Dealer
An Autobiography
© 1995 John Howard (Jack) Swanson

Cover design by Becker Graphics

Book design & production by Deborah Fisher
Mill Valley, California

Editor, Laurel Olson Cook
A Way with Words
Sausalito, California

Vitality Publications
111 Maiden Lane, Suite 400
San Francisco, California 94108

Cataloging-in-Publication Data
ISBN 0-9646946-0-3
LCCN 95-60996

First hardbound edition 1995
10 9 8 7 6 5 4 3 2 1
Printed in United States of America

　　1. Swanson, John Howard.　2. Art dealers—United States—
Biography.　　　I. Title

N8660.S93S93 1995   709.2
                                        QBI95-20275

This book is dedicated to
Lieutenant General F.E. Leek, U.S.M.C. (Ret.)

"All objects point to the ultimate, but the difference between an ordinary object and a work of art is that the ordinary object is passive in its pointing toward the ultimate, whereas the work of art is active. The aim of a true work of art is to give a form to what escapes definition. This leads to the aesthetic experience, a timeless moment."

—Jean Klein, *I Am*

"DELAY IS THE WORST FORM OF DENIAL."

A saying displayed in every one of my galleries over the years.

Contents

Preface

Although this book is a true account of my experiences and adventures, I have changed the names and disguised the identities of some of the people involved to preserve their privacy. Any similarity between the fictitious names and those of living persons is, of course, entirely coincidental.

I'd like to thank Norman Singer for helping me organize and outline the book. Thanks also to Heide Walsh and Karen Jakobovits for their editorial assistance and educated support. I am especially grateful to my wife, Eileen, and friends for helping out and putting up with me.

Permission to quote a passage from Jean Klein's *I Am* was generously given by Third Millenium Publications.

1

Introduction

Most collectors of art sooner or later think about finding a public place to exhibit their collections—either for sale or just display. My galleries supported my habit of collecting art and my love for the people who create it. When I started my first gallery in 1970, I certainly did not know a great deal about the art world, but I was aware that as an entrepreneur I could try to join an established structure of old-line art galleries, art schools, academia, and museums or I could invent a new organization.

I chose to start a new grassroots method of selling to the public those works produced by emerging California artists. There were some happy circumstances that coincided with my going into business for myself in San Francisco in the 1970s. One was the phenomenal number of young tourists who were relatively affluent due to America's post-World War II economic boom. Others were the advent of jet travel and the credit-card revolution.

I was a high school dropout from rural South Texas and a former Marine who eventually graduated at twenty-six years of age from the University of California at Santa Barbara in 1967. At age twenty-eight I decided to open an art gallery in San Francisco with an investment of $168, all of which I plunked down on some frames for various paintings placed with me on consignment by local artists. The $168 down payment on the $1,000 worth of frames was all my credit card would allow at the time.

I had had some exposure to the art world in my college art history courses in the early 1960s, and I had hung out at some art galleries in Santa Barbara. I also had met a few sculptors and painters at the Sunday outdoor shows along the beachfront in Santa Barbara. It was a time of artistic awakening and creative production among the youth of America. All art forms were being explored and artistic expression was a big part of the '60s revolution. Everyone dressed differently, expressing in their attire a new world view—flower power—and art was definitely "in." It seemed like everyone loved art, from the old masters to the funky creations of the bohemian baby boomers.

I moved to San Francisco in 1968. I had wanted to stay in Santa Barbara, but I couldn't see much future there jobwise. I decided to "go where the fishes are," as my dad had admonished me. San Francisco was a wild place for a young man: one of the most beautiful places on earth—bright lights and big city. Every nationality in the world was represented. I remember sitting with a friend one night in the barroom of the Top of the Mark, a restaurant atop the Mark Hopkins Hotel on Nob Hill, and looking out the window at the panorama of lights and masses of humanity below. I vowed to whip this town and make it cough up the success that I desired. I didn't know how or what I was going to do careerwise, but I knew there was an answer out there somewhere.

My college degree was in Middle Eastern History. No job possibility there, so I decided that sales was the place for me. My first day on the job was a shock, because I was given a phone book and told to start cold-calling anybody, everybody, or any group in the Yellow Pages, such as doctors, lawyers, or clothing stores. Somehow I expected life to be simpler and more structured, but I persevered and chipped away at the work world of downtown San Francisco.

After a year and a half of selling insurance, life was going well. I started making good money and was able to get a great penthouse apartment on Telegraph Hill in a good part of town near Coit Tower. The apartment had a 360-degree view of San Francisco, including the bay and both bridges, and I could see Sausalito across the Golden Gate and Berkeley and Oakland across the bay to the east. I purchased the obligatory red sports car.

But I still wasn't happy in insurance sales, no matter how much money I was making. I seemed to spend all my spare time and money in San Francisco art galleries. People thought I was extravagant in purchasing art by local artists. I kept waiting for God or the powers that be to point me onto the right career path, and I became more and more frustrated waiting for the call. Then one day my lovely Japanese-American girlfriend (Honolulu-born-and-raised) pointed out a "help wanted" advertisement in the *San Francisco Chronicle* for a salesman in a well-known art gallery. I answered the ad. I got the job.

The gallery was run by a P.T. Barnum type of fellow; I'll call him Lou to disguise his identity. Lou had been an olive oil importer and owned a kosher foods business. Somehow, he started buying and selling inexpensive European paintings as a sideline. The U.S. dollar was very strong in Europe at the time and he could get really good artwork, some of it original, some of it mass produced, at the merchandise marts in different major European and American cities.

Lou opened a small gallery in San Francisco and expanded into selling oil paintings by local artists. When I met him, he had two galleries in the city and had started selling limited-edition prints by internationally known artists. The prints sold well. Realizing their appeal to the public, Lou decided to expand his business. He was one of the first to produce Salvador Dalí prints in large quantities.

In making prints, the artist ordinarily etches or draws on a metal plate, smooth stone, wood, or silk screen, then uses it to print a limited quantity of pictures, each of which is signed and numbered. Lou made a deal with Salvador Dalí through the artist's business manager whereby Dalí would sign thousands of otherwise blank sheets of lithograph paper, draw on some metal plates, and send the sheets and plates to Lou in San Francisco. Lou set up a workshop, acquired a hand-powered printing press, and put etching plate and presigned paper together. Voilà! Dalí etchings signed by the artist. But the lack of supervision by the artist and the easily copied pencil signature left a lot to be desired regarding the authenticity of the artwork, its quality, and the number of pictures actually printed.

I remember one Salvador Dalí edition of a suite of four or five images published by Lou. He had commissioned Dalí to draw some San Francisco scenes from a batch of postcards he had sent the artist. Dalí sent him back some copper or other metal plates with scenes etched on them. Presumably they were by Dalí, but he might have hired an artisan to execute the etchings. Lou apparently thought that the San Francisco scenes needed some pizzazz, because he hired a couple of local artisans to color the sepia and black-and-white creations. He then advertised the prints as original hand-painted etchings, numbered and signed by Salvador Dalí.

During the next two decades this practice of using presigned paper for editions of prints became a billion-dollar scheme, with many variations, including the outright forgery of famous artists' signatures and the churning out of hundreds of thousands of photomechanical reproductions printed on presigned blank paper. It was probably the largest, or one of the largest, art frauds ever perpetrated.

Salvador Dalí was a willing participant in this charade. The extent of his participation is illustrated by the number of blank sheets of paper he would have to sign for a single edition. If the edition quantity of Lou's original hand-painted Salvador Dalí suite was a thousand, and each suite consisted of four prints, at least 4,000 presigned sheets of paper would be needed. In addition, many more might have to be used for proofs and to replace damaged prints. One of Salvador Dalí's many business managers estimated that Dalí signed 350,000 blank sheets of paper. Dalí was paid something like $40 a signature and, with helpers on both sides of him, he was reportedly capable of signing 2,000 sheets an hour for $80,000. That was pretty good hourly pay. Dalí became an industry unto himself.

After Lou got his Dalí manufacturing operation up to speed, he was able to expand his business into a chain of galleries, and his success attracted other business people and would-be art dealers into this netherworld of "print-them-yourself, never-run-out-of-merchandise" deception.

Lou, however, never cashed in on his innovation, which would later turn into a monster. He got involved in a messy divorce and lost his business in the early '70s. Other people went wild with his pioneering scheme. They churned out a presigned paper blizzard. The bubble burst in the late 1980s and early 1990s. This huge art fraud and its collapse have been exposed in detail by a Honolulu investigative reporter, Lee Catterall, in his book *The Great Dalí Art Fraud and Other Deceptions* (Barricade Books Inc., 1992). It makes great reading. Mr. Catterall lists almost every publisher and dealer known to have been involved in the scandal. He also documents how a number of famous artists were unknowing participants in the scam and how their signatures were used without their authorization on prints that were misrepresented and sold to an unsuspecting public.

I started working at Lou's gallery at the time the Dalí scheme was beginning to take off. Although I was good at selling art, I stayed only about six months, because I didn't like the direction in which the company was moving. I had no way of knowing what would become of Lou's idea, but I felt something was amiss and didn't want to be associated with it. I started thinking about how I could open my own gallery and sell only original art by live artists, preferably local. Selling works from the past struck me as a bad idea, because there was a limited amount of that type of art available. Authenticity would also be a problem, and I wouldn't be helping any of the long-departed artists.

I made up my mind to set a date for starting a gallery featuring California artists whom I knew personally. I envisioned a partnership between the artists and me. They would create the art, and I would do the sales and administrative work for them. The idea of independence and going into business for myself was not well received by my girlfriend, her family, or—for that matter—my family. My girlfriend thought I was nuts, and my family was not supportive. One of my rich relatives gave me a long lecture on how I should strive for security and stay where I was so that I could always be prepared to support my aging mother.

By this time I had met a lot of San Francisco artists and had my eye on some locations for the gallery. I talked to a few landlords about rent, deposits, and other mundane but necessary aspects of business. The fact was, though, that I didn't have any money for the first and last month's rent. I couldn't even dig up money for a phone system. But I was confident that something would turn up. Finally, I hit on a perfect place for a gallery. It was an old lumber warehouse in a well-traveled tourist area near San Francisco's Fisherman's Wharf. It wasn't on the wharf, but close. It was on Beach Street between two new exciting shopping areas that had recently been created out of two old complexes of brick buildings. One complex had housed a cannery, and the other the Ghirardelli Chocolate Factory.

The old lumber warehouse was occupied by a store that sold European, mainly Scandinavian, furniture. I saw that the store wasn't doing well, and I approached the owner to let me use the walls for artwork. The store was mostly outdoors, with a lot of sky showing above the hastily erected walls within the huge building. The owner said that I could hang my paintings on the walls for 10 percent of my sales. He would also let me use his phones and deposit my credit card sales to his account. From the deposits he would take out the rent and commission, then give me the rest.

I was ecstatic. I quit my day job at Lou's gallery and set December 15, 1970, for the opening of my place. The night before, I went out and celebrated my good fortune at a restaurant in Sausalito across the Golden Gate Bridge.

Well, to say that I jumped the gun on the celebration is an understatement. When we opened the roll-up doors, rain and fog swept right into the building. I discovered that the overhead lights, which were sixty feet or so up in the rafters, pretty much constituted the available lighting. There was a space heater in a makeshift office used by the owner of the furniture store and his stockpersons, but there was no heat for the patrons. I was freezing in my three-piece suit.

So my first day was a bust. I was rained out, fogged out, and cold. I think I went home and cried. However, I hung in there. I put in some outdoor gas space heaters, built some walls for the paintings, and set up lighting for the show rooms. I didn't hesitate to have the work done, even though I didn't know where I would get the money. Somehow, though, I always sold enough art to pay the bills.

The first month I made $2,000 in sales, which wasn't very much. In January I brought in $4,000, and the next month $8,000, the next $16,000, the next $30,000, the next, $60,000 and June was a $100,000-in-sales month. I then bought a building in Sausalito and started another gallery. By the year's end I had opened four different galleries: one downtown on Sutter Street, one on Fisherman's Wharf, and one in Sausalito, as well as the big gallery between the Cannery and Ghirardelli Square. Not bad for a boy from South Texas. I always knew that I would make a million before I was thirty. I just hadn't had a clue to how that was going to happen until it hit me in the face.

After starting my first gallery in 1970, I went on to open and close nineteen more at different locations during the next twenty-four years. I had a chain of seven galleries for many years in the '70s and '80s. I even opened two galleries in Washington, D.C. My corporation normally supported a staff of sixty or more people—plus selling, promoting, and paying the bills for a legion of artists. I usually handled the work of fifty or more artists living in California. Others came from all over the globe. Since San Francisco is a port of entry from the Orient, artists streamed in from China, Japan, Korea, Vietnam, and the Philippines. Europe was also represented by Germans, Russians, French, Britons, Italians—you name it. They had heard correctly that the Bay Area was a good place to make a living and a vibrant place to live.

The majority of my artists were self-taught and did not care to join the academic art world or the "vanity galleries," most of which were run by rich doctors' or lawyers' wives. When I started my gallery, I sought out artists who lived in Northern California and were painting or sculpting art that appealed to all walks of life. Two of my criteria for accepting artwork were that the artists must be willing to sell their creations at a reasonable price and that the core value of a work be its beauty. Even if the work was abstract expressionism, it had to be aesthetically pleasing. I never went for the holocaust art that would scare the hell out of you or depress you. That could be left to the coffee-shop and grunge people.

One of the first artists I carried was a feisty eighty-year-old named Benjamino Bufano. He was only about five feet tall, but thought on a monumental scale. I had bought a lot of his work from various galleries and thought he was one of the greatest artists I had met. Bufano, who became a legend in San Francisco, passed away before I opened my gallery. I made a great deal of money by selling his art, but I always had a macabre feeling about not sharing it with him. So I made a mental note to never sell work unless I knew the artist personally, and to make sure that the artists I handled were alive so that I could pay them directly for their creations. Most of the works sold at my galleries have met those requirements.

Scouting for artists to stock my increasing number of galleries became a full-time job—I was on a hell of a wave. Since things weren't as spiffy as they became in the '90s with all the malls and boutiques, I was able to spend comparatively little on decor. My first big gallery in the warehouse lent itself to pegboard walls. I put pegboard everywhere.

Long before I thought of opening a gallery of my own, I had done a lot of reading about the origins of the retail gallery. Apparently it was introduced in the early twentieth century. At the time there were some antique and decorating shops and estate-sale outlets, but no art galleries where you could go to experience the creations of local artists. One of the first real galleries representing living artists whose work had not been commissioned was opened in Paris by Daniel Henry Kahnweiler in 1907. Kahnweiler had been raised in a prosperous Jewish family and educated to follow in the family tradition of working in the stock market. His uncles owned gold and diamond mines in South Africa. So he was well connected. After a brief stint as a stockbroker, he realized that the securities business was not for him.

He had been collecting Japanese woodblock prints, which were the rage in France and elsewhere in Europe at the time. Kahnweiler felt that perhaps a small rented shop on one of the Paris side streets would be a good place to set up a gallery and sell art to wealthy people he had met through his family and in the stock market. When he set up shop, he bought some burlap to put on the walls for a decoration and to serve as a backdrop for his woodblock prints and some local artists' works that he fancied.

A mecca for artists from all over Europe, Paris attracted many shining lights. One of the first artists he decided to show in his burlapped gallery was a very young and unknown Spaniard, Pablo Picasso. Kahnweiler had been introduced to Picasso at the artist's studio just as he was finishing his first cubist painting. Kahnweiler knew he was witnessing genius and decided to show Picasso's work to his well-heeled friends.

Kahnweiler found many such starving artists in Paris in the years between 1907 and the First World War. His discoveries included Modigliani, Vlaminck, Derain, and Braque, as well as Picasso. He had amassed quite a personal collection of these young artists' works. By the time war broke out in 1914, he hit a rough spot in his luck. Kahnweiler was of German Jewish descent and had never bothered to become a French citizen, so he had to flee France when the First World War began. All his possessions were confiscated and sold by the French authorities for almost nothing. His outstanding collection of twentieth century artists would bring tens of millions of dollars today.

Before opening my first gallery—when I was just thinking about doing so—I considered decorating the walls with burlap, as Kahnweiler had done, and trying to sell works by established artists. But I realized that if I dealt in old masters, European impressionists, or modern artists of world renown, I probably wouldn't find many people who could afford to buy and collect their work. That would certainly be true for the huge middle class, which had disposable income but not the wealth or expertise required for museum-quality art. They were the people I wanted as clients.

I began to see that there were legions of artists, recognized or unknown, who were alive and well and living in the U.S.A. While attending college I had met a lot of artists, many of whom sold their work at outdoor shows on the beachfront in Santa Barbara. I had also met quite a few artists in San Francisco while hanging around galleries. An idea began to crystallize that there was an almost unlimited number of talented, working artists in Northern California who needed representation. Bang, another idea just popped into my head. The artists didn't like to sell their own work, even though many exhibited at outdoor shows which were usually organized by artists' guilds and cooperatives. Ordinarily, the artists had vans or station wagons and would make some pegboard wall-like stands on which to display their paintings and prints. I called this movement the "Pegboard Revolution."

I saw the opportunity to gather a number of these talented flesh and blood artists under one roof where I could market their work, which they didn't want to do or would be better off not doing. I knew I could have my pick of artist partners for my new venture if I paid them fairly.

My concept of handling the sales and administration work for the artist has succeeded like a champ. Most artists are not good at both creative production and business. There are exceptions of course, but I have found that a true artist cannot maintain a high level of sensitivity and also deal with bankers, landlords, lawyers and the inevitable lawsuits, managers, sales employees, bookkeeping, local, state, and federal taxing agencies, and irate customers, all of which are endemic to the business world.

My galleries were in the forefront of the development of a new type of retail art industry, one that brought original art to the American public. Since 1970 I have dealt with and personally represented hundreds of artists and have hired about 2,000 sales employees. It seems that wherever I go in the world I run into people who have worked for me, and most of them thank me for what they remember as one of the greatest times in their lives. I have made quite a few of my artists wealthy and some famous. I successfully dealt with the vicissitudes of recessions, various and sundry lawsuits, temperamental artists, an ever-changing labor pool, ex-wives, landlords, the government, and a diverse clientele. Despite all those go-go years of the '70s and a couple of recessions, I am able to state unequivocally that none of my checks ever bounced and that I don't owe anybody a dime.

2

A Texas Childhood

My first memories are of being put in an orphanage in Houston, Texas, at age three. I didn't know what was happening, but I was glad that one of my sisters was with me. My mother, Ann Williams, had four children: two boys and two girls. A couple of years after I was born, she went through a divorce and had some health problems that hospitalized her. She felt that she had to give up her two youngest children in the hope that whoever adopted them would provide them with much better lives.

Years later, when I was a grown man, I received an account of my biological father from Ann Williams. I had gone on a trip to Texas after graduating from college, and I decided to drop in on my mother in Houston. She told me that my father, Ed Williams, was a smooth-talking Southern boy who drove trucks for a living. He was half Cherokee Indian and of German/Scottish/Irish descent. He loved the ladies and drink. After he divorced my mom, he remarried a girl named Opal and sired three more children. It was a jolt to find out about Opal and the kids. I was able to find her while I was in Houston and she told me that after she split up with Ed Williams she had given up all three of her children for adoption. It must have been the times.

Alcohol and hard living had ruined both of Ed Williams' marriages and brought him to an early death. The knowledge that drinking had been disastrous for my real father has always made me leery of getting too fond of distilled spirits. I wonder if my dad's Native American ancestry had anything to do with his weakness for booze. (Someone told me that since I'm one-fourth Cherokee I might be eligible for a free year-round fishing license from the government. Too bad I don't like fishing a little more.)

I was three and my sister Sally was five when we were faced with the abrupt change in our lives. I adapted to the orphanage more easily than Sally did, who was old enough to know what was going on. Sally never adjusted to the change. I remember my sister's protective attitude toward me in the orphanage when it was beginning to look bleak for us. We were just a couple of kids in a whole colony of children who needed a home. After eight or nine months, the staff showed some interest in us. Then a nice, well-dressed lady came to visit us and afterwards brought her husband. Being no dummy and a tad precocious, I waved a scissor-like signal to them and made damned sure that they knew I wanted them to take me home.

It turns out that they wanted to adopt my sister and me. My most vivid memory is of leaving that cheerless institution on a bright summer day. They put us in the back seat of a 1941 black Chevrolet. I remember looking out the rear window and thinking how glad I was to be going to a new home. Seeing the orphanage disappear in the distance and the dust thrown up by the tires was very comforting.

We hit the jackpot of the adoption sweeps as it were. Our new parents were an older couple (my new mom had gray hair) who couldn't have children. Right away I realized that these people really wanted me. They even let me choose my own name. They gave me a choice of either my original name, James Henry (Jimmy), or my adoptive father's, John Howard Swanson. I chose to be John Howard Swanson Jr., with Jack as a nickname.

My sister also took a new name, changing from Belle to Sally. We began to realize that our parents had a funny way of speaking—both were from the North; they were Yankees. My adoptive mother, Constance Sutton Bull Swanson, was forty-five-ish, five-foot-two, blue-eyed, and pleasingly plump. She came from a wealthy background. Her New England family traced its lineage to an English ship that landed in Boston in 1635— she was a ninth-generation Bostonian. Her father had been a Yankee Clipper sea captain at the turn of the century. His last name was Bull. Her mother, who lived with her, was from an old-line Back Bay Bostonian family named Sutton and had been a real beauty in her younger years.

My new mom had never been that attractive, and even complained to me later that when she was young her widowed mother outshone her to some of her beaus. But Constance Sutton Bull Swanson was very brainy and excelled in school. She was one of the first of her Brahminic class to go to work, becoming a nurse in 1919. A strong, articulate woman who had the best vocabulary I ever ran across, she put her career ahead of marriage and childbearing. She was very successful in her medical career, rising to superintendent of nurses at a children's hospital in Chicago.

Constance moved to Chicago because her only brother moved there, had started a paper-manufacturing business. Richard Bull Sr. had a pedigree of family gentility, received a Harvard education, and married well, but had no money to speak of. His star rose when he and his best friend, Harry Calvin, were among the first to see the potential of the cardboard box and to manufacture the cartons. Eureka, they were rich!

When Constance moved to Chicago, she lived with her brother, his wife, and four children and helped raise her nieces and nephews. It was the "Roaring Twenties" and Chicago was a huge, wide-open city. She lived life to the fullest, until a tragedy changed everything. Her brother died in his forties from appendicitis and some medical mishaps. He died intestate and left no provision for the care of his mother and his sister. However, his wife, my Aunt Sally, married her husband's business partner Harry Calvin, and the family business prospered. (The paper company Richard Bull Sr. and Harry Calvin built is still alive and well, and heir Richard Bull Jr. can boast of a $250-million-a-year company.)

Harry Calvin was a great man and bona fide WW I hero. Harry Calvin won every medal but the Medal of Honor (he was nominated for it, though). He has been one of my idols

since my folks first took me to Winnetka, Illinois, to meet
the Bull side of the family. I must have been five or six when
I met Uncle Harry. He lived in a mansion next to the Indian
Hill Country Club in Winnetka. I remember that he was
rather profane and bombastic. He took a shine to me (seeing
a kindred soul, I think) and gave me one of his golf clubs,
a putter. I wish I still had that putter. It was one of the
nicest presents I ever received. In my mind he was always
my proverbial rich uncle.

My mother decided to leave Chicago after her brother's
death. A married couple whom she was very close to
had moved to Houston, Texas, where both were staff
physicians at a hospital. She accepted a job as
superintendent of nurses at the children's hospital in
Houston and, with her mother in tow, started a new
life in wild and woolly Texas. It was there that she
met her future husband, Dr. John H. Swanson. He was
a Professor of Chemistry at Rice University, but he
wanted to change careers and was completing a
curriculum in dentistry. After they married, just before
the Second World War, he started a dental practice
with money he borrowed from my mother's family and
he set up house with his wife and mother-in-law. (My
mother later pointed out that he never repaid the debt.)

They say opposites attract, and that must have been
the case. No two people were ever more dissimilar than
my future parents. My dad-to-be, John Swanson Sr.,
was a big, burly six-foot, 250-pound Swede, raised on
a Minnesota farm by parents who came over to America
in the 1890s and never lost their Swedish accent. The
only thing that this newly married couple had in common
was their love of medicine. John Swanson had plenty
of Nordic gray matter. No one who ever talked to him
was left unimpressed by his awesome thought processes on
just about any subject. But in dress, temperament, and
demeanor, he never strayed far from the farm. He spent his
adult life in academia and in the dental office, but spent
his summer vacations every year in Minnesota visiting relatives
on their farms. One of his peculiarities was that he never

cottoned to the idea of indoor plumbing. During all the time that I knew him he invariably availed himself of the nearest bush. He might not have been perfect, but I sure was glad that he took in my sister and me.

My first few years with the Swansons were idyllic. We lived in a small town outside of Houston. Our house was on a twenty-acre patch of land, and my new dad was in his element in this farm-like setting. He brought in some bulldozers to clear the land, set up chicken coops, and bought some goats. Ever the scientist, he even found a strange-looking spider and sent it off to the Smithsonian Institution. It turned out that the spider had never been discovered or classified, so they named the creature after him, with some Latin thrown in.

I remember carefree days with my new family. However, I tried to stay out of my new grandmother's way. She must have been 80 years old, and was a tough old bird. One time I was crawling around with my toy gun, sneaking up on a Japanese entrenchment and yelling out for more ammo, more ammo, and I don't know why but she asked me if I knew what *ammo* meant. Of course I did, but we always seemed to have a touchy relationship. She did a few favors for me though: She made sure I went to the Episcopal Church and continually asked me to become an altar boy when I was old enough.

I loved my new life. It included collecting chicken eggs to earn a nickel; it was right out of Huckleberry Finn. One day during my collecting I fell down and knocked out two front baby teeth, thereby extending my baby-talking stage another year or so. It was great living in a coastal Southern town—no school, no shoes, and no orphanage.

When we were young kids we spent many summers driving up north across the Ozarks to Minnesota. We got to know our Swedish aunts and uncles and a whole lot of cousins. When we grew into our teens, we found there were some perks for not being blood cousins of at least a few of my Yankee relatives.

After we acclimated to our new life, and the Second World War was over, we took our first road trip to Minnesota so that Sally and I could meet our aunts and uncles and cousins on the Swanson side. I got a view of the harsh life of a working farm in the North. There was also a trip to Winnetka, Illinois, to meet my mother's side of the family, the Bulls.

As I have already pointed out, I was quite taken by my uncle by marriage, Harry Calvin. Uncle Harry and I maintained our bond of friendship based on some unknown chemistry, until he passed away from emphysema in 1968. He had been gassed by the Germans in the First World War and was plagued the rest of his life with lung problems. Though I was only five or six the first time I met him, I was extremely impressed with this uncle. I wanted to be just like him. Uncle Harry never seemed to be hesitant or uncertain about things. I figured that men like him sure must save an awful lot of time by never hemming and hawing or putting matters off until later.

I could not have been more pleased about my adopted family. But slowly a few dark shadows appeared. I was as happy as a clam, but my sister wasn't adjusting. Our biological parents showed up at separate times for a visit. Since Sally was seven or eight years old, she certainly remembered them and a different life. I think my birth mother tried to get us back, but she was not in the same position that our more affluent adoptive parents were. Sally was just not happy and she started doing some off-the-wall things. For example, when we had arguments she seemed to overreact. My father, "Doc" Swanson, might have saved my life one time when he walked in on one of our fights and Sally was drawing a bead on me with his .22-caliber rifle. She caught hell for that, and I have never forgotten the look in her eyes. I still own that .22-caliber rifle. I'm glad she didn't pull the trigger.

It must have brought back some horrible memories for Dad, because when he was a young man he had shot his brother in the head. His brother lived, but was the only one of five children who didn't go to college. He stayed on the farm, married, and raised a passel of great kids. He never forgave my dad. I have always suspected it was a Cain and Abel story, but never asked anyone about it.

During the early years of my boyhood I had a fairly tranquil existence. There were some changes that required adjusting to. When I was six years old my parents decided to move 400 miles south of Houston to Brownsville, Texas, a border town on the Rio Grande. Site of the first battle of the 1846-1848 Mexican-American War, the city also had the dubious honor of having the last battle of the Civil War fought on its outskirts. The Confederates won the battle, but found out later that the war had been over for several weeks.

I understood my parents' decision to pull up stakes. My dad thought it would be a good career move; he would be one of the only dentists in the area. But I had to make all new friends. As it turned out, most of them were of Mexican descent, the ratio of Latinos to gringos in Brownsville being about ten to one. In Houston I had come into contact with very few Mexican Americans whereas now I had my first taste of how it felt to be part of a minority. But within a very short time most of my best buddies were Hispanic, and I no longer thought of the relationship as a novelty.

The town itself offered an easygoing kind of dual culture: It was American, but it was also Mexican. There were certain parts of town where the pungent cooking odors would almost convince you that you were deep in the heart of old Mexico. I started first grade in Brownsville and remember lining up before the palm trees in front of a tiny schoolhouse to pledge allegiance to the flag and sing Army songs, such as "The Caissons Go Rolling Along." It struck me as strange that there were older Mexican boys in our class. They were put in with us to learn the rudiments of English. One boy was nineteen.

I liked school and my first-grade teacher. I guess we all remember our first-grade teachers. Even though I haven't seen her for a million years, I remember that Mrs. Graham was a very straightforward schoolmarm, and one of the first things she told her new students was that the most useful phrase

in the English language was "you all" or "y'all." She was a
zealous disciplinarian, and favored the old ruler-over-the-
knuckles trick.

Mrs. Graham also used to pin notes on my shirt
when I got embroiled in the pecking order of the school
yard. Since I was a minority and a new kid on the
block, I had to learn how to defend myself. I recall
that an older boy was giving me a hard time. He was
from a migrant farmworker's family and extremely
poor. He ribbed me about how his Mexican ancestry
made him tough and that "gavachos" (an ethnic slur
meaning whites—a little more derogatory than gringo)
like me were wimps. I snuck up on him during a lunch
break and walloped him on the noggin with a two-
by-four. That was good for a few whacks from my
teacher and another note pinned to my sleeve.

It was during the last part of the second grade that
the contentment I enjoyed since living with the Swansons
crumbled into little nervous pieces of anxiety and pain.
Like so many other youngsters my age during the
1940s, I came down with polio. I was walking home
from school one day when my legs suddenly gave out
and I couldn't take another step. I had to sit down
by the side of the road and wait for someone to rescue
me. Around dusk my mother drove by looking for me.
Neither one of my legs had any feeling.

As a result of the polio I lost more than a year from my
life. I never went to the third grade. I was paralyzed from
the waist down. If my mother hadn't been a trained nurse,
I might have remained crippled for the rest of my life. But
for a year or more my mother applied hot compresses to
my legs every day—morning, noon, and night. She even hired
some college boys to come in and help her. The hot compresses
were the only known remedy for the disease. I didn't understand
what was happening and was scared. Terrified of the future
I faced, I sunk into a deep depression. I owe my recovery
to the iron will of my mom; she never let up on physical
therapy.

Once my mother saw improvement and that I was regaining some movement, she allowed me no wishy-washy self-pity. Funny thing is that once you are an invalid you begin to be afraid to return to the world. You are also afraid of what will happen if you fail to meet expectations. My mother saw me wrestling with a neighbor one day and realized that I had some use of my legs, even though disuse had wasted away my muscles. She focused her indomitable will on me and made me get up and walk—then and there. It scared the hell out of me, but I was more afraid of displeasing her than concerned about my physical or psychological infirmities. I got up and walked. I needed help, but I was on the road to recovery and was able to enter the fourth grade on crutches. I became pretty skilled in the use of those crutches—in fact, they were useful against bullies and unfriendly types. My mother kept disciplining me like a top sergeant until I was able to walk under my own steam.

I was so determined to recover completely that from then on I followed a strenuous regimen of calisthenics and other exercise. Roller-skating was one of the only forms of group exercise available, and it turned out to be a fabulous way to rehabilitate my legs. I started out pushing myself backwards— it made for a cushier fall. I'll never forget the rinks and how cute the little Texas girls were in their jean shorts. In the late 1940s and early 1950s, girls didn't have the fancy sports clothes they have today. Checkered calico blouses and cut-off jeans were the rule. I also reentered the mainstream at school, playing sports, hunting lizards and horny toads, and joining the Cub Scouts.

That early scare has stayed with me all my life. Even now if I wake in the dark of night and my legs have gone to sleep, I break out in a cold sweat. I am haunted by the memory of that childhood year as a cripple.

The joy of my recovery was marred when I suddenly realized how long my parents had been having marital difficulties. Now that I had time to notice, I realized that they were fighting a lot. I don't know all the details, but the fighting escalated to screaming and physical abuse. My dad was a big man and normally a good-natured Swede.

He would laugh heartily, his head thrown back, and usually swept those around him into his mirth. But he also had a terrible temper, which he was never able to master. *Mercurial* is a good word to describe his personality—he could be laughing one minute then, if something hit him wrong, look out. The veins in his head would start pulsing and all 250 pounds of him would become agitated and his face would turn red and blue.

My parents' personal problems might have triggered a need for change. We moved from Brownsville 700 miles north to an East Texas oil town named Kilgore. It had a population of about 10,000 and the distinction of having more continuously pumping oil wells downtown than people. Churches were even moved over a few feet so that more oil wells could be drilled. Kilgore was a boomtown, with more millionaires per square mile than any other place on earth.

It may have been the boomtown mentality that led me to use a tray of gold pellets from my father's dental lab to salt my make-believe gold mine in the gravel driveway behind his office. I was out back playing in the dirt and rocks and had this great idea of pretending I had a gold mine. Of course, I needed gold. In the middle of the game my dad came out and asked me what I was doing. It didn't take him long to figure it out and realize that we were not going to find all the gold pellets that he used for fillings. He stuck my body through his legs, head first, leaving my rear as a stationary target, and beat the shit out of me. When a 250-pounder loses his temper, beware. I have to say that he rarely lost his temper with my sister or me, but the few times he did—ouch! I carried a grudge for years over a few of those spankings, even if they didn't go over the line to abuse. The helplessness and hurt pride fueled resentment and a craving for revenge.

Kilgore was a great place—lots of hustle and bustle— and it seemed to be just right for Pop, as I called my father. He was the only dentist in the area. The weather was quite different from the climate of South Texas. It actually snowed in the winter (700 miles north of the border town we had left), and the temperature sometimes climbed to 120 degrees in the summer. The ethnic makeup was different also. There were no Hispanics, but a large black population. Bordered by Louisiana and the deep South, East Texas was segregated.

The change in scenery didn't do much good for my folks' marriage. They kept on fighting. A few times it got so serious, with hitting and kicking, that Sally and I hid under the bed. It even crossed my mind to get the rifle out and protect my mother. Her Victorian background had something to do with their problems, I think. For example, my parents had separate beds. The fact that her mother was living with them didn't help. On the other hand, when there is an abusive situation adultery is often a major factor. That proved to be the case with my dad. I found out years later that when we moved to Kilgore he had an affair with his nurse, a very healthy young black woman. Eventually, my folks realized that they could not go on living together. One night after dinner my mother gathered Sally and me to her and said, "Daddy isn't coming home anymore."

I was shocked, but relieved. I don't know how it affected my sister, but she was already showing signs of rebellion and a proclivity for going a bit beyond the normal. She had run away from home a couple of times, taking a cardboard box full of clothes with her.

So my folks split up for good. Yet even after the divorce they remained linked by a fierce kind of love-hate relationship. They never seemed to get over each other. They carried on a life-long feud, with insulting notes and court battles. But one day many years later my mother wistfully mentioned to me that it was their thirtieth wedding anniversary.

When I realized that I would now have my mother's full attention, I got over the rift in my life very quickly. There was something great about being the man of the house. But some harsh realities were confronting the reduced family. My mother decided to move back to Brownsville. She was forced to seek work after a thirteen-year hiatus, and found a nursing job at a public clinic. I was glad to be going back to the border and the subtropical ambiance.

Money was very tight when we got back to Brownsville. Nevertheless, because my grandmother was infirm and had to be placed in a nursing home, my mom needed to hire someone to look after Sally and me if she was going to support the family. Through a friend she met a couple from Mexico City who wanted to become U.S. citizens. The couple, René and Carmen Naranjo, had moved to Matamoros, Mexico, a large city across the border from Brownsville. René and Carmen wanted to change their lives. He was from a lower-class Mexican family and had earned his living as a masked wrestler, until he was unmasked in the ring and he had to seek a new line of work. Carmen was from a wealthy family and had many well-to-do relatives who were giving her flack for her lifestyle. She thought that it would be a good idea to put distance between herself and her childhood home. They found jobs as managers of a supposedly first-class hotel in Matamoros. However, when they arrived there they were aghast to discover that the hotel was a whorehouse. That's when they decided to emigrate and start over. Thank God they did. They saved Sally and me from becoming latchkey kids.

After renting a tiny house for a while when we moved to Brownsville, Mom found a more suitable house that had a small apartment attached to the garage. René and Carmen moved in and became part of the family. They couldn't have children, but my mother was able to help them adopt a child after they had lived with us a number of years. My mother took a job as a county nurse and had to travel all over South Texas bringing modern medicine to sleepy little towns. She had a little black bag and drove her 1950 Ford to wherever she was needed, treating the sick and serving as a kind of Texas-style Florence Nightingale.

The last dot on the map in Texas, Brownsville is the southernmost point in the continental U.S., and seemed to be about fifty years behind the times. I remember my mom driving us out to the beach in the early '50s and on the way we saw cowpokes riding herd on a bunch of steers. They still had their lariats, side irons, and Winchesters in saddle holsters.

I don't know how my mother did it, but she had to make some major adjustments in her life, what with her work and being the breadwinner. My father took a typical wounded machismo stance on alimony and child support. He felt that since his ex-wife came from a well-to-do family, she should hit them up and not depend on him for money. Although he was ordered to pay only $37.50 a month for child support, he refused to send a cent. His attitude kept them in continual court battles. (It seems some divorced couples thrive on the bitter energy that litigation engenders.) One thing that came from all those court proceedings was a deal about custody. The court said that Sally and I would spend the winter school months with my mother and the summers in Kilgore with our dad. What a deal! I loved it. Sally and I were quick to figure out how to maximize the situation by pitting one parent against the other.

My mother had found a great career in nursing. She loved to work with children and was able to bring immunization against a variety of diseases to the lower Rio Grande Valley. She had to go out into the fields and minister to poor families who lived in mud huts, sometimes sixteen or more people to a dwelling. Usually, she had to take an interpreter with her, because she never mastered Spanish. Her New England accent seemed to get in the way. I still wonder what she thought of the extremely rural and ultra-Southern area.

Brownsville was a provincial Confederate port during the Civil War. The South tried to export cotton to European markets from Brownsville. The Yankee blockade of ocean ports stopped almost all shipping between the Confederate states and Europe, and the Rio Grande was one of the few avenues open. Some of the land barons in Texas became immensely wealthy from this trade. The giant King Ranch was put together at that time, and even today when you drive through South Texas to get to Brownsville, you have to go through the ranch, which stretches eighty miles from one end to the other with no gas stations in between.

Although its population was almost completely Hispanic, the area along the north bank of the Rio Grande was included in Texas when it won its independence from Mexico in 1836.

But just because the government was under Texas and, after 1845, U.S. jurisdiction, doesn't mean that the social order reflected Anglo values. The town had a 300-year history of Spanish and Mexican influence. All the upper crust of the town was of Hispanic ancestry.

In fact, disputes between Mexico and the U.S. along the border between Texas and Mexico continued until our own time. In 1914 Pancho Villa and his army rode through Brownsville and shot up the place, and General John "Black Jack" Pershing led an expeditionary force to Brownsville in 1915 to protect the border. Boundary disputes with Mexico were not fully resolved until 1970. I firmly maintain it was our victory in WW II and unquestionable military superiority that finally brought about the settlement.

Brownsville was an interesting fusion of two cultures. My mother was always a bit shocked by the annual celebration of Jefferson Davis' birthday. The Cameron County health workers got the Confederate president's birthday off, and not Abraham Lincoln's. There were no statues of Union leaders in rural South Texas. However, the extreme Southern bias had begun to change. After WW II, particularly during the Eisenhower presidency, many Northerners moved to South Texas. Pan American airlines used Brownsville as a "last-chance" fueling stop and an embarkation point for flights to Central and South America.

My childhood in Brownsville was a wonderful time. I was a dutiful, easygoing fifth and sixth grader. I walked or rode my bike to school every day. My best friend was Perfecto Garcia, a rotund kid, who was very conservative and a good student. Then, in the sixth and seventh grades, I went through an important personality change. I began to see that the older kids my sister hung around with had cars, frequented beer joints, and went over the river to Matamoros to party. It dawned on me that there was something going on between boys and girls that I might not understand but that seemed to have an irresistible pull.

In the seventh grade, my dutiful behavior at school began to change. I developed a strong aversion to studying and shifted my focus from climbing the academic ladder and adhering to socially acceptable behavior to materialism and immediate gratification of the senses. My transformation into an anti-academic rebel had more or less snuck up on me. While I still saw myself as a good kid, some of my close friends started telling me that I was changing. A big turning point in my eleven-year-old life was when I decided that my Schwinn bicycle was passé. The answer was to get a motorcycle.

A fateful decision had been reached. I went downtown to the Sears store and put a down payment on a little red motorcycle. It was my first major purchase and my first experience with monthly payments. The salesman never asked about parental consent, he just wrote the purchase up and gave me the receipt for the down payment. I didn't know how to ride my new toy, but didn't let that faze me. I just pushed my prize to my house a few miles away and waited on my front lawn until someone on a motorcycle came by. I ran out and flagged the rider down, asked for insights on the operation of an internal combustion engine, and received pointers on how to ride my new passport to distant places. I bounced off a few curbs and suffered a few scratches on man and machine, but got the hang of it in short order.

Getting to school was going to be a lot easier. I couldn't wait to show off my glistening red motorcycle. After school, on one of the first days I rode my shiny toy, I went over to the parking area and found that some sneaky son-of-a-bitch had kicked my cycle over and filled the gas tank with sand. I learned that there were drawbacks and possible penalties for being different from the group. You have to be careful if you dare to stand out.

Now that I was motorized, nothing was quite the same for me again. It changed my relationships with friends, who were still peddling their bikes or walking to school. My new-found gasoline-powered transportation gave me a freedom and power I never imagined before. I could cover vast distances in minutes. I also learned about the consequences of a lack of parental control. If my folks had been in on the decision, I probably wouldn't have been able to sell my Schwinn bike and the rest of my childhood might have turned out to be quite different. My mother wasn't overjoyed about the fait accompli, but shrugged it off and said that I would have to earn the money to make the payments.

The monthly payments necessitated quick action. I found employment with the *Brownsville Herald*. A paper route was just the thing—it was like a commission job. You earned according to your ability to expand your route. I just took off, even recruiting neighborhood boys to help me as I branched out all over town. I got my lieutenants to deliver the papers, while I solicited subscriptions for my profitable and ever-increasing business. You would think that the newspaper would have been very happy about my sales ability, but no.

One of my first lessons in social reality and the man-made limits that are thrown up in front of anyone trying to make a living was when my route manager told me that he was limiting the size of my route. He said that I should make only so much and no more. I just smiled and didn't listen, nor comply. They even wanted me to turn over some of my accounts—I refused—and due to the fact that I kept no written records I was irreplaceable, for the time being at least. Still, it was a shock and gave me a sobering insight into the social order we call business. There are checks and balances that are unarguably necessary to run a newspaper, but I found out there were also petty jealousies, incompetent supervisors, and mendacity. My favorite part of the newspaper business was collecting all the money every Saturday—I was rolling in cash. I paid off the cost of my motorcycle quickly, and began to finance my experiences outside the home.

After getting used to the new-found freedom of being motorized, it occurred to me that there was some territory on the other side of the Rio Grande River that I had heard people talk about: the forbidden fruit, the *zona rosa*, known as Boys Town, the fabled red light district of Matamoros. How could I resist? I was growing fast, the blood was pumping through my veins, and I wanted to know: what, I had no idea, but I wanted to know.

Thirteen may seem a bit young, but many people maintain that the heat in southern climes matures people beyond their years. I was about to embark on a hell of an adventure. I was spending the night at my friend Neil's house and, as luck would have it, his folks were out of town. We started on the "what-do-you-want-to-do" routine and the answer was to jump on my motorcycle and find Boys Town. It had been rumored that this pleasure district on the outskirts of Matamoros consisted of some 10,000 souls dedicated entirely to the needs of men. The Mexican government condoned and encouraged it, providing medical supervision and requiring all prostitutes to have official papers and physical checkups. Neil and I jumped on my cycle and headed across the bridge into a foreign country, one that I had been to many times with my family but never unchaperoned. I still had braces on my teeth and sported a crew cut, which was in vogue in the '50s.

We crossed the bridge and found directions to La Zona Rosa. When we got there we were amazed at the size of the district. There was a main street and what seemed like unending side streets, with innumerable bars and nightclubs, all announced by gaudy neon lights and glittering light bulbs. We were scared, but determined to press on. We walked around in the side streets, not brave enough to venture into the bars and mix with the crowds. The district was packed. I had a few bucks, and we started to negotiate with the girls sitting outside their stalls, cubicles that were house and workplaces combined in a few square feet of space.

There were all kinds of Mexican women—different shapes, ages, skin color, hair color, and every one of them knew that we were "cherries." They offered a variety of business propositions; we smiled, pushed them away, and kept wandering the streets. There were Mexican cops everywhere, with their bus-driver-type military hats, and "45" automatics stuck in their belts. They made us feel safe and in danger at the same time. The streets weren't paved, so there were giant chuck holes on every road. The taxis were bumper to bumper, brakes squeaking and engines roaring. This was truly Dodge City—cowtown, boomtown, anything goes.

I finally picked a lovely señorita who had long since lost her favored place in a swanky bar and wound up on the side streets, pretty much the two-dollar window. I bargained with her to get the best deal and, when I felt that the price was right, I stepped inside her stall. Neil was making his own deal close by. The cubicle was evil-smelling and without electricity, candles providing barely enough light to illuminate the picture of the Virgin Mary on the wall. There was no running water, only a washbowl and pitcher. The girl explained the different choices available and the additional charges for extraordinary creativity. It was less than romantic, what with her giving me a checkup for venereal disease and a sponge bath. But I wasn't about to back out. Carnal knowledge was my desire. It didn't take long—the girl was obviously a professional with a lot of on-the-job experience.

Neil had made his own deal nearby, and his story was the same as mine. We met outside in the cold winter air in just minutes. But at least we had something to talk about— and a new avocation. As we headed back across the bridge to Brownsville, a few thoughts hit our wicked little minds. We had just risked life, limb, and property for knowledge of the flesh. We now felt that we were older and wiser, men of the world. When we returned to Neil's house, we laughed our heads off and let loose disparaging remarks about the grossness of Boys Town. But then we were struck with a frightening thought: what fatal venereal disease might we have caught by doing it with a professional? Amazing what a few pesos could buy. We got out a bottle of rubbing alcohol and generously doused our private parts all over. It burned so fiercely we yelped and rolled around the front yard, laughing, screaming, carrying on like a couple of hyenas.

After waiting a few weeks to make sure none of our most prized equipment had fallen off, we hungered for more of the same, but this time we vowed to go into one of the fancy bars. Henceforth, my buddies and I were never at a loss for somewhere to go. I became familiar with Boys Town over the next few years, slowly but surely selling off a valuable coin collection. For many years, I lied to my dad, assuring him that, yes, I still had the silver dollar collection he had given me.

My sister, Sally, could have used a bit more direction at this time. At fourteen she could pass for twenty-one, and she took to running around with a tough group of teenagers. She spent little time in the classroom and appeared to be headed for big-time trouble. My mother couldn't control either of us and agreed to have Sally live with my father all the time. But Sally continued to play with fire, leading a purely physical existence with no thought of the future.

3

The Last Days of Innocence

When I entered junior high school I quickly became aware of social classes, and saw that there were powerful groups I'd have to contend with. I observed different factions forming on the school yard. There were the do-gooders and the very rich kids who hung around the front of the school. They were ever-so-correct in the way they dressed: the boys always wore slacks that were a little short for them, and the girls always seemed to be decked out just so. There were the more or less regular boys and girls who wore jeans and more casual clothes. Then there were the Mexican gangs, the jocks who were high school age but still in junior high, and gangs of poor white kids (usually the kids of the shrimp boat fishermen from the coasts of Georgia, Mississippi, Louisiana, and Texas). Most of the students were Hispanic; we Anglos were in the minority. Although I didn't feel any racial overtones in the relationships we had, I was concerned to see gangs forming from the different barrios and poorer sections of town.

I lived in an area called Riverside, a rather modest neighborhood. Right next to our house was a shantytown that the very poor—mostly illegals from Mexico—called home. You could throw a rock from my backyard to the Rio Grande. Any time I walked down to the levee I could watch the so-called wetbacks wading across the river.

By the time I hit the eighth grade in 1954, like most kids, I was blending in, playing football and coping as best I could with the obstacles put in front of me. Common were petty conflicts with other guys over territorial rights—whose girl was whose, for example. I learned that if you had a fight with a "dude," especially if he was from a Mexican gang, you were not just starting something with an individual, you were starting a long-running family feud that could be detrimental to your health. We are not talking about a few bumps and bruises or loss of face if you didn't win. This was big time.

It did not take me long to get into some scrapes. My biggest problem was with the Mexican gangs. Every time I flirted with some cute Hispanic girl, for example, there would be a fight. After I had my motorcycle trashed, I began to realize that if I was going to live to a ripe old age I was going to have to get some bodyguards—which is what I did right after a hair-raising incident that happened one afternoon just as I was leaving school.

When the school bell rang, I walked out of my last class and was met by a whole army of Mexican kids with evil intent on their minds. A kid had warned me that he was going to get his cousins on my case for something real or imagined that I had done to him. Well, you haven't lived until you are surrounded by a few hundred hostile Hispanic kids. I'm not exaggerating. Here I was in the school yard, and my only option was to leave books, motorcycle, friends, etc., and run for my life.

The screaming, yelling mass of humanity was armed and dangerous; chains being the weapon of preference. With no time to think, I ran like hell, looking back over my shoulder to catch a glimpse of weapons, rocks, and chains in the hands of my persecutors. Adrenaline is a great thing: I outran the whole bunch of thirty second cousins and, a few blocks across the school yard, found refuge in a corner market store. Panting, I explained my perilous position to the owner and had him call the *policia*. The gang milled around outside, taunting me (the *gavacho*) to come on out. The police came and I escaped unscathed. But I had learned the danger of being a lone individual. I had also become very aware that my language skills were deficient; I couldn't speak Spanish worth a damn. I knew all the curse words, but they just got me *into* trouble, not out.

By the time of my next altercation I had found a bodyguard who could speak Spanish fluently. I had seen a buddy of mine conduct himself rather well with the old fisticuffs. I had watched him roll down an embankment and beat the shit out of some kid and, at that moment, I knew I had found my man. I made a deal with him then and there that I would provide the transportation (I was the only one around who had wheels) if he would act as my personal bodyguard. He took the job and we have remained lifelong friends.

He was instrumental in my retaining my looks and health when we got to high school. Willie wasn't real tall, but he seemed to make up for it by growing out instead of up. He made me think of a Tasmanian devil. He had a certain look in his eyes that said "don't mess with me."

Sure enough, within days of our pact, some group of guys—Anglos this time—decided that they were going to kick my ass (as the saying goes). I alerted Willie and we met the miscreants at a prearranged place. Willie took care of those guys with a few one-two punches. It soon got around school that I was off-limits unless they wanted to deal with Willie.

Willie was part Anglo and part Mexican, and spoke the dialect of the street. He lived in a rough neighborhood and knew most of the gang leaders from his side of town. Under Willie's tutelage, I became streetwise. I also found out you could *negotiate* your way out of a lot of political mistakes.

In the midst of all this learning about how to maneuver around Matamoros and keep my scalp attached to my head, I was still signed up for Boy Scouts and Sunday School. I was just a regular kid. My grandmother had passed on, but I kept my promise to her and attended the Episcopal Church on a regular basis. I met a lot of wonderful people at the church. We had an older congregation, many of whom were Anglos who had come to our semi-tropical region to retire. You could live well in Brownsville in the '50s. A gardener got $10 a month and a full-time live-in maid earned $30 a month.

The Episcopal Church, or Church of England as it is called, was somewhat elitist in its membership. The well-to-do Yankees from the East Coast and many prominent people in Brownsville, Anglo and Hispanic alike, belonged. The Episcopal Church had all the opulent trimmings of the Roman Catholic Church with none of the dogma. It seems that Episcopalians didn't let religion mess with their lives too much.

I loved the pomp and circumstance of the candlelit ceremonies and the robes worn by the ministers. As an alter boy I carried the cross down the aisle each Sunday to the solemn organ music, sometimes at both the 7:00 A.M. and the 11:00 A.M. masses. I loved the musty smell of the church and putting on my vestments. I became close to the minister, Reverend Albright, who impressed me with his very correct and conservative demeanor. He smoked a pipe and he had graying, wispy hair, and a very Anglican sense of style.

The church arranged field trips for the Sunday School classes. I remember on one of these outings going to a large ranch—thirty or forty thousand acres—owned by one of the parishioners, a very rich lady. We got to watch the cowboys castrate the young calves and brand and tag the yearlings. We even got to swim in the ranch's freshwater tanks (of course with the strict provision that we would exercise restraint).

My sister and I spent our summers in Kilgore with our dad. Our stays were enlightening, as they exposed us to different lifestyles. My dad had an office downtown on Main Street. He lived in the back of his office and, to accommodate us, he put two fold-up beds in a room that served as his laboratory where he made dental casts and dentures. It also served as a kitchen. Whenever I slept late I would wake up and find some of his clients sitting back in the bedroom/lab waiting for their turn on a back room dental chair that was reserved for "colored." The African Americans had to come in by the back door entrance. I argued with my dad about this unjust practice. His response was to get all huffy and indignant. He said, "That's just the way things are in these here parts," and that if a man wanted to practice dentistry around here he "couldn't rock the boat."

Close to the office were fast-food drive-ins. We loved the burgers and our daily job seemed to consist of bumming enough money from dear old Pop to keep us in munchies and out from underneath his feet.

Pop was your original absent-minded professor. He left money all over the office and never remembered where he had put anything—a happy circumstance that kept me in the clover. To give you an idea of how absentminded he was, I saw him walk outside many times without shoes and get halfway down the front walk before realizing something was amiss. Then he would turn around, stuff his feet into some shoes, and go on about his business.

My dad's personal and professional life kept him so occupied that he was unable to supervise us, which was all my sister needed to make some bad choices that would have lifelong consequences. She seemed to seek out lower socioeconomic types to hang around with. I remember one event that exemplified both the trouble she was heading for and my dad's rather violent way of dealing with family problems. My dad's temper and the Texas barbed-wire mentality of protecting what's yours with a gun or your "dukes" led to quite a scene.

Sally was around fourteen years of age at the time and her looks and figure were far more mature than her mental abilities. She had conned my dad into letting her spend the night at a girlfriend's house. Her friend was a bit wild and the girls had honky-tonking on their minds—not staying home playing with dolls. Sally had her girlfriend's father call to assure my dad that he would keep an eye on the kids and all would be well.

For some reason Dad got to worrying about whether Sally was really staying at her girlfriend's house. Perhaps he received a phone call letting him know that Sally wasn't where she was supposed to be. It was late at night—midnight or so—when he told me to get in his old Willys jeep with him: we were going to check on Sally's whereabouts. (The old jeep was the same vehicle that I had learned to drive at age nine, the same vehicle that had carried Sally and me to Minnesota and down to South Texas so many times.)

We drove outside of town to the girlfriend's house. The summer nights are hot in East Texas, usually in the mid to high eighties. When we pulled up to Sally's friend's house, her father came outside to see who had pulled up in his drive at that hour. The man insisted that the girls were there. But my dad was piqued and demanded that he produce the girls. It soon became painfully clear that the man had lied and there was no telling what the young girls were up to.

My dad was pushed out of shape, to say the least. The magnitude of the lie and his concern for Sally were more than Doc Swanson could take. Fists, arms, and elbows flew. As the dust swirled, the lights of the jeep illuminated the scene and I looked on from the passenger seat inside the car. Pop seriously out-classed his opponent, who finally cut and ran toward his house, yelling that he was going to get his gun. Pop jumped into the jeep and shifted into first, grinding the gears and heading straight for him. My dad ran right over the "son-of-a-bitch." We just kept on going, leaving the poor bastard in the dust. As we headed home, nobody spoke.

Sally showed up the next day, with much trepidation, I'm sure. It wasn't a pretty sight when my dad was through with her. I don't know what injuries her girlfriend's father suffered when he was run over by my dad, but no litigation resulted from the incident. (Of course, that was in the '50s before lawyers turned into man's worst enemy.)

There was some fallout from the event, however. It seems that the man Pop had literally flattened had a son away in the Army. When the son came home from the Korean War he showed up drunk at my dad's place a few times, challenging him to come out and fight. My dad just ignored him, but he did keep his P-38 German Luger well-oiled and loaded.

Pop made a Machiavellian deal with Sally. Carrying on the custody feud, he promised her a new car if she stayed in Kilgore. (In Texas you could get a driver's license at fourteen.) Pop knew that my mom wasn't having an easy time of it with Sally and would give in to having her under his control. Big mistake. He also bought her a wardrobe that made her seem older—she looked and passed for twenty-one. She started hitting the bars and honky-tonks. Fast living and some bad influences led her to brushes with the law. Before the year was out, she got into some serious trouble, and when she was fifteen my father and I went to visit her over Thanksgiving at a reform school for young women in north Texas.

I don't know what she did, but it must have been horrendous if my folks couldn't persuade the state to take an alternative measure. It was an eye-opener for me to see my sister incarcerated. When I visited her, I was struck by the subculture represented by the girls that I saw locked up. They were a hardened bunch; their vocabulary would have made a drill instructor blush. They had a gang-style caste system in which each girl considered herself part of a particular family and each had a designated position in it.

I felt bad for my sister, and held my dad responsible for dangling the custody carrot in front of her. I now knew how it might feel to have a crazy aunt in the basement. At least I knew I didn't want any of my friends finding out about Sally, although I was sure they would. She didn't straighten out any after getting out of the "home for wayward girls." She showed up in Brownsville for a short time when she hit sixteen, but by that time I didn't have too much to do with her, except get into fights with some guys that saw fit to disparage her in front of me. There were some rough elements in town that I never knew existed until they materialized with my sister in tow.

Ever in a hurry to get out from underneath our folks' control, she finally outdid herself when she hit sixteen. She ran off to Reynosa or some such border town and got married. She married a kid a year or two older than she was. He worked on a shrimp boat. (Brownsville called itself the "Shrimp Boat Capital of the World" at this time.) I knew my new brother-in-law's younger brother; he was a classmate of mine, and that just got me in more fights and left me in the unenviable position of again trying to defend my sister's name.

The guy Sally married was a pretty nice kid. He was real skinny, and had slicked-back straight blond hair styled in a duck tail. I doubt that he had finished the seventh grade, but his mom thought he hadn't done too well by marrying Sally and even mentioned to my mom that she questioned whether my sister was a virgin. Since this lady was now more or less family, my mother tempered her remarks and mumbled something about how she had strong reservations as to whether her new son-in-law was a virgin himself.

Before Sally got into serious trouble with the law, we had some good times. One summer when I was thirteen and she was fifteen my dad took us up to Minnesota for our annual sojourn. Sally and I took turns driving Pop's Willys across the Ozark mountains in Arkansas heading north to Minnesota. Pop brought along a girlfriend, Effie Millam. She was also his nurse. Effie was mostly of Cherokee extraction, very beautiful and exotic looking. She was also very kind. She had never been out of East Texas so she got on our cases because Sally and I were so blasé about the trip.

We also brought along a friend of my sister, named Jackie. Cute as they get in East Texas, she was ripening into a fine young woman and had a pert and sassy manner. I sure was smitten with her, as any male would be. Having been initiated into the solemn brotherhood of sexual pleasures, I couldn't believe my luck having to spend a couple of weeks rubbing shoulders with Jackie. Jackie's mom worked in a honky-tonk, and even though she wasn't of loose morals, she had a way of talking that was part come-on, part put-down, and, all in all, very worldly. It may not be true of all girls raised in and around a honky-tonk crowd, but Jackie had "it's possible" written all over her.

When we got to Minnesota we visited various aunts and uncles. In Austin, we dropped in on one of my dad's sisters, Aunt Mary. My Aunt Mary and my dad had a thing: they just seemed to get on each other's nerves—fast. It was automatic. I would say hello to my cousins Mary Sue (my favorite—she was my age and very cute) and John. Invariably, in the middle of our warm reunion, there would be a commotion. We'd hear Aunt Mary and my dad (known as Uncle John to my cousins) having an argument. My dad would stand up and announce that we were leaving. One time we left after only fifteen minutes.

After Aunt Mary's, we headed for the family farm in Buffalo where the Swanson family had grown up. The farm was owned by my Uncle Morris, the only one of the five children to stay on the farm and not finish college. Uncle Morris had been shot in the head by my dad when they were kids. It didn't affect his thinking ability, but somehow it became an impediment when it came to following his brother and three sisters.

This extended Swedish family exemplified the closeness and upward mobility of the immigrant. Since farming was always hit and miss, there was never enough money to go around for my dad and his sisters to attend college. So they made a pact where one would attend college and then help the others to go. One of my aunts never married, giving up much of her youth to advance the status of her sisters and brothers. My dad started college in his teens. He would attend school for a year and then work as a farmhand to help his younger sister get into college. It was this kind of thing that brought the siblings so close together that nothing could break their familial ties.

We were not the only ones to descend on the farm that year. All my aunts and uncles and their broods were there, and everyone was excited to see everyone else. I climbed out of the Willys and greeted my younger cousin Jan (Uncle Morris' son). I was pretty proud of my mature status and height—about five-foot-nine then—so when I popped out of the car and saw Jan standing in front of me, a full six-foot-three, I couldn't take it. I attacked him then and there. We rolled around in a furious tussle before someone broke us up. He forgave me later, but he must have thought he had a pretty weird Texas cousin. Our Minnesota cousins thought Texas was still the wild west and expected us to carry six-shooters. We might not have lived up to some expectations, but Sally and I certainly left an indelible impression on them during this trip.

Sally was a wild fifteen-year-old and, I found out later, had propositioned a couple of her northern kinsmen. She may have had some success but not everyone gave in: twenty years later one of the cousins told me that he had been tempted by my sister (amazing what can happen when the kids are sleeping out in the barn; must be something in the hay) but that he was so put off by her behavior that he held on to his virginity until he married.

While Sally was becoming notorious in family circles, I went on to bigger and better things after my fight with Jan. My Uncle Morris had a hay machine that picked up the cut hay and used a conveyor to drop the hay on to a horse-pulled wagon. One day a group of us kids were inside the wagon as it was being loaded with the newly mown hay. My job was to use a pitchfork to push the hay into different parts of the wagon. We were going merrily along; I was doing my job with the old pitchfork, when—thud! I knew instantly I had hit flesh. It was a sickening sound. My fork had hit one of my girl cousins, fortunately in the derriere. We took her back to the farmhouse and my father hastily drove her to town for some medical attention and a tetanus shot. Not much harm done, but if Carolyn has forgiven me, I bet she has never forgotten me.

This trip was eventful in other ways, too. My father scandalized the family by bringing a woman friend with him and then demanding to sleep in the same room with her. Then my sister's friend Jackie fell off a farm horse and broke her arm. I became very solicitous of Jackie, even though her accident interfered with my amorous intentions. The good part was that in helping her put on her sling from time to time, I would get a glimpse of her upper torso. She had hurt a few ribs as well, and, of course, I was there to help when we wrapped her chest area with an Ace bandage.

As if all that was not enough, I added one more war story to the books that year. Uncle Morris had to get the loose hay from the hay wagon to the inside of the barn. His practice was to put some ropes under the accumulated hay and, hooking a line to the hay, pull the hay high in the barn. Once it was high enough the hay would travel down another line to the far end of the barn where someone would pull the trip line and the hay would crash down in a pile. A load of this piled-up hay weighed a couple of tons. When I was manning the trip line, I had figured out that if I pulled the trip wire about halfway, as the hay was zipping down the rope to the end of the barn, the speed and trajectory would make it land where I wanted it.

One day I dared my cute cousin Mary Sue to stand on top of the hay mound and try to jump out of the way just as I released the trip rope. She took me up on it and, as I had surmised, had no idea of my intention to let the trip wire go at the halfway mark. Bingo! I let the hay fly and she was hit mid-stride trying to escape a grassy entombment.

By the time I and my other cousins reached the hay mound, all we could hear were muted cries of "help me, help me." At that point, I panicked and dove into the haystack and started pulling hay off of her. It seemed like an eternity but finally I found a foot, then more of her. I had just got her upright and was trying to help her button her blouse when in walked my dad. He quickly figured out the scenario and spent the next half hour chasing me, from time to time kicking my rear end. Mary Sue joined that ever-increasing group of those who would remember me.

Many years later I went to her fortieth birthday party in Los Angeles where she had moved to pursue a public relations career. She had become very successful. During her obligatory speech during the party, she acknowledged that it was nice growing up with cousins who were adopted because it allowed you to fantasize about them romantically. I agreed completely.

4

A Walk on the Wild Side

After this vacation was over, I went back to Brownsville and my sister stayed on with my dad. The '50s were in full bloom and we both felt the blood pumping through our teenage bodies. I never spent any time with my sister again, but the whirlwind of economic expansion and the musical revolution muted these changes and we followed our destinies. If the '50s were to be defined symbolically, they could be summed up by the automobile. America was on the move— industrially, it was at the top of the heap.

I didn't know very much about why the U.S. was on top, but I knew we won the war, we hadn't been bombed, and our people weren't trying to get out of the country. I saw a lot of folks trying to get in. In 1955 when I turned fourteen, car styles changed dramatically. All of a sudden they sprouted fins. In '54 the fins were controlled little bumps, but in '55, wow! Fins were out there. To my eyes, these style changes were intense, beautiful, and exciting.

With my whole being, I wanted a car and a license to drive. No one had given me any static about driving my motorcycle without a license. My mom said that I could borrow her car (a 1950 Ford V-8 stick shift) the day I passed my test. I couldn't wait. I made a date with a cute young thing for the weekend following my fourteenth birthday. This girl was the best thing I had ever seen, and I just knew if I could pick her up (without her parents around) I would be set for life.

Have you ever noticed, things never turn out perfectly? Well, I failed that driving test four or five weekends in a row. I never did get that date and I probably lost out on a great love affair. The driver's license testing person was a tight-lipped sucker who took perverse pleasure in poking holes in my program. But I finally passed and life really opened up for me then. It was expensive for my mom. I hate to think about how many cars of hers I wrecked. I loved her '50 Ford with the V-8 engine. It was her prized possession. It wasn't a fancy car with fins, but it didn't take me long to be able to peel rubber in all three forward gears.

In no time, I was speeding over the International Bridge to Mexico. I still had the crew cut, braces, and angelic smile. I'd pick up a bunch of my buddies, make them pitch in a quarter or so for gas, and we would cruise downtown and then head over to Mexico. By this late date in life I was smoking full-time and had acquired a tolerance for beer. When we went to Mexico we didn't always head for Boys Town. Sometimes, because of monetary concerns, we would order tacos from street vendors and just hang out and drink beer.

With the price of beer at 10 or 20 cents a bottle, a gang of us guys could eat and drink all night for a few dollars. The bars always had juke boxes with Mexican and American selections. The stylistic revolution in automobiles was eclipsed by the revolution in music. In '55, rock and roll hit its peak and, as they said, the hits just kept on coming. It seemed like every week there was another monster hit song or group or singer. Elvis took over the consciousness of all teens. When I saw nubile teenyboppers come unglued every time someone played a rock record, it didn't take me long to join the revolution. Right after I got my driver's license I was at a girlfriend's party, my first high school party, and someone played Jerry Lee Lewis' "Great Balls of Fire." Listening to it, I knew my future was going to be wonderful and exciting.

As I began high school in 1955, things on the home front were pretty cool. My mother had settled into her nursing job and had only me to contend with at home. She was devastated about Sally getting into so much trouble. I saw her break down completely a few times over Sally's behavior. It must have been hard for her to face family and friends.

I tried to be a dutiful son. I still wonder what went on in my mother's mind—if she ever thought about the heartache she let herself in for when she adopted us. I'm sure she didn't know about my nocturnal jaunts to Matamoros. But she was painfully aware of her lack of control over her teenage son. She would forbid me to go out, and I'd go anyway. The first time I pushed my cycle down the driveway, waiting until I was out of earshot to start it, I was elated that the wrath of God hadn't blown me to kingdom come. If my father had been around, I'm sure I couldn't have taken such license, especially since he outweighed me by 100 pounds.

High school was a lot more work than I expected. It took a little getting used to. I gravitated toward the "car boy" type that hung out across the street from the school. I even signed up for auto shop to get closer to what I considered the greatest thing in the world, the car. As I learned more about cars, I began to yearn for my own. I began casting about for something cheap. Voilà—I finally found an affordable rather beat-up junker. I negotiated a deal on this bucket of bolts called a "Crosby." I think the Crosby Motor Company had long since gone out of business; the car I bought had been a lame attempt to be the first compact, fuel-efficient vehicle of its kind. It was small, but styled like a station wagon. Well, for $50 I was not surprised that it wasn't in running condition. I got a couple of friends to push this baby to my house. Once I got it running, a bunch of us started hanging together.

We were a tight-knit group. Gas was 25 cents a gallon and so were Marlboros and Camel cigarettes. We would squeeze five or six guys in this little bitty unreliable mode of transportation and off we would go. Sometimes when we hit an overpass or the ramp to the International Bridge to Mexico, everyone would have to pile out and push. We had a ball.

But I still buttered up my mom trying to stay on her good side so I could borrow her more reliable wheels. I tried to come home fairly close to the time she asked me to. It didn't always work out that way. She had this little Chihuahua dog that never liked me—ever since I rolled over on it one night when it was sleeping in my bed. This yappy little thing weighed about two pounds but was still the best watchdog in town. I could never sneak into the house late at night without "Tiny" yapping her head off. The light would go on in mother's room and I would get the summons, "Jack, come in here."

She lent me her car for important occasions, always with the understanding that I wouldn't take it across the river. Sure, I didn't *intend* to, but from time to time I succumbed to the majority—and off we would go to *Foco Roco*, the red light district in old Mexico.

One night a bunch of us were wandering around this tourist haven checking out some of the floor shows offered in the swanky bars. Sometimes the bars would feature some dated, black and white, dirty movies. It didn't matter that the film was of rather low quality or grainy; the "participants" did things I hadn't imagined were possible. As we got ready to hit the road, we returned to where I had parked my mother's car. I jumped in, hit the old starter button, and nothing—it wouldn't start. Here we were in Boys Town where the policemen looked like refugees from a Banana Republic. I remember one of these cops had one eyeball that was completely white and he appeared to drool.

I had visions of Armageddon when my mother found out her car was with the Mexican authorities in a quaint little settlement outside Matamoros. We opened the hood and found out some rat had disconnected the spark plug wires. A few days later an upper classman at the high school told me that he and some guys had recognized my car and decided to play a practical joke on me.

Overall, my first year of high school was pretty uneventful. I played football on the J.V., became a regular at the detention hall, and made some new friends. I started to go steady with a little Mexican gal, Helen Carrol. She was one of the "in-crowd" people. Her mom dressed her up all "fou fou" and made sure she went to all the right parties—or gave them. We would go to movies and I would spend the entire time trying to maneuver my hand around her padded bra. These little victories were just as thrilling as my experiences with the "professionals" on the other side of the border.

After my freshman year was over, I went back up to East Texas for the summer. Now I was fully grown—around 150 pounds and five feet ten-and-a-half inches tall. My lanky frame, dark brown hair, blue eyes, and square jaw seemed to open a lot of doors for me. My friends all acknowledged there was never a dull moment when I was around, and if I said something was going to happen—it happened.

When I got back up to Kilgore, I started hanging out at a honky-tonk right outside of town, a place called the "Honey Dew Drive-Inn" where carhops would fasten your food tray to your car window. They were the principal attraction. Elvis, of course, was on the juke box, and every time his songs were played all the girls would squeal. My buddies and I really enjoyed Memphis style rock and roll but it disconcerted us that Elvis was getting that kind of attention. We all swore that if he ever made it down our way we were going to cut off his family jewels. I loved the Honey Dew Drive-Inn. The owner was a great big lady named Tommy. She ran the place with an iron hand. Her husband, Kenny, was a rather short guy who just saluted and followed her orders. Tommy took a shine to me and became my surrogate mom.

I soon got a fancier motorcycle and started wearing a motorcycle jacket and a white T-shirt, and I took up smoking Lucky Strikes or Camels, fancying myself as Marlon Brando or James Dean.

I sometimes blame a lot of the trouble I got into as a kid on my life below the border and the temptations so readily available there. However, I soon started having a few problems with the law up in East Texas. I ran with a pretty normal group of guys. None of us were taking college preparatory classes and none of us were planning our futures. All we thought about were cars and girls. Everyone and his brother's uncle as we used to say, seemed to be buying new cars. The '55 Chevys, '55 Ford Victorias, the sassy Buicks, Oldsmobiles, Pontiacs and the Cadillac El Dorados were everywhere.

As for the music, Buddy Holly was hot, Little Richard, Chuck Berry, Elvis, Jerry Lee Lewis, and on and on. Who could think about school? I just figured that it would all work out. Meanwhile, we'd suck up Lone Star beer and decide what to do with our free time. There were drive-in movies, roller skating rinks, and some swimming holes and lakes we'd go to. Kilgore is pretty country; the soil is iron-rich and red to the eye, and the town's rolling green hills are covered with pine trees.

One night a bunch of us decided to liberate some watermelons from Farmer Jones' field. We were sneaking through the corn field, climbing over barbed-wire fences, and about to pounce on the sweet melons. Boom, someone— I'll never know who—opened fire on us with shotguns. Now I knew how deer and rabbit must feel. We froze, for a split second, then survival instincts took over. We scaled the fence much faster this time; I hit that barbed wire going full tilt— ouch. When we had all piled into the car we headed straight for the Honey Dew Inn. Tommy patched me up, cleaned the wounds, and laughed like hell.

Around this time I pulled off one of the stupidest things I ever did. Bored one night, a gang of us decided to rob a fruit stand. The plan was to create a diversion by banging on the side of the stand, distracting the proprietor so that one of us could grab a few watermelons. We should have stuck to the open fields. When my buddies skidded to a stop at the fruit stand, the nut in charge came out waving what looked to me like a very big handgun. (It was probably a .22.) Seconds later, the police came, hauled us off, and called our parents. My dad was getting used to these nocturnal calls. Lucky for me he was on good terms with the local judicial authorities.

There were a few more scrapes with the local constables. The one that prompted dear old dad to ship me back to Brownsville was the time I was arrested for possession of a stolen .22-caliber rifle. This 300-pound lady constable came by the house and literally threw me in the back of her police car. When I saw there were no handles inside, I quickly agreed to turn over the rifle. Thank God I didn't have anything to do with stealing it. Those boys were caught and went off to reform school.

Back in Brownsville I quickly realized that I needed a source of income. I was too old for a paper route. The lure of easy money got me to thinking about the stories I had heard that a "hard-working lad" could make a lot of money working on the shrimp boats. Quite a few of my school mates' fathers were shrimpers. They were a hardened bunch—heavy drinkers, uneducated, often from the deep South. Crackers from Georgia and Louisiana Cajun French constituted a very large part of the workforce. These guys made good money during the summer fishing season but had to make do with slim pickings in the winter time.

The coastal fishermen had discovered that the shrimp were more plentiful at night, so for a week or two at a time they slept all day, mended nets in the late afternoon, and started fishing when the sun went down. They would haul the fishnets up a couple of times a night.

One of my heroes at this time was a Georgia boy who came to Port Brownsville in the early '50s. He had stolen a shrimp boat in Georgia and wound up in Brownsville during a boom in the shrimp business. In just a few years he had made a bundle, enough to acquire a fleet of boats. He actually sent the stolen boat back and paid off his startled creditors.

After hanging around the house awhile, I got bored and decided that action was required. I packed my stuff in a cardboard box, left a note for my Mom—something to the effect of "gone fishing"—and hitchhiked to Port Brownsville, about twenty miles away. I was big for my age, easily passing for sixteen or older, and I was a clean-cut kid with braces. I was also a fast talker. I asked around if anyone knew of a berth for an able seaman (albeit a novice) and what the going wage was.

I was told that pay was on a commission basis. The crew— the captain, rigman, and header—got 50%, 30%, and 20%, respectively. The captain navigated and gave the orders, of course; the rigman handled the nets and winches; and the header cooked, washed dishes, pulled the heads off the shrimp you caught, cleaned the deck, and did all the shit work. Sounded neat to me.

I walked up and down the docks. There were hundreds of fishing boats, usually trawlers 60 to 80 feet in length. I went from boat to boat until a young captain said that he needed a hand and would give me a try. Under twenty-one, he was the youngest captain in the fleet, but evidently he had proven himself to the fleet owners. We headed out immediately. There were three of us—the normal crew. We headed out of the jetty to open water. Before it was even dark I could no longer see land. Holy Shit! The old sphincter muscles were working overtime. All the while, the guys were poking fun at me, saying "If you're not seasick by now, by god, you probably aren't going to get sick."

By the time we were well into the Gulf of Mexico, the vessel was lunging up and down and side to side. Well, I got sicker than a dog. I hung onto the wooden rail for dear life. Thank God, it was the last time I ever got sick on ship.

The next night we dropped the nets overboard in Mexican waters. You have to fish shrimp close to shore because your nets have to drag the ocean bottom to scoop them in, and there is just so much cable that you have available. Dragging the ocean bottom means you pick up a lot more than shrimp. All the debris goes back into a pouch-like portion in the back of the net. When you haul out and have the nets over the stern of the boat, you pull a ripcord and let the accumulated mess (fish, shrimp, crabs, junk, turtles, mud and gunk) hit the deck.

As low man, I was elected to sort through it all and pile up only the shrimp. Once we had accumulated enough, my job was to pull the heads off each and every one of the little bastards. This was tough work. Not only was it always at night, but sometimes rainstorms would maul the boat. The trawler would be gyrating side to side at an alarming rate, the cold rain would be coming down, and there I was, using a wooden rake to pull another pile of shrimp over to where I was sitting on an old soft drink box. While I was massacring the crustaceans, I would often look at the pilot house and see the captain and rigman looking at me sympathetically from their nice dry digs where they drank their warm coffee. Rank had its privileges.

That first trip out was a humdinger. We started fishing our second night out and by a happy freak of nature we ran into this motherlode of shrimp. I had never seen a live shrimp up close before, but there I was, staring at millions of the little buggers. We caught so many shrimp, all on the small side, that I couldn't possibly pull the heads off all of them. I yanked the heads and legs off the larger ones but most of the catch had to be shoveled into the refrigerated hull of the boat. After the next night of fishing, we had damned near overloaded the boat and I was afraid we would sink. The captain headed for port. We got in and unloaded at the company cannery where after a few more hour's work, I was issued a check in the $600 range. I was rich. I grabbed my stuff and headed for home. I tried to scrub the shrimp juice from my hands, which were cracked and gnarled from the constant wet and heavy work. As I reacclimated myself to solid ground, my plan was never to look at another shrimp for the rest of my life, although I was tickled about the money in my pocket.

I went out and played some pool; the table kept rocking with the rhythm of the boat. That night I asked my mother if I could borrow her brand-new 1955 Plymouth. She had just splurged on this beauty. It had huge fins and pushbutton automatic transmission. Reluctantly, she agreed, but only if I promised to be home early and fill the tank up with gas. I rounded up some of my buddies to celebrate my good fortune. None of my friends had jobs so having gone out on a shrimp boat made me a big shot.

It didn't take long for the wad of greenbacks to burn a hole in my jeans. We hit a few bars across the river and, after a few drinks, decided what the hell? Let's see what's happening in Boys Town. Although I had been to sea for only three days, it seemed to me a very long time. So, after we had downed a couple of Cervesas, we agreed that we were tired of the "back alley" variety of hookers we had been going to and that we should go "top line." The top of the line was in the $16 to $20 range. Since I was the only one with any money, I agreed to foot the bill. I was really on top of the world. Happiness abounded, money changed hands, time flew, and at the end of the night I had gone to bed with a bunch of different gals. Around 2:00 A.M. I realized it was time to gather up my buddies and pack it in.

We got in the car with its new-car smell and headed home. On the way home, a sheriff's car signaled us to pull over. I panicked; this didn't fit in with my plan. I was driving, of course, and obviously I had had a lot to drink. So instead of pulling over, I stomped on the accelerator. That sheriff chased us all over. I finally lost him by turning out the lights and doing some daredevil antics. Finally I pulled into an orange grove and he whizzed past.

I spent the next hour or so driving around Brownsville, without the headlights on, depositing all my friends to their respective abodes. I got home without being apprehended, and I pulled into the garage. Once again, Tiny barked and woke up Mom. "Jack, come in here." After I slipped and fell on the throw rug in her bedroom, proving how sober I was, I trotted off to bed. I woke up in the early afternoon with a hangover and the horrible realization that I was broke, cleaned out, busted. Not only that, I had forgotten to fill up the car with gas.

When my mother came home from work I made a tactical error; my timing was very bad. It was probably the hangover. I explained that my beat-up old Crosby didn't work and that somehow, I had lost, at any rate was no longer in possession of, my windfall shrimp money. I asked to borrow some money and her car. My mother was already not too happy with me for taking off on my fishing expedition without her approval. She had been worried sick. So not keeping my word and "coming in at all hours" was the last straw.

Mom said, "If you're old enough to make a man's wage, then you should have given some thought to helping out around the house and to my upkeep." I had never thought of helping out at home. It dawned on me that she was right. She said I was grounded and she wasn't going to give me even one thin dime to get a milkshake.

The next day I packed up my gear in a cardboard box and hitchhiked back out to the port. I went from boat to boat until I found another boat, another crew. This time I could say I was an experienced hand and get a better percentage of the catch. My new captain was a grizzly old dude with red hair and the toughest beard I ever saw. The rigman was a short, wiry little guy with a toothless smile. He had some great war stories about the South Pacific. Seems like his Southern accent almost got him killed a few times because sentries couldn't understand him; he had problems with his r's. For some reason these two rough-and-tumble shrimpers took a shine to me and treated me like family. They were pretty tight when it came to spending money on provisions; we would go out with three or five days' worth of grub on a fifteen-day trip. As soon as we ran out of store-bought food, we would either start eating fish or start trading some of our catch with the Mexican shrimp boats (which the Anglo shrimpers called *poncho* boats) for food, cigarettes, rum, and coffee. The poncho boats, generally small boats holding large crews, went out for a day at a time.

Lucky for the captain and rigman, I wasn't asked to cook. I learned how to gut fish and I appreciated the great Mexican cooking I had been used to at home, but I didn't have a clue about how to cook anything myself. One day I found a can of peaches. We had been out for a week or more. I was hungry and I gulped them down. Well, the captain and rigman took me to task for my greediness and thoughtlessness in not sharing. I took their point and started being more of a team player.

We would stay out for a week or two at a stretch, long enough to fill our boat with shrimp or run out of diesel fuel, whichever came first. Diesel fuel was 10 cents a gallon back in those days.

When we hit port and I got paid, the first thing I would do is hand over my paycheck to my mom. She would dole out a few bucks here and there. My friends were unhappy about my new-found frugality. Quite a few of them ended up getting jobs on the boats in the coming years. Even with the little money I had, I soon managed to get on the best-dressed list; I wore pink and black shirts, grew my hair out and slicked it back, and finally had my braces removed.

Shoveling ice to cover the fish in the hold of the 85-foot trawler had filled out my physique.

I didn't spend any time at home for the rest of the summer. I just hung out at the boat and helped out with its maintenance and general upkeep. We would usually stay in port for two or three days and then head out again. When we were in port I acted as chauffeur for the captain and the rigman. They would get their paychecks and I would drive them to the bank where they would cash them. They made a lot of money during the summer season, thousands of dollars a trip. Every time we hit port they would start drinking and carrying on. More than once I had to stop the car and race across the flat and dusty Texas landscape to ground one of their paychecks that had blown out the window.

These guys had great cars. The one I loved most to drive was an Oldsmobile '88 Cutlass-Supreme. What a bomb! It was a smooth V-8 with muscle. I would stay sober and drive them "over the river" to—you guessed it—Boys Town. I saw how the old guys partied and how they threw money around. For years I thought I was one of them. It finally dawned on me one day that I wasn't, but I sure had fun pretending.

By the end of summer I had enough moola to buy a real car. First I bought a '52 Oldsmobile. Neat as it was, it was not my dream car. Once school started I met a sailor who was stationed at the nearby naval air base; *he* had the car I wanted. I traded him my Oldsmobile and some cash for his Black 1950 Mercury with a hopped-up 1955 Chrysler engine and all-white, custom upholstery. Jesus, it was hot.

That black 1950 Merc was identical to the car used by James Dean in the 1955 movie *Rebel without a Cause*. To say that I identified with the Dean character is an understatement. I even wore a red windbreaker like James Dean did in the movie. I can't think of that car and not reflect on how much I invested in it, not just time and money, but how much of my self-image I projected onto it. That car represented everything of value to me at the time.

I also won a lot of drag races with that car. Every weekend, I and a bunch of my friends would be out raising hell and dragging for cases of beer, and more. I expanded my circle of friends around then. I started running with a school chum I had known from first grade on. He was Hispanic, of Mexican and French lineage. Gaston is still one of my best friends today.

Gaston came from a large family, solid middle-class. He spent a great deal of time at my house and would barely stifle a laugh at my mother's Bostonian ways, especially when she would ring her little bell for the maid to prepare and serve different courses at mealtime. I would just about die of embarrassment, especially since I knew there was no such formality at Gaston's home where, even if they were short on food, his folks would give me the last tortilla in the house. I also spent a lot of time over at Gaston's house. His dad was a really soft, thoughtful man who was a surrogate father to me.

Gaston never acted as a bodyguard like Willie, but he performed the same function many times. Like Willie, he spoke Spanish and had a very level-headed and conservative way about him. But in other ways we were all completely opposite. Gaston would always call for cool heads to prevail, I would always be the instigator for action, and Willie would always hope that negotiations would break down.

One time I had to call in *both* Willie and Gaston to get me out of a scrape. My mother was away on a trip with one of her rich relatives and had left me home alone. This was a green light for running amok, of course. Somehow during this time I had displeased a Latino gang leader named "Angel." This guy was a bona fide young ganglord in our part of the world.

I don't remember all the details but I remember that I had gone to the local movie house (the Majestic Theater, easily the fanciest edifice in town) and had heeded the call of nature during intermission. While pursuing nature's call, I heard a noise behind me. I turned to see who or what it was. To my amazement this large, upstairs balcony restroom was filled with brown-skinned Mexican kids. They were affiliated with Angel's gang that hung out in my neighborhood. The leader, one tough little hombre, stepped forward and said, "We're going to kill you."

I felt my hair stand straight up. Every gland in my body kicked in a ton of juice. I pulled a blackjack (a homemade club—an iron pipe wrapped with black electrician's tape) from my back pocket and fought my way to the door. I surprised myself and them by getting away unscathed. However, that episode started a feud with the Ramiranio gang from a barrio bordering my neighborhood. That's where Angel came in.

Angel was the leader of that close-knit area. So, he decided it's over for me and called in a bunch of his compañeros to surround my house. They called for me to come on out and repeated some phrases about killing me. I wasted no time in calling Willie and Gaston. They showed up in fast order and started negotiating; all the while I kept my finger on my .22-caliber rifle. After much name-calling, pushing, and shoving by Willie and calm cajoling by Gaston, the Ramaranio gang and Angel decided to let me continue to live. It was important to defuse this type of feud because, sooner or later, they would have gotten me. Gaston and Willie still marvel to this day about how I used to get myself into such dire predicaments.

Gaston and I cut quite a swath through the women folk at the high school. He was exceptionally handsome—dark curly hair, big brown eyes, and the look of a person you could to trust. He never said anything without thinking it through. We were opposites.

When we got to the tenth grade we took a lot of the same classes. Auto mechanics filled up our morning schedule. I, as always, brought my car into the auto shop to be worked on. It was great having a reliable car. Pretty soon we were driving to Corpus Christi (about 160 miles north) to meet what we regarded as more exotic girls. (Somehow they just seemed more interesting if you weren't raised with them.) Ironically, I met a girl in Corpus through an Episcopal Church group. I had become close friends with the couple who sponsored this group and used to stay with them when I went to Corpus. These people were very kind to me and, even though I didn't spend that much time with them, I wrote Christmas cards and corresponded with them until they passed away many years later. I could always count on them for sound advice at important milestones in my life. For me, this girl was a dream come true—a good-looking girl I could take across the border and wine and dine legally. I would take her to intimate little clubs a few blocks over the bridge where mixed drinks were 35 cents. We would dance all night for five dollars. I even had her come and stay at my house for the weekend with my mother as an eagle-eyed chaperone.

Living in the lower Rio Grande Valley, and especially in Brownsville, lulled me to the reality of race relations. Since Anglos were in the minority in Brownsville and there were zero black people, I had just not given racism much thought. However, on one of my trips to Corpus Christi to go to a football game with my new-found, long-distance girlfriend, I had my eyes opened. She informed me that my friend Gaston wouldn't be welcome in the bleachers with the Anglo kids.

Well, that was the end of that romance. I was flabbergasted and hurt beyond words that she would take such a stand. She knew and liked Gaston; it seemed he was all right down there on the border but not with her friends up the valley in Corpus. I was soon to find out that this division between Latinos and Anglos was the norm outside of the lower Rio Grande Valley.

Having a fancy customized car, however, did wonders for my love life. If Corpus was out, there were still lots of local gals and the ubiquitous drive-in movies. Dating took on a whole new meaning at those double features where I'd struggle undoing the fasteners on many a bra. Even worse, it was the day when girls and women wore girdles, and those contraptions were impossible. I don't even want to guess how many nubile young things escaped my amorous designs. Not that I was counting or anything like that.

There were two or three different levels of girls in the gene pool in Brownsville. There were the extremely Catholic religious types. If you dated them, your chances for mutual satisfaction were slim. Most of these girls were more afraid of what their parents would do to them if they gave in than with any case I could build for physical fulfillment. There were the middle-class Protestants, usually Anglo gals that didn't hold to such a strict moral code, but if you were going to get intimate you had to be going steady—and closer relationships usually meant marriage in the 1950s. Thank God there were exceptions to these morally upright types, but they were certainly in the minority and, hence, more sought after—meaning that if the sweet young thing was desirable to me, then I could count on a lot of competition.

Another problem with high school girls was that, regardless of the grade they were in, you could never be sure of the age, size, and temperament of their boyfriends or would-be suitors. One day I was hanging out at the Eagle's Nest hamburger joint across from the high school when I spied the girl of my dreams. In other words, she was cute, and she was alive and well. I smiled, she smiled, but, alas, our love was not to be. Her boyfriend, I found out, was this mean little bastard I had met on one of the shrimp boats. He was a couple of years older than I and was about the toughest dude in town.

Soon after my flirtation with his girl, I and a bunch of my compadres were hanging out at our favorite drive-in diner, the Oasis. It had a big old neon palm tree out front. We were sitting around listening to Elvis blaring from the outdoor speakers of the juke box when a group of shrimpers pulled up to the Oasis and I heard myself being called out to fight by the boyfriend of the girl I had flirted with at the Eagle's Nest. Oh boy! I didn't have my bodyguard on hand, and even if I did it wouldn't have helped; these guys were huge and numerous (a couple of carloads full).

I was soon surrounded by some twenty-year-old guys with about nineteen-inch necks and receding hairlines. With Elvis in the background ("One Night with You" always seemed to be playing at these times) I had to fight it out, toe to toe. I did a whole lot better than I had anticipated against this pint-sized bully, and he was surprised. I couldn't really press for a decisive victory because of his menacing buddies, standing at the ready, but before the dust cleared I knew that it was going to get around town that you "don't mess with Swanson." Funny thing about the blows you take in a fight. You really don't feel pain when you get hit; in the heat of the moment your reflexes take over. It always surprised me what I was capable of in these situations. The Oasis was such a stable part of my life that friend or foe could count on finding me there. Consequently, it was the site for a lot of confrontations. I never went to the Oasis thinking that I would get into a brawl, but quite often things would just happen.

One time at the Oasis I mentioned to a shrimper friend of mine, Blacky, that some guy I didn't even know had given him an unsavory look. Blacky was Louisiana French—lithe and handsome to the point of being damned near beautiful. He had strong blue-blue eyes, and jet black hair. A lot of the Cajun shrimpers down South had that raven black hair. I certainly didn't expect what would happen because of my offhand remark. Blacky jumped up, grabbed the guy I had pointed out, held him in a vise-like grip, and commenced to beat the ever-loving shit out of the poor innocent bystander. Besides surprising the hell out of me, it revealed a side of Blacky that I would see more and more of in the ensuing years. He hurt this guy bad. This bone-crushing violence wasn't just a fight; his behavior was pathological. Over time, I had to put distance between us.

After this fight was over, we all piled into our vehicles and split before the cops showed up. After some of these incidents, the local cops started dropping by my house on Riverside Drive. I remember one night after some brawl at the Oasis we had all jumped into my hot-rod Merc to "get the fuck outta here." I was hitting about 110 miles an hour down the old Port Isabel Road when I heard the ding, ding, ding, of the railroad crossing signal. Red lights were flashing and the alarm sounded, but it was too late to slow down or change direction. We missed that train by milliseconds— one more coat of paint, as they say. It's hard to breathe with your heart in your throat.

During the school year I began to see cracks in my academic record. All this running around wasn't doing much for my educational future. My "eat, drink, and be merry" attitude got me thrown off the football squad and the only reason I was passing English was because my youthful, full-bodied teacher had the hots for me. Other than that, I wasn't doing too well, except in auto mechanics. Another obstacle to my education was that I still needed money for racing my car, so from time to time I would skip school and go out on a short fishing trip. I continued this way for the next two years. My mom kept ragging on me about grades and future, but when you're going a million miles an hour, the future seems nonexistent.

I spent another great summer on the boats, having adventure after adventure, mostly off the coast of Mexico. The beauty of that mountainous coast can't be adequately described. We would anchor off the coast every morning and watch the sun come up. We'd talk on the ship-to-shore radio to other shrimpers, usually linking up at an anchorage where we would tie our boats together. Besides the trading, bullshitting, and conviviality associated with being "shipped out" in foreign waters, there was danger. Crewmen from the Mexican gunboats would board us from time to time, steal our shrimp, and generally harass us for fishing in their territorial waters. They probably had a point, but since it was our livelihood we saw them as Mexican bandits.

We would sleep most of the day tied up or anchored out next to a reef. These reefs in the Gulf of Mexico around Tampico or Vera Cruz were circular reefs in salt water—so clear and blue you could see the beautiful tropical fish and multicolored coral on the bottom of the ocean. I would usually try to take a swim in the afternoon before pulling up anchor for another night of commercial fishing. I would jump off the side of our 85-foot trawler, assuming that a rope or tire tied to the side to serve as a bumper would be available to get back on board. If not, there was always the anchor chain I could use to shimmy back on board the shrimp boat.

One afternoon as the crew slept, I jumped over the side for a swim and to check out the reef lagoon. When you're in the water looking up at the boat it seems huge and you feel pretty tiny. Well, this particular day, there I was bare-ass naked, and what do I spy? A long, silvery barracuda! I sure churned that water as I headed for the boat with speedy intent. I made it to the side only to find that there was no rope to hoist myself up on. However, my self-preservation instinct must have been riding high because I managed to leap straight up out of that water to grab hold of a tire bumper that, under ordinary circumstances, would have been beyond my reach.

Now that I had put in a few miles as a shrimper, I began to realize that my ideas were useful and that the captain and rigman were ready to listen to my advice. The captain put me in charge of additional crew that we would occasionally hire on for a trip. Some of these hired hands were WW II vets or soldiers-of-fortune types who didn't cotton to taking orders from a youngster like me. I had to stand my ground and be willing to back up my orders with force. All of this was a bit dangerous on the open ocean in the black of night on the back deck of a boat miles from shore with no witnesses. My captain and rigman backed me up as far as the chain of command went, but they knew the rest was up to me.

When I came home from fishing trips in the summertime, I continued to hand over most of my paychecks to my mother and I kept to the routine of being the designated driver for my captain and rigman. They came to rely on me, and they threw around a lot of money. We usually spent our shore leave across the river in Mexico. Things were mellow in "Margaritaland" as long as the money held out.

After hanging out in Matamoros for a few years, I began to get to know the locals fairly well. I had favorite hangouts where the bartenders or proprietors knew me by name or sight, and I had grown attached to some of the young señoritas that had become part of my south-of-the-border life. I remember one Latin gal I had a crush on. Uneducated and poor, she had turned to the "sporting life" because she was in need of a costly operation. I don't know if she was able to get rich quick and get out as she planned, but I hope she did. This girl was a spitfire. She found me flirting with another girl one night and flew into a jealous rage. She jumped at me and tried to scratch my eyes out. It took two people to pull her off me. I learned a very valuable lesson—be careful of girls who have a fiercely possessive nature.

My sixteenth summer was going to be my last summer on the water. By 1958 I was an old hand on the boats. I had fantasies of captaining my own boat someday, maybe even of owning a fleet of boats. Being the lowest man on the totem pole didn't dampen these grandiose dreams. Even though I was now an experienced hand, as the youngest, I was still called on when there was a tough or dirty job. If the light on the top of the mast went out, I was the one to climb up the mast pole where I would hang on for dear life as the boat rolled and shifted from side to side. I would look down to see the deck and the top of the pilot house, then an expanse of water on one side, then the deck again, and another expanse of water on the other side. Apart from such dangerous jobs, I also had to clean all the fish we caught. We pulled up some carp-like fish from the ocean depths. One weighed in at 700 pounds. I cleaned that mother by inserting a butcher knife at one end and hitting it with a hammer, then gutting it from stem to stern. We traded this fish to the Mexican poncho boats for cigarettes and booze.

Strange creatures inhabit the ocean depths—giant manta rays, ten feet across the back not counting the tail, and giant turtles weighing a ton. We tried not to kill the giant turtles because we knew that they were an endangered species. We'd get them off the deck and over the rail by using a rope and a winch. We did eat a few smaller turtles, even using their eggs to whip up some pancakes.

By now, I was making a man's wage and I was given more responsibility at the helm. I was taught the rudiments of navigation and quite often was called upon to stand watch while the captain and rigman slept. Sometimes, while traveling along the Mexican coastline, I would take the ship off auto-pilot and head to land seeing how close I could get to the shore without mishap. We had fathometers so I could calculate our depth and location on the charts. I played it safe most of the time, but I'm glad that the captain and rigman never awoke to some of the close-ups I managed off the Mexican shoreline.

When school started in my junior year I was mentally primed to forge on academically. But with the kind of life

I had been living, interest in learning, at least school learning, just wasn't there for me. I started cutting school classes and hanging out at the port. I couldn't see where I needed any more book learning, not when the material world beckoned. There was a revolution happening in Cuba that was capturing the imagination of the Caribbean. Fidel Castro was leading a group of youthful guerrilla fighters to throw out a corrupt dictator. I started formulating a bold plan to hijack or steal a fishing trawler and head for Cuba. I figured that I could join Castro and help liberate the island. I also saw a chance to follow in one of my hero's shoes—the guy from Georgia who stole a boat and went to Brownsville to make his fortune, and then sent back the stolen boat.

In 1958 to 1959 our border town was swamped with Cuban militiamen trying to recruit soldiers for their cause. These revolutionaries cut quite a romantic figure in their green utility Army jackets and caps. The more I saw of them the more I wanted in on the action. Attending school just got more and more unappetizing.

I still went to church on Sundays when I was not out on the boats. Many a time I would show up for 7:00 A.M. mass on my way back from Matamoros after being up all night. I would roll up my blue jeans, put on my vestments (which covered my clothes) and march up the aisle with the cross. The Reverend Albright knew about my antics but had taken a shine to me. He always called on me when he needed an altar boy for weddings or funerals, the latter being the mainstay of his official business. Since we had a lot of "snow birds" in our congregation, I was called on to walk in front of a lot of caskets.

The Reverend Albright treated me as an adult. He filled me in on the politics of the church, or at least the domain that he was a part of, and the juggling act one had to put on to appease different factions within the congregation and the church bureaucracy. He even asked for my advice from time to time. He had his heart set on being the Episcopal Bishop in Cuernavaca, close to Mexico City.

Reverend Albright and I saw a lot of one another at this time, as there were a lot of funerals. When the church service was over (the Episcopal service is short and sweet) I would ride in the Reverend's car to the cemetery where he would say a few words over the casket. On the caravan to the cemetery, the Reverend and I would catch up on current events and almost invariably, he would tell me some of the off-color jokes that would be making the rounds at the time. When we arrived at the gravesite, he would once again assume his solemn composure and recite the "ashes to ashes, dust to dust." After the next of kin and friends left the scene, the coffin would be lowered—or they would try to lower it. The mechanism almost always stuck and I was the one who had to get on top of the coffin and jump up and down until it sank to the bottom of the pit. Then someone would pull me out of the earthen hole ready for the car ride back to the rectory.

The Reverend Albright always showed up when I got into trouble with the authorities. My mother would call him, sometimes at odd hours of the night and he would drive downtown to retrieve me from the police station. Most of my transgressions were minor, such as racking up 18 speeding tickets one year, drag racing on city streets, and fighting, of course—which he would characterize as "kids will be kids."

One of my more memorable busts was when a friend of mine ratted on me. I had accidentally wrecked his motorcycle and he had been holding a grudge about it. He owned a vintage Indian motorcycle, in the 600-lb. range with a motor that looked like a V-8 car engine. Indians and Harley-Davidsons were similar; if you owned one of these cycles, you were somebody.

Well, my friend lent me his Indian and one day after I revved up the engine and hit second or third gear, the unthinkable happened. The throttle stuck! There I was on top of the largest vehicle on two wheels going 60 miles an hour on a dead-end road. I couldn't go left or right, there was no time to turn off the engine, and the brakes wouldn't stop it. I crashed. The bike was almost totaled. I hit the dirt and rolled over and over. Outside of a few dings and gashes, I was not too badly hurt.

I helped pay to fix his motorcycle. But it seems my neighborhood buddy never forgave me. The vendetta came about this way: A couple of my friends and I had concocted a story about possessing a mythical potion better known as "Spanish Fly" that was supposed to have a cataclysmic effect on feminine libidos. If you slipped one of these pills into her drink, she would turn into a sexually insatiable nympho. What we didn't tell anybody is that we had shaved the "B" off some Bayer aspirin and wrapped these now plain white pills in paper packets, ready for sale. We let it be known that we had a supply of Spanish Fly pills and were willing to part with them for a price.

It turned out to be a lucrative business. During study hall one day, this guy, still upset about his Indian motorcycle, sent me a note asking if I had any of these Spanish Flys. I took the opportunity to write back a lengthy explanation, quite graphic as I recall, of what one could expect from the object of one's affection after she consumed just one of these little white pills. My nefarious friend arranged a buy and kept the notes.

That afternoon, who do I see walking down my driveway, but my favorite plainclothes detectives from the Brownsville Police Department. Yep, they hauled me off to the pokey on suspicion of selling illegal drugs. My sainted mother had to come get me. Much to my chagrin they showed her my school notes and the so-called drugs that I had sold. As it turned out, they had to let me go when the police lab discovered that the magic pills were store-bought aspirin. I'd been telling them that all along, but I began to realize that these police goons viewed me in a different light from the way I viewed myself. I saw my behavior as good clean fun; they saw it as adding up to jail time.

Considering the discomfort and disruption it must have caused him to keep coming to my rescue, I was very surprised that Reverend Albright stuck by me. He appeared to appreciate my zest for life, and even asked me once if I would take his son, a classmate of mine, to Mexico to show him the sights. (The kid never did go with me, but when I saw him, four years later, he had turned into a handsome and together young man—without my help.)

School definitely was not going well in the autumn of my junior year. By this time, I was cutting class for many days in a row to take the occasional fishing trips I needed to earn transportation money. This action brought on a face-to-face clash with the high school principal, Mr. Finch. Mr. Finch was a much decorated WW II marine who had fought it out hand-to-hand with some Japanese soldiers in the Pacific theater of the war. Mr. Finch didn't take it lightly that I was disruptive in class and was now ditching school.

My science teacher, Mr. Smith, had been giving me a hard time about my lack of attendance and my clowning around when I did show up for class. One day I saw Mr. Smith waiting at a stoplight when driving home after school. I jumped out of my car, ran up to his vehicle and tried to pull him out of his car. He managed to escape my revenge by quickly locking his door and speeding off. To me, this was more of a prank than anything else. Mr. Finch, however, didn't see it that way. He was crazed.

The next school day he had me hauled into his office and, his face beet red and his bald head shining, actually challenged me to a fight behind the gym. Amidst saying he had "had it" with me, he kept babbling about his experiences in the war in the Pacific. Discretion being the better part of valor, I declined the invitation. He left me with the warning that if I missed any more school, it was finito, over: I would be out for good.

That experience did nothing to restore my interest in school, and it wasn't long before I was back out to sea. This time I stayed away for thirty days. Needless to say, as soon as I went back to school I was marched down to the principal's office. The principal and his aides escorted me to my locker and cut off the lock. Then they confiscated all my books and personal belongings and physically ejected me from the building.

Free at last! . . . or was I? I wasn't upset about my new status but it didn't sit too well with my folks. My dad, who was in Kilgore, couldn't quite grasp my not finishing high school. He had graduated from high school at age thirteen and had earned a master's degree from Northwestern University at age nineteen. My mom just accepted my new status with confusion and dismay. I wasn't too bothered with this turn of events and just kept on working the commercial fishing boats.

But there were some drawbacks to my full-time employment. I was now expected to pay my fair share for my upkeep at home. I also lost touch with my school chums. Since I wasn't with them in class anymore, I wasn't up on their lives or school news. I drifted toward palling around with the guys working the boats. Some were good guys but some were rather unsavory.

After a few months of being a full-time shrimper, I took a good look at my life and didn't like what I saw. I soon began to hate the work and the lifestyle. Working the boats in the winter didn't bring in much money and there were occasional cold fronts that made even these southern climates damned miserable. Slowly I began to realize that there was no real future in what I was doing.

I finally started to think long-term and came to the conclusion that even if I applied myself diligently, and even if I wound up owning a whole fleet of shrimp boats, it just didn't appeal to me as a lifetime career. I could observe that these guys I worked with had no real home life. They were always breaking up with their wives and girlfriends, they were usually drinking and brawling, and, physically, they were aged well beyond their years. The wild idea I had earlier of pirating a boat and heading for Cuba was shot down by Castro turning Communist. Thank God.

In the throes of deciding what my next move should be, my sister showed up in Brownsville again. She was divorced from the young shrimper she had married and was now a free agent. I got word from some of my friends that she was pregnant. Being incensed about my sister's situation, I decided that a shotgun wedding with the other half of the romantic equation was in order. I got my shotgun, literally, and set out to right any wrongs—or else. As luck would have it, the father turned out to be a stand-up guy and, without any prodding from me, up and married Sally. Sally gave birth to a baby boy and my mother had her first grandbaby. I prayed that this would have a stabilizing effect on my sister.

I was well aware that Sally and I had not turned out the way my mother had wanted. And I realized that neither of us had done her standing in the community any good. I also knew there was a big world out there and that I wanted to see it.

I had met some sailors at Port Isabel and hung out with them at the naval air station, listening to their stories of sailing the seven seas. I got the impression that their life was laid-back and romantic—nothing like working on a shrimp boat. To me all they did was hang around in their barracks listening to the radio, smoking cigarettes, and waiting for payday.

John Wayne's WW II movies had given me another view, especially one where he was in the Marine Corps and landed on Tarawa, a Japanese-held island in the South Pacific. John did a masterful job on those Japanese defenders and made me want to be a part of an outfit like that. Another film that had impressed me in those years was *Sayonara*. Michener's saga about post-war Japan and American occupation forces whetted my interest in Oriental culture and the exquisite sensitivity of Japanese women.

After some informal research, I got the notion that if I joined the service, especially the Marine Corps, I would probably be stationed in Japan. (Of course, if anyone had told me at the time John Wayne's real name was Marion and that he never served in the armed services or in combat, I would have attacked them then and there. It would have been like spitting on the flag.)

While I was contemplating how I was going to get the hell out of town, I continued my dissolute life. It was fun to cruise around in my customized black Mercury. When I rolled past a group of high school girls, they would scream and make a big fuss. I was a hero to a lot of the young high school guys, who feared me and revered me at the same time. It was a pretty heady experience. At seventeen, I thought I had been everywhere, done everything. I even had developed stomach ulcers, which the doctors linked to my chug-alugging tequila. I didn't exercise at all—I'd hop in my car just to go across the street. Even though I knew I had to change the direction my life was taking, it took a drunken car accident to make me admit it.

5

U.S.M.C.—The Turning Point

I will never forget that fateful Saturday night. The memory will remain etched in my mind forever. It was early March of '59. I was dragging home in the early morning hours after being up all night raising hell in Boys Town. There were a few things on my mind and I had been trying to drown them out with a bottle of tequila. I wasn't fully aware of it but I had several unopened bottles of the stuff rolling around on the floor of my 1950 Mercury two-door coupe.

Aside from being under the influence, I was driving home in a cold and rainy winter storm. The rain was coming down at a slant, but I didn't pay much attention to it. The alcohol in my system made me feel invincible. I followed my usual pattern, turning onto the main road that led to my house. Typically, when I got onto this road, I would put my car through all the gears and go 70 or 80 miles an hour before slowing down to take a left on the side street where I lived.

Obviously, my timing was off and, before I realized it, I had reached the street where I was supposed to turn. Cursing, I slammed on the brakes. Because of the rain and the slick roads, the wheels locked. My car started to skid. I turned the steering one way, no response; I turned it the other way, no response. The car just continued to skid. Immediately up ahead I saw a huge palm tree looming very large in my immediate future. As if in slow motion, I saw myself getting closer and closer. The rain was coming down harder than ever, the windshield wipers were clapping back and forth, and I knew I was going to hit that tree, head-on, at the speed of 60 or 70 miles an hour.

I made a split-second decision. I jumped into the back seat a fraction of a second before I hit the tree. The impact was so tremendous that it shoved the engine straight through the front seat. If I hadn't been in the back seat, I would have been killed instantly. For a moment of trembling shock, I just crouched there. It was about three in the morning. Neighbors began rushing out of their houses and I heard voices saying, "What's going on out there?"

The front of the car was elevated and stuck to the palm tree. As a couple of men pried open a door to extricate me from the wreck, a bottle of tequila rolled out of the car and hit the ground. Someone asked if I wanted an ambulance or the police. I sobered up fast and said, "No cops, just help me push this heap off the tree and to the side of the road."

I wasn't hurt, but my car was totaled. I didn't have any insurance and, as far as I was concerned, I didn't have any future. A few of the men helped me pull the car off the tree and push it to the side of the road. I walked, unsteadily, the remaining two blocks to my house. By now my mother had grown so conditioned to my late comings and goings that she no longer awoke when I came home late, regardless of the announcements made by her mighty mouse of a dog.

When I awoke the next morning, I realized that life as I had known it was over. Number one, I had no wheels. Number two, I didn't want to go on being a shrimper. In fact, I had developed a real aversion to shrimp. Number three, the cops told me to get out of town. It was a good thing I had been impressed by those John Wayne movies because they said to join the military "or else." As an added incentive, they intimated that if I joined up, they would seal my police record or even destroy the whole file.

Although I didn't know then how much I had romanticized the legend of "the few, the proud, the MARINES!" I did join. My dad had always said that if you played ball for the L.A. Rams or were a Marine, you had made it as a man. The clincher was the Marine's dress blue uniform. Once you compared the Navy sailor suit and dixie cup hat, as far as I was concerned there was no contest. What I did not suspect was the pain involved in earning the right to wear that fancy uniform.

The morning after the accident I trudged down to the Marine recruiter's office in downtown Brownsville. (Naturally, I had to walk the few miles to the recruiter's office.) When I got there, a Sergeant Chisholm had me fill out some forms making sure I could pass certain written exams. Sergeant Chisholm was a wily old salt, and his sales pitch was designed to make me question whether I was "man enough" to sign my life away for a four-year hitch with Uncle Sam. He even went so far as to promise me that if I signed on the dotted line he could have my record erased (sealed) at the police station.

I went home that evening and informed my mother of my bold plan. Despite her anguish about my leaving home, I thought I sensed a sign of relief in my mother's face. She said that she would sign as my legal guardian and give her consent to my joining the military. It didn't occur to me that my mom probably knew a little more about the Marines and what I was signing up for than I did, and was probably praying that the strict discipline would do me some good.

One thing I have to say about Constance Swanson is that for all the turmoil and grief I put her through, she was always on my side. She never wavered. Her love was truly unconditional and I believe that stood as the cornerstone or foundation of my better thoughts and decisions.

After I signed up and was given a date to proceed to a regional office in San Antonio where I would be given a physical and be sworn in, I got together with my buddies Willie, Gaston, and others. They were shocked and not too sure that I should make this momentous and irrevocable decision. There was sadness and melancholy in our conversation over beers at our favorite bar in Matamoros. I didn't know if I would ever see these guys again, but I knew the dye was cast.

When it was time to go to San Antonio, my mom drove me down to the bus station and waved good-bye to her prodigal son. After passing the physical I and a bunch of other guys were sworn in. I was now Private Swanson. I was flown to the Marine Corps Recruit Depot (M.C.R.D.) in San Diego. I was all puffed up with my new importance.

When the four-engine propeller-driven plane arrived in San Diego, I got off the plane and walked around the airport. I was surprised at the multitude of sailors all over the place. There were millions of them in their brand new suits and white dixie cup hats. I was in my civilian clothes but felt every inch the Marine. I pushed a few of these lowly swabs out of my way. This was my first trip to California and I didn't know that San Diego was a predominantly Navy town and the home of the Seventh Fleet.

After inquiring where Marine personnel were to check in, I walked outside and found a green truck with a Marine insignia. I was told to climb aboard. I had expected a bus. This was more like a dump truck with no tarpaulin cover or roofing. There was a gang of us new recruits holding on for dear life to the sides of this multipurpose vehicle as we drove the few miles to the Marine Corps Recruit Depot. The Depot was adjacent to the airport where planes were taking off night and day over the base.

Later, I would regard those flights as the free flying over the not so free. But at this point I was still on a high of gleeful anticipation; I didn't have the slightest idea of the fierce regimentation I was in for. This was a time for dwelling on the novelty and prestige of wearing my uniform and impressing the hell out of the local girls. Looking back, I can't believe I had never asked anyone about what went on in boot camp.

As soon as we arrived at the base, we all looked up at a billboard next to the entrance. It had a large skull and crossbones emblazoned on it. For some reason it succeeded in striking horror into my heart. Was it the shape of things to come? Months later I looked at the billboard again and realized it had been a public service announcement warning about drinking and driving; it didn't have anything to do with the Corps.

Once inside the gate, the truck stopped in front of some Spanish-style stucco buildings. We climbed over the sides of the truck to our new California reality. The first thing we saw was an enormous drill instructor; he must have been six and a half feet tall. He was wearing the regulation khaki shirt (emblazoned with rows of medals), green winter-wool trousers (with creases sharp enough to cut), and a "Smokey the Bear" campaign hat (held firmly in place with a leather strap across the back of his shaved head).

This symbol of authority immediately started yelling at us; he had a vicious look of hostility on his face. Being that we had just arrived, I was a little bewildered about why he seemed so pissed at us already. The drill instructor ("D.I.", as I would soon say) started mouthing off some vile obscenities: "Okay, you no good motherfuckin' maggots" (*maggot* seemed to be his favorite word), "it's my job to square you assholes away and try to make honest-to-god Marines out of you shit birds if I have to kill you to do it!"

I seriously wondered if the guy was sane. No one had ever called me those kinds of names before and I wasn't sure how to respond. I wasn't happy and I wasn't about to take all this abuse lying down. As the D.I. started to line us up in neat rows, I gave him a dirty look or two. Big mistake! He came over gave me a lot of "in your face" promises of dire punishment if I didn't go along with the program. I wisely kept my mouth shut.

We were then herded into some barracks where they proceeded to hack off all our hair. It was a very emasculating experience. It's amazing how much of your self-image is tied up in your hair. Your hair—how much you have, the color, and the hairstyle you wear—classifies you. It states your age, your individuality, and your socioeconomic class (real or affected). At first, it was funny to see all of us shorn like sheep. The humor quickly faded when we were issued green utility uniforms with no regard to fit. We could trade for a sized one later, we were told. At this point, we were a sorry lot—and we all looked alike.

From then on, everything I felt, heard, and was subjected to was in sharp contrast to my former life of margaritas, señoritas, and rock and roll. I began to wonder if it was too late for me to smile, apologize, and run like hell in the opposite direction. It soon dawned on me that in becoming a Marine, I had signed away what I thought were my inalienable rights of freedom.

First on the D.I.'s list of tortures was endless nonstop marching or running. I hadn't walked anywhere since getting motorized at age eleven. Now here were all these unsmiling drill instructors ordering me to march like some kind of wind-up toy, even when there was clearly no place of interest to go. We were formed into squads and platoons and taught to distinguish between our left and right foot. We could never be alone. If we went anywhere, it had to be on the double (running) and we had to say "sir" preceding every utterance, every statement, or every question. "Sir, yes sir!" Some of my fellow look-alike privates decided they had made an error in judgment and took the first opportunity to close down mentally. They just climbed the fence and went AWOL. I thought about it, but it seemed too drastic a step. And it would be unpatriotic. Anyway, I didn't want to embarrass my folks by becoming a fugitive from the military.

The worst of it for me was having all these barking strangers telling me what to do. Until now, I had never been seriously disciplined or ordered about by anyone. That, plus the lack of privacy in the barracks, really put me in a low mood. If you were a new recruit in the U.S. Marine Corps, no matter what you did you did it in plain sight of everyone. If you left your Quonset hut at night to go to the privy, you would be stopped by guards saying, "Halt! Who goes there?" You would stop to identify yourself and then proceed. Guards were everywhere; it was beginning to get claustrophobic.

Because of my deep resistance to taking orders (ancestral blood memory, I'm sure), I was in trouble from the start. The first time one of the noncoms (corporal rank and up) shouted at me, calling me *maggot*, etc. and demanding that I salute when addressed, I refused and gave him a dirty look instead. From then on, the lines were drawn. It became general knowledge that this Texas boy—meaning me—was going to be a real hard-ass.

Whatever I did, it was wrong. Whenever the D.I. wasn't yelling filthy insults at me, he chose some other form of punishment that convinced me he couldn't be playing by the book. There were countless times when, with little provocation, he'd just haul off and hit me about the head and shoulders and send me sprawling to the ground. As I kept picking myself up I thought, Jesus, if this keeps up I'll be dead in a few days. Nevertheless, I had a strong patriotic urge tugging away at me. I kept telling myself that John Wayne must have started this way so I had better hang in there.

After a few weeks of this daily restructuring of my world view, I was getting in better shape. I would rise every morning before the 5:00 A.M. wake-up call to wrap my ankles with Ace bandages. My ankles were not up to the daily punishment of running six miles before breakfast and then many more miles during the day. I suspect my bout with polio had something to do with my ankles taking the brunt of the pain. All I know is that I was reduced to tears a few times from the sheer agony of it.

One morning my platoon was heading over to the obstacle course where the routine was to run the course with pack and rifle. The pack weighed 70 pounds and the M-1 rifle, 9.6 pounds. The course entailed running, scaling fences, climbing ropes, jumping ditches and leaping over walls. There was one wall that tilted backwards and was just high enough that you had to run at it and try to glance off it sideways; if you were lucky you would reach high enough to gain a handhold on the top. Once you got your hand on the top of the wall, you could pull yourself up and over.

Hoping to impress the powers that be, I ran wildly at the tilting wall. I hit it full speed and flattened out against it like a cartoon character, before sliding slowly to the ground. I knew I had kicked the wall with my left heel but in the heat of the moment didn't think about it. It wasn't until the next day that I realized something was definitely wrong. As I limped along in formation, the D.I. came over and smacked me a few times to get me up to speed and to put a stop to my "malingering ways." By afternoon I had to report to sick bay. My leg had swollen up and I couldn't put any pressure on my left foot. (The left leg was the one affected by polio years earlier.)

An X ray revealed a broken heel. It called for a cast, which meant I would have to be transferred immediately to a special training platoon for the recuperative period. Since a broken heel can be slow to mend, I was told I could expect to be there for a month or so. Upon recovery I would be given a new platoon and graduate from boot camp a month later than my original group.

When I hobbled over to the special training platoon I soon realized that this wasn't going to be a walk in the park. It seems like they sent a lot of "shit birds" and "fuck-ups" to this outfit. The purpose of the special training platoon was to square away the recruits who didn't make the grade or fit in. The Corps wanted to weed out those people who were not physically or mentally fit. All day and usually into the night there was constant harassment, inspections, and a poke, poke, poke by the D.I. in charge. I'm sure even the D.I.s didn't relish riding herd over these boys who were somehow defective. As I remember, the only time we had to ourselves was when we lined up for roll call. The D.I. would give us the okay to light up a cigarette. If he was in a good mood he'd say, " The smoking lamp is lit." Even the nonsmokers lit up, since it was our only freedom.

Lucky for me I wasn't classified as a "screw-up." The poor bastards who had been sent to the special training platoon for other than medical convalescence were in deep shit. They were harassed unmercifully by the supervising officers. Sometimes they would take the recruits out on a run and make them hold heavy foot lockers over their heads; at other times, it was water buckets filled with sand. I even saw the D.I.s tie ropes to any recruits who couldn't keep up with their peers. If a recruit fell down during these runs, the D.I. would bark a few commands and the platoon would run right over him. Most people got out of the way but some did not.

After a month or so I was on the mend and ready to be assigned to a new platoon. Going back to basic training looked good to me after my detour in the special training outfit. Starting out fresh and repeating those tough first few weeks wasn't all bad. On our fourth or fifth week, we were bussed to a rifle range camp, Camp Roberts, now the site of the University of California, San Diego. It was pretty country and there was a tent camp to accommodate all the neophyte sharpshooters.

A few days before we were shipped out I had been assigned to mess duty. My job was to crack open hundreds and hundreds of eggs and throw them in a vat so the cooks could serve us up scrambled eggs in the chow line the next morning. I was doing a masterful job until I stopped to help a comrade at arms with a large carton that needed to be put in a refrigeration unit. He stepped ahead of me into the walk-in freezer and I followed blindly behind him, running smack dab into the step-up part of the freezer and putting a dent in my shin. I rolled around on the floor in pain knowing I had done serious injury, something you know by the tears in your eyes. I knew it.

I was afraid that if I told my superiors I had injured myself, they would send me back to the special training camp. I sure as hell didn't want to go back there, so I kept quiet. The next day I was on the bus to the rifle range. When we got there the D.I.s gave us a guided tour of the whole camp. They made us carry our sea bags (crammed full of everything we owned), crouch down, and walk like ducks. We walked for miles.

When the day was over, my wound had gone full bloom into a nasty infection. My foot swelled up so much they had to cut my boot and trousers off me when they got me to the hospital. The broken heel was a real inconvenience but this gash went right to the bone. When I got to the hospital, I had to wait an hour or two before they would dare take care of me. The Marine Corps doesn't have its own medical staff; they rely on the Navy to provide all the doctors and nurses, and they look down on the Marine "boots." Making you wait was the least of the contempt with which they treated you.

When my turn finally came around, I was brought hobbling into an emergency-type room. The naval corpsman assigned to provide paramedical help took a look at my festering wound, which by then had turned black. He called in a doctor who was amazed at the severity and the extent of the infection.

He then informed me that what we had here was gangrene, adding, "If you want to save that leg, we will have to operate immediately." "Okay," I said.

The next thing I knew, the doctor disappeared and the corpsman was preparing me for surgery. "Where's the surgeon?" I asked. The corpsman explained that he was it. They didn't waste real doctors on recruits. He gave me a rolled-up towel to bite on while he anesthetized the area by passing a device that looked like a fire extinguisher over the wound. With a quick pass of the dry ice cylinder, he began to cut a hole in my shin area the size of a silver dollar.

Well, the anesthetic wasn't working. I began to sweat like a pig and freeze at the same time. I was on fire and I was cold. I was shaking like a leaf. Time stood still while he scraped and scraped and scraped. I knew that even if he was successful in containing the gangrenous infection, I was going to be "fucked up" for a long time. The corpsman packed the gaping hole with some treated gauze and bandaged the wound. All the time I was biting down on the towel he had given me to stuff in my mouth.

After surgery I was admitted to a hospital ward reserved for Marines, mostly M.C.R.D. recruits. I was told I would be in the hospital at least six weeks. After being examined by the Navy doctor in charge of the ward, I was told that I might lose the leg. I was put in a traction-type device designed to keep my leg elevated, and told I would be given four penicillin shots a day—at 8:00, 12:00, 4:00 and 8:00.

I was furious that I had not been operated on by a surgeon and I certainly hadn't cared for the corpsman's attitude. The threat of being a peg-leg had me in shock and turmoil. It looked as though my life might be over before I had a chance to go in search of the Holy Grail.

The next day I was fully bedridden. I couldn't even go to the head without help. The Navy doctor in charge of the ward and his hospital nurse come over to my bed to check my chart. Then he surprised me by saying, "Private Swanson, since you happen to be in a ward populated exclusively by your fellow Marines, we've decided to put you in charge of them."

I mumbled, "Huh?" and I pointed out that I was in traction, I was still feverish and, probably most important, I was just a recruit private. Not only that but how could I be in charge when some of the patients were of higher rank and almost all of the hundred or so men were immobile? The doctor said he had faith in me and my ability to keep order in the ward. I was to assign duties, such as head cleaning, scrubbing and waxing the floors, dispensing medicine, and generally keeping track of the patients.

Why they saw me as a capable leader I couldn't figure out, especially in the condition I was in. But mine was not to reason why. I was in charge and that was that.

Hanging around in a hospital ward is akin to prison. You can look out at the world passing you by and reflect on all those workaday people going about their daily activities. In the Marine Corps I was beginning to learn a lot about the military mindset and here in the hospital I was observing how human beings dealt with infirmities of all kinds. I saw hundreds of men come and go in the hospital ward; some were there for serious illnesses or injuries, and some for congenital imperfections that rendered them incapable of completing boot camp. Some were seasoned soldiers who had drinking or drug problems. Being around a diverse section of humanity representing every ethnic background, religion, and social class certainly gave me a perspective on society I hadn't had before. I saw us as all locked up together.

My leg wasn't getting better. I had to soak my wound every day in a poisonous purple liquid. I was given every sort of pill in addition to those four penicillin shots a day. After awhile there was nowhere on my rear that had not been repeatedly punctured. It got to the point where if I got one more shot I thought I would freak out. Luckily, they stopped the treatment. The gangrene had affected the bone. The doctors were unsure of my prognosis. It was clearly up to a higher power to decide the fate of my leg.

Running the ward, as it turned out, saved me from focusing constantly on my own problems and how my medical condition was going to affect my future. I began my "tour of duty" by doing whatever chores the doctors or nurses needed done. We had all kinds of barter gigs going and, since I was in charge of dispensing medicine, including sleeping pills, I became quite powerful on the ward. I soon encountered the resistance I expected to my being in charge. Realizing I would need some coercive force to manage this particularly sensitive situation, I did what I had learned to do years ago: I set up a cadre of bodyguards, picking the biggest, ablest, and meanest men as my representatives.

One of my enforcers was a tall (six-foot-six-inches) skinny orange picker from California. He had occasional seizures when under too much stress and was in the hospital for observation. He claimed it was an automobile accident that caused the problem and gave him the facial scars we could all see. He was one of our local ward heroes because his last seizure had been brought about by a very unlucky drill instructor he had beaten the hell out of, along with a few more of his type who had tried to break it up.

I witnessed a seizure or two of his. It appeared that when he snapped, all of his strength would flow to his hands and he would become so powerful that he could bend steel bars. Under the most benign conditions, Slim was not an easy fellow to restrain but, luckily, he was devoted to me. Slim made a perfect bodyguard. In return he had my assurance that he would not get any shit details.

While I was in residence we had a few suicide attempts to clean up after. The guys' favorite way out was to slit the wrists in the white tiled shower room. Another choice was to drink poison. A couple of guys drank the same kind of purple medicine I used for soaking my leg; they didn't die but they were a little the worse for wear. The suicide attempters were quickly hustled out of the hospital and then given a medical discharge under what was called a "Section Eight."

After a few weeks of medical incarceration, I seemed to be on the mend. My "smoking lamp" was always lit, I ate three meals a day, and my leg was showing improvement. All during those weeks of convalescence, however, I harbored a hatred for the Navy corpsman who had performed what I regarded as a Mickey Mouse operation on my leg and shin. I swore that if I ever got out of boot camp, I would hunt that butcher down and strangle him with my bare hands. But, despite his clumsiness, the guy did manage to get all of the poison out of the wound. What saved me then was the four booster shots of penicillin I got every day for weeks.

When I was released from the hospital, the fact that I could actually walk without limping convinced me I was in prime condition to continue my training. But, acting under orders from the Marine Corps' top brass, an officer approached and said, "After your surgery and long hospitalization, you probably want your release from the Corps; am I right?" "No, sir. If it's all the same to you, I'd like to stay on and finish my training." The officer pointed out that the Corps had already invested a small fortune in me and that, if I wanted out, they were prepared to give me an honorable discharge. He didn't add the words "just get rid of you," but I caught his meaning. I thought it was damned unfair of the Marines to blame me for a couple of accidents. And besides, I couldn't go back home and face my mother and all my buddies and tell them I couldn't make it or had been thrown out of the Marines for being accident-prone. What would my father think? Although he had been writing me, he had shown little support; he even wrote once that he didn't feel I was man enough to make it through boot camp. With these thoughts running through my head, I began to plead with the lieutenant to give me one more chance. He finally agreed.

Once again, I had to start my training from scratch. I was sent to a platoon that had just formed. Standing among all these raw recruits in their spanking new uniforms, there I was with my washed-out old-salt outfit. I had even spit-shined my boots until they looked like mirrors. My new D.I.s took one look at me and flipped. They saw me as a potentially bad influence on their charges. First, they beat the shit out of me. Then, they made me scrub my boots with a brillo pad. Generally, they did everything in their power to get me to quit. I'm proud that I never fell out on a run or a forced march. I stuck with it.

Luckily for me, the true test of a Marine was to become an expert rifleman. The opportunity to become familiar with firearms had been one of my various reasons for joining the

Marines. I had already handled guns back home, so when my new platoon got to the Camp Roberts rifle range, I knew my salvation was at hand. Our platoon had another guy named Bob Swanson who was known to the brass as the "good Swanson," but that all changed when it became obvious that I was a natural with a rifle. The so called "good Swanson" couldn't qualify and he became a liability to our outfit. I qualified as an "expert" and ultimately became the best shot in the whole battalion.

Almost overnight my status changed from camp shit bird to heroic sharpshooter. Now my superiors could take credit for having a real champion in their platoon. In the Marines, this kind of expertise meant a lot. By the time I finished basic training I was promoted to private first class and awarded my first stripe. This was much closer to the triumphant movie scenario I had envisioned for myself when I first thought of joining up.

By the end of six months I graduated. It was a formal graduation ceremony replete with military bands, parades passing in review, speeches, hats thrown in the air, and families in attendance. My mother very happily flew in for the festivities, but not my father. I don't know why he didn't show. Maybe he didn't want to see my mother, maybe he couldn't afford the trip—whatever the reason, it hurt not having him there.

After six months behind barbed wire, I was ready for some R & R, but it was not to be. My orders were to go directly to Camp Pendleton Marine Base. It was about an hour's drive north of M.C.R.D. A few hours after graduation, I was on a bus heading north. Camp Pendleton meant another month of advanced infantry training—more running, calisthenics, and special weapons training. My steady aim and expert marksmanship continued to hold me in good stead with the professional gyrenes and I really enjoyed the hand-to-hand combat training and boxing.

Pendleton was the home base of the First Marine Division. There were 40,000 men on the base. Advanced infantry training was harder than boot camp, but I was finally given a ten-day leave before I was to be shipped off to foreign shores.

After all the months of training, it was wonderful to get leave. I went straight to Kilgore to see my dad for a couple of days, before going on to Brownsville. After six months of early to bed and early to rise, good healthy food and rugged training, I was in great shape. I could now run twenty miles with pack and rifle and had earned the right to wear the Marine insignia—globe and anchor with an eagle perched on top.

When I got home my dad suggested we take in a movie in the neighboring town of Longview after he closed up shop. Around sundown we left with his long-standing girlfriend, another nurse. Mrs. Savage was a fine "widow woman" who had successfully raised six sons and one daughter. Her sons had joined every branch of the armed services.

My dad let me drive and off we went. I was in my dress-green winter uniform with my PFC chevron proudly in evidence. Dad's car was a fast, 1957 V-8 Studebaker with fins. It was the top of the line Golden Eagle, whose styling was ahead of its time.

As I was driving carefully down the highway, glad to be alive and really enjoying driving again and, especially, not being under military supervision, we came upon some traffic congestion due to road construction. My father, not too comfortable with someone else driving, started yelling at me to slow down. About the second time he yelled at me, all the pent-up anger I felt for him welled up and exploded. I slammed on the brakes. Tires screeching, the car skidded off the highway onto the dusty shoulder of the road. I jumped out of the Studebaker, slammed the door hard, and yelled "get out of the car." I was filled with murderous intent and resolved to settle this old score with my dad.

He and his girlfriend gave me a piercing look and Dad reached over and locked the driver's side door. They let me stand there until I got control of myself. I finally got back in the car on the passenger side; Dad was at the wheel and Mrs. Savage sat between us. After that episode, I didn't go to see my dad for about ten years.

Once back in Brownsville, I made the rounds to show all my old buddies how good I looked in my uniform and military hat, to catch up on the gossip and goings-on, and, of course, to give the local gals a look at the whole new me.

It was great to see my mother and be able to tell her about my experiences in boot camp. I finally had done something for her to be proud of. I also took advantage of my new-found prowess in hand-to-hand combat to beat up on a few of my old enemies. Sweet revenge. I even wound up with a cute blond I pried loose from one of my male targets.

Money was tight for a young Marine. No one had warned me about the low pay. I was making about $60 or $70 a month, even with my promotion. Off the base, just my basic upkeep and a few meals would wipe out this pittance fast. I had made more money in two weeks shrimping than I now made in a year. Still, I duly impressed my old buddies Neil and Willie and a couple of others, enough so that as soon as they graduated the following summer they joined the Corps. They thought if I could make it, it must be a breeze. I smiled reading their letters from boot camp. I even sent cookies to Willie. The D.I.s love it when a "maggot" gets cookies from home. I know because Willie's mom had sent me some cookies while I was struggling though boot camp. They made me eat every one of them, then and there, as I was running in place in a bucket of water. Then I had to run a few miles to a dipsy dumpster and throw away the package. I never found out what they did to Willie, but I'm sure it was memorable.

At the end of my leave, I took a Greyhound bus (welcome to the real world, Private First Class Swanson) out to El Toro, a Marine Corps air base near Anaheim, California. There I was given my first assignment: I was to be shipped off to Japan. My ship was scheduled to leave the port of L.A. in a few days.

Just before I got on board, I did call my dad to let him know I was headed overseas. (I had a feeling that I might not be coming back. There had been a lot of scuttlebutt about outbreaks of Communist aggression in Korea, Pakistan, China, and India. To a melodramatic seventeen-year-old, my chances of getting killed seemed huge.) My dad told me that he couldn't talk long—something about the cost of a long distance phone call, and, by the way, he just heard that my sister Sally had run off on her baby boy, leaving her husband to raise him. I was stunned. After all Sally and I had been through, I never imagined she could do something like that.

Outside of this family fiasco, I couldn't believe my luck. When I joined the Marines, I had a gut feeling that I was going to be stationed in the Orient, probably Japan. It was so romantic and exciting, I could hardly stand it. I felt that I knew the culture from medieval times. It was almost a past-life thing, even though I didn't believe in past lives—not that I had given it much thought. According to my understanding, life was a one-shot deal and in the end you were sternly judged by a patriarchal guy with a white beard, and you didn't get another chance.

All I knew was that I had dreams that included visions of misty, old-world oriental cities with intricate, maze-like, meandering streets dotted with houses made of wood, paper, and bamboo. If I hadn't joined the Marines I could have lived my whole life without ever having the opportunity to visit Japan. And now here was Uncle Sam, providing me with this seaworthy magic carpet, a troopship, all expenses paid. It was the answer to this young Texan's dream. Like John Wayne, I too was off to start a brave new adventure, and maybe even get the girl in the end. On board the troop ship, I used to sit out in a lifeboat late into the night smoking Pall Mall cigarettes, and dreaming about the mysterious Orient. The adventures I foresaw would later come true.

The voyage across the Pacific took about thirteen days. My shrimp boat experience served me well: While my shipmates spent most of their time throwing up, I sat around chatting with the old "gyrenes," as they liked to call themselves. I loved listening to their war stories from WW II and Korea. Those who had spent many tours in the Orient talked about "getting a ranch" as soon as they landed in Japan; in Marine talk, that meant finding an amenable Japanese girl and shacking up in some apartment or house a little way out of town, comfortably away from the base. That scenario seemed ideal to me. I couldn't wait to get there fast and start "ranching."

The old salts with a couple of hash marks on their uniform sleeves (each stripe on the lower sleeve represents a three- or four-year tour of duty) told me how much the Japanese women loved "Amelican Malines," not just for our money but because we treated women with more respect. They also talked about the flourishing black market and the enormous profits that could be made selling contraband goods. Profits and women, what more could this strapping seventeen-year-old adventurer ask for?

The voyage served as a kind of training course for me, giving me an idea of just what to expect when I landed in Japan. I spent many a moonlit night planning how I was going to prosper in the "shadow world" of the black marketeer. The newness of it all was staggering; it gave me a feeling I was living in another century. I was living a South Texas version of Marco Polo, with visions of exotic conquest in foreign lands.

As the troop ship neared the Japanese coast, we began to see the characteristic bows and sails of Chinese style junks called *sampans*. My heart pounded. We were close and getting closer. We landed in the Japanese port of Yokohama. As our ship pulled into the harbor, clearly visible were the WW II fortifications our boys would have had to take by force had the war not been ended by the atom bomb fourteen years earlier.

As we disembarked from the ship, we were taken to a military base and given our new duty assignments. Unfortunately, things had a nasty habit of not turning out the way I wanted or expected. Here I am in Japan, on my dream assignment with my orders processed, and where was I assigned? To a Marine air wing squadron in the Philippines. Crestfallen, I realized I would have to put all those impossible dreams on hold for a long time.

I was in Japan for one day, just enough time for a fast look at Yokohama's terrain, buildings, and people. Then, along with other Marines, I was bussed to Tachikawa, a nearby Air Force base, where we were put on a prop-driven DC-3 plane of WW II vintage and flown to the Philippines. We were loaded off the troop plane in Subic Bay, 50 miles from

Manila, at 2:00 in the morning. The temperature was over a hundred degrees and it was extremely humid. It was the kind of air you could breathe through a straw, and there we were, in full-dress winter green uniforms, drenched in sweat. Welcome to your new home!

I kept wondering if a war had been declared behind my back. Why were we here? True, the year 1959 was mostly a time of peace, but many cold-war scares and rumors had been circulating about. There were fuming conflicts between Taiwan and Communist China at this time, as well as border disputes between India and China.

We were billeted in newly constructed, air-conditioned Navy barracks on the base for a night or two. At night, they let us hang out at the enlisted men's club, a big Victorian building on a mountainside overlooking the harbor of Subic Bay. The naval base and air base was immense. When you looked over the harbor, you could see that it was one of the largest protected natural harbors in the world. The whole Seventh Fleet seemed to be in port. I soon realized that there were thousands and tens of thousands of Navy swabbies and only a few hundred Marines.

After a few beers at the enlisted man's club (The "E" club, I started to get into the swing of things, literally. The next morning I had a gargantuan hangover and I could hardly see out of either eye.

We were rustled out of our fancy living quarters, loaded into huge cattle trucks, and driven to the top of a mountain where we were surrounded by thick, impenetrable jungle. The only hint of civilization we could detect was a bunch of pre-WW II huts propped up on stilts. I found out later that the Japanese soldiers had lived in these huts after they had been liberated by the Filipino and U.S. forces in 1941.

"This is where you guys will be staying," announced the Navy yeoman who had driven us up the mountain. I was having strong doubts about the shoddy accommodations when the wise guy added, "You didn't really think we'd let you slobs stay down with the Navy personnel, did you? No way!" Then he broke up laughing, climbed into the truck, and headed back down the mountain to civilization.

I had wanted adventure: it looked like I was up to my eyeballs in it now. We were assigned bunks and given bedding and mosquito netting. I thought the bugs were big in Texas! In these tropical islands of Mindanao, they were huge. I still didn't know why I was here or what an "air wing" of the Marine Corps was all about. But by now I knew you didn't ask questions; you accepted your fate and made the best of it. Someone was always around to remind you that everyone in the Corps had signed up voluntarily.

I was assigned to the motor transport outfit, not a duty I had requested. I would probably be driving a truck, which I had to admit was about the only thing I could do that they could use, despite my gradual discovery that my sense of direction was faulty. After getting settled in my living quarters, I was given a ride down the mountain to peruse the Marine portion of the Naval air base and check out the motor transport section. When it got dark that night I noticed Filipino guards walking around with German Shepherd guard dogs. I was informed that if those dogs ever got loose, I should drop to the ground and cover my jugular. It seemed that without the guard dogs and our own Marine sentries, complete trucks and even cranes would be dismantled and made to disappear overnight. I wish they had stolen the tire irons and pickaxes used to fix flats.

As it turned out, since I was the newest addition to the motor transport, I was to have the shit-bird job of busting tires. They handed me a pickaxe, a couple of tire irons, and told me I'd learn as I went. The trucks were 25-ton gasoline tankers and 18- wheelers. The tires on these babies were bigger than I was. When you popped a rim off the tire, it would pop straight up in the air. If you were unfortunate enough to get in the way, you wouldn't have to worry about tire shop detail anymore.

I got so good at it that they kept sticking me with this backbreaking duty. The tire shop was near the bay, which meant that the sun reflected off the water onto the white rocks that covered the area and cooked me every day, at 120 degrees or more. My nose and the back of my neck blistered and peeled on a regular basis. I even got a dark tan through my T-shirt. I still have scars on the back of my neck from this posh duty station. Each morning I would pray that the old gunny sergeant would assign me to a different work detail. No such luck.

At the end of my shift, I would return to the barracks where we routinely used bayonets to poke holes in the floor to let out the accumulated rainwater—to find a pygmy, *negrito,* sleeping in my bunk. I would have to chase him out of the hut and delouse my bed before I could even lie down. Looking out into the jungle, only yards away, you had no idea who or what was out there. There were a lot of monkeys about; some of the guys even kept them as pets. They were filthy little bastards, cute in a frightening, human sort of way. At least they ate all the bugs in sight.

When I was busting those huge truck tires, I started thinking of ways to get out of this rugged duty before I had a sunstroke. My only relief came at night when the guys and I could dress casually in our civvies, Filipino shirts with fancy embroidery, and take a bus down the mountain to the nearby town of Olongopo. This Sodom and Gomorrah town of the Philippines had a population of 100,000 indigenous people. There were hundreds of whorehouses, strip joints, pawnshops, and bars of every description and illicit preference.

For me, it was almost like being back home in good old Boys Town, except that it was a lot bigger and I had to contend with thousands of sailors. The swabbies were recognizable because all sailors on liberty had to wear their uniforms. Almost every time I hit Olongopo I got into a fight. We would be in a bar, drinking San Miguel beer (General MacArthur's family owned the brewery) and a fight almost always broke out. If I wasn't fighting with the Navy boys, one of my own kind would invariably start something. I learned to watch for flying beer bottles and glass ashtrays. Those ashtrays were dangerous; I have scars on the back of my head to prove it.

Sometimes the officer in charge of our motor transport outfit would come into the bar where a bunch of us Marines hung out and yell, "Marines, follow me." We would all pile into taxis waiting outside—the taxis were open, long-bed

jeeps decorated in a garish manner—and speed to the other
end of town and jump into the fray. It was great. On occasions
like these, the M.P.s would come with guns and nightsticks
drawn and try to break it up. There were some great escapes,
up and over fences, and climbing out windows.

The girls were plentiful and reasonably priced, one more
reminder of my life in Matamoros. Filipino girls were an
exotic kind of a cross between Oriental and Spanish. The
more light-skinned Spanish-looking ones were on the top
of the social scale. I should say that I was awfully lucky in
that never in my life have I caught a venereal disease. Thank
God. I remember one time in Olongopo I took a gal home
and jumped into bed with her, ready for a tryst, when she
pointed to a fresh puncture mark on her derriere. She informed
me she had the clap and that sex was out. Besides dampening
my ardor, it reminded me that I was going to have to be
real careful.

The Filipinos spoke a native dialect called Tagalog. To
my utter surprise, all of their curse words were the same as
Mexican Spanish. All in all, I felt right at home. The people
I met were warm and, for the most part, laid back. Their
mañana attitude could teach the Mexicans a thing or two.
Only if you insulted their religion did you have to watch
out.

One time I was playing pool for money with some buddies.
I was trying to make a winning shot and I made the sign
of the cross hoping for divine guidance. The whole bar went
silent. You could hear a pin drop. Seems I had seriously
blundered: I had made a religious sign in an inappropriate
place (a bar) and for an inappropriate reason (pecuniary gain).
This grizzled old dude came over to me, his gun and holster
visible under his jacket. Smiling and revealing his gold teeth,
he said, "You'd better leave." Realizing I was on shaky ground
and had just committed a cultural faux pas, I and my buddies
beat a hasty retreat.

Even though we'd go to Olongopo at night, we were
almost never given overnight passes and we were warned
about taking any sightseeing tours of the countryside. The
Communist insurgents, called HUKS, were in control of the

roads. I don't know if they were really Communists, but that's the way they were described by the powers that be. After all my tire-changing experiences, I was hot to take up my rifle and have a go at these banditos. I wasn't a warmonger, but once again my future was looking grim.

One morning as I was hanging around the motor transport office waiting to be sent to the tire shop, a senior noncom yelled out, "Does anyone here know how to drive an 18-wheeler, jet fuel tank trailer?" Even though I had never been inside the cab of a diesel truck and didn't have a military driver's license, I yelled "Yo!" The Sergeant Major told me to jump in this monster truck and trailer and take it to the fuel storage tanks, fill it up, and go down to the flight line. I jumped in and, with gears grinding, managed to get the hell out of the motor transport yard. Before the day was over I got the routine down pat and talked the office clerk into issuing me a license with the highest truck limit, 25 tons. From here on out, I was driving everything the military had, from 18-wheelers to fork lifts. The tire shop became a bad memory.

It turned out that the "Motor T" office clerks pushing the typewriters were buddies of mine—same age and rank bracket—and I found out that they were able to schedule who worked where or what received priority for shipping by truck. I also found that out of about 80 guys in the motor transport outfit I was one of the few guys with a stripe on my shoulders. Other than the honchos in charge, what we had here was the largest concentration of misfits ever assembled in one place. Most of them had been busted down in rank. The outfit seemed more like the French Foreign Legion, except that it was peopled mostly with farm boys from Georgia, South Carolina, and Mississippi with "19-inch necks." I was the only one that hadn't been busted and I had the smallest neck. It was fun to hit the town with this bunch of desperados. They didn't care about the future and they weren't afraid of the M.P.s.

In town, you could hardly see the buildings through the mass of humanity in little blue sailor suits with white hats. Although the unwritten rules were that Navy and Marine personnel use separate whorehouses and bars, it rarely worked out that way. But when one branch of the service failed to respect the turf of the other, a bloody battle would be the catastrophic result.

It was during these fights that I began to suspect that maybe I wasn't as tough as I thought I was. After a few drinks, I was positive I could whip any ten Navy guys, but the reality was that I was spending way too much time on my hindside. It also became clear that I was being picked on by some of the 19-inch-neck Marines who felt that they would have no trouble clobbering me into the dust. These fights convinced me to sign up for some self-defense boxing classes given on the base. It wasn't until later when I was finally assigned to Japan that I took this training seriously and began boxing on a team.

Meanwhile, weeks were turning into months in the Philippines. Even though I was driving trucks most of the time, there were still some times when the higher powers made me use my back. If there was nothing to do, they would have the lowly private-first-class types move boxes from one side of the motor transport yard to the other. One time I went to get a fork lift to facilitate the move. The top sergeant just smiled and told me we shouldn't waste the gas. The prevailing line of thought was "a bitching Marine is a happy Marine."

I didn't know how long our Marine Air Squadron was going to be in the P.I., but I knew that I wasn't cut out for this grueling work and sweating my rear off in the steamy Filipino climate. One day I saw something that told me help might be on the way at last. I noticed a huge black limousine drive by with all the windows rolled up. Since it was high noon and 120 degrees at the time, this told me that whoever was inside was reveling in the joys of air conditioning. I knew there had to be some way I could get behind the wheel of that car chauffeuring some high-ranking Marine officer sitting in the back seat.

At that time I didn't know anything about the higher command structure. When you're busting tires day in and out, that doesn't concern you very much. After some snooping around, I found out that a corporal had this august job of driving the C.O. around. He didn't mingle with us low-lifes, which explained why I hadn't noticed him. I started asking around about how I could get this job when, serendipitously, the corporal had an accident that broke his leg. To my great joy, the sergeant major tracked me down and said, "Swanson, go put on your best uniform and report to headquarters. You've been chosen as Colonel Andrew's new driver."

The colonel was an imperious looking guy in his late forties. He was the highest ranking Marine officer on the base and a highly decorated Marine aviator. His job was to make sure that our air group and four or five squadrons of jet fighter planes were combat-ready. As our air group moved from island to island in the Pacific, it was up to him to organize the ships that would carry the men and materials to the next destination. It was a big job, and if he excelled in this duty he would be assured a general's star at the end of his tour. The colonel also had the power to order the use of nuclear weapons. Our air wing always kept two jet aircraft, armed with atomic bombs, running at the flight line so that, if ordered, we could strike anywhere in the Far East.

The colonel seemed to find me a lot of fun to be around, both because of my enthusiasm for getting things done and because I reminded him of himself when he was young. Right after I started driving for the colonel, our air wing squadron got orders to move out. We were to be stationed in Taiwan, an island off the coast of China, where at that time there were rumblings of war. The Chinese Communists were using aircraft and long-range artillery to shell the offshore islands of Kwi Moi and Matsu, trying to take them away from the Taiwanese government.

I was sent with an advance team to help prepare a tiny air base named Ping Tong. My job was to help set up living quarters and amenities for my colonel. The landing craft we were on had a top speed of about three knots and so it took a couple of weeks to get from the Philippines to Taiwan—a very slow boat to China indeed. As we were poking along in the South China seas heading for the seaport of Kowshung, we were buzzed by Chinese Communist MiGS. For a second,

I thought we were history. Of course, then I still believed in Pax-Americana and felt that if we were fired on we would be avenged.

When we got to Taiwan I was again met with as many new sights and smells as when we had landed in Japan and the Philippines. We were transported from Kowshung to the Ping Tong air base and I was amazed at the crush of humanity we saw en route. The Taiwanese had not yet been motorized and they rode bicycles by the hundreds of thousands. Our truck drivers had to lean on the horn and move very slowly so as not to squish anyone in the two-wheeled throngs.

As I said, I was the advance man for the colonel and his staff. My job was to make sure he had proper living accommodations, transportation, etc. I was only a PFC with one stripe, but I was fully empowered to commandeer any materials I needed to complete my assignment. I had to deal with the Navy, Marines, and the Chinese military. Pretty heady stuff for an eighteen-year-old. With no sergeant or officer around to supervise me, I had to make things happen on my own. I began to see the power I had when I started to invoke the colonel's rank and commanding officer status. Since I was the only motor transport person, I was put in charge of setting up a motor transport operation on the base until our Marine air group showed up a few weeks later.

If I needed trucks and jeeps I contacted the Chinese Marine detachment and they handed them over, complete with drivers. Once I set up a temporary Motor T outfit, I was told to oversee the building of an airstrip and to make the improvements needed for our F8-U fighter jets to land safely at the Ping Tong air base. Talk about flabbergasted. What did I know about building airstrips? To complete the runways, I worked my Chinese laborers day and night. My work crews soon started dwindling in number; some had to be hospitalized. They were not used to working long shifts. Their nutrition wasn't the same as ours and their custom was to work only a few hours at a time. I quickly received more people and managed to get the job done.

When the colonel flew into Ping Tong, I went back to driving him around; that was how I started seeing who and what was outside the base in the exotic civilian world on this island fortress. The C.O. had to meet with a lot of bigwigs, and it was an eye-opener to see how the high-ranking officers lived. If the colonel stayed in some swanky hotel in a large city, so did I. I might have the room in the basement, but it was still high-class stuff, and I wanted more.

The town outside the Ping Tong air base was different from Olongopo in the Philippines in that it hadn't seen American military personnel and so it wasn't set up with camp followers. One of the things I did while I was overseeing the base renovation was to organize the Chinese drivers into a nighttime bus shuttle into town. I charged a nominal fee. I really did well when the jet squadrons showed up. Even the pilots were required to pay. No one dared to complain to the C.O. for fear that I might have some influence with him and that I might be able to adversely affect his career.

One nice thing about working for the colonel was that I had to be on call 24 hours a day to take him anywhere he wanted to go. This meant that I got my own all-purpose liberty card and was not subject to checking in or out with the sergeant major in charge. The only other person who did not have to answer to anyone regarding his comings and goings was the C.O. himself.

The freedom of having no one to check in with meant that I wouldn't be put on any work details, guard duty, or other grunt job. Prior to having a liberty card, I would be chosen for a whole host of back-breaking jobs. I remember being put on guard duty for the 12:00 midnight to 4:00 A.M. shift, a long haul when you have to work the next day. The jet planes rolled in with some new air-to-air missiles called sidewinders. It was part of my assignment to help guard these missiles, which were America's secret weapon—one the Communist powers didn't have and were determined to steal. As I walked back and forth in the shadows with my rifle at the ready, I would always expect some enemy ninja to come up behind me and slit my throat. We were on a war alert and the rumor was that anyone caught sleeping on guard duty would be shot. It's amazing what your imagination can come up with when you are all alone, seemingly a million miles from home, walking guard duty on the graveyard shift.

I remember an incident that happened to me in the Philippines while I was walking guard duty around an armory building housing all our rifles. We stored our weapons to keep them from being stolen by the *negritos* or Filipinos, who seemed to have free reign of the base. On the black market, our American rifles were worth about 700 to 800 dollars (a year's pay to a PFC).

One particular night I was given the graveyard shift and told to guard the armory with my life, literally. Here I was in the middle of a hot humid jungle, dark as pitch, with exotic birds calling to one another in the night and monkeys swinging from vine to vine. I walked around with a 12-gauge shotgun, fully cognizant that if a HUK guerilla or even some black marketeer had half a chance, I could be a goner.

Nervously, I walked my rounds with no Marine personnel within hearing distance, when what do I hear but a very loud "fuck you." My hair stood straight up and my heart stopped as my hands and arms were wildly trying to crank a buckshot round into the chamber of the 12-gauge shotgun. As I strained to see my foe, expecting a multitude of attackers, I saw instead a very large lizard; it was at least a couple of feet in length. It looked like an iguana, and it belched out another garbled "fuck you!" After the shock wore off, I cracked up. Thank God I didn't shoot that son-of-a-bitch. I would never have lived it down.

By the time the air wing squadrons arrived at Ping Tong I had become close to the Chinese servicemen assigned to work for me on the airstrip. Some of these men were officers in the Chinese Army; many were university educated and spoke English. I was amazed at the disparity in our pay structure. Even as a private first class I made more in a month than they made in a year. I had met men who were officers in the Chinese Army or Air Force applying for menial jobs on their time off. The Chinese officers enjoyed taking me to outlying towns and exchanging knowledge about our respective cultures. They seemed to appreciate that I didn't put on the air of superiority they had encountered in American officers.

Besides familiarizing me with their local customs, my new Chinese friends introduced me to the night spots off the base. I frequented one high-class nightclub that catered to an older and more elite crowd than I was used to. Taiwan wasn't anything like Olongopo or my Mexican experiences. As soon as you got away from the tawdry bars and camp followers that are ubiquitous wherever military bases are located, it was apparent that the Chinese culture was rather straight-laced.

One night at this club I was introduced to an exquisite Taiwanese girl by the name of Charmaine Chung Yu. Damned if I didn't fall in love for the first time in my life. True, I was only eighteen, but I knew it was for real. I had never experienced such feelings before.

Charmaine was breathtaking to look at; her figure was voluptuous and petite, and she was extremely well-educated. She spoke Russian, English, Japanese, and various dialects in Chinese. I discovered that she was from a well-to-do family. (Her surname brought looks of surprise to the faces of my Chinese friends.) She was a year or two older than I and, as I found out later, her ambition in life was to marry an American and become a U.S. citizen.

The mix of being in the exotic Orient, the war scare with mainland China, and this gorgeous girl at my side had my blood pumping faster than it ever had. Now it became clear why I had signed up. The Chinese plum wine and the stir-fry wok cooking wasn't bad either. Of course, there were some dark sides. I saw poverty that was startling. Taiwan was trying to feed millions of people who had fled the mainland and, as a result, there was a severe food shortage. You didn't see any dogs or cats on this island for that reason. Even the rats were not safe from the hoards of hungry people. I was increasingly aware of how privileged life was in the States.

Charmaine and I spent every spare moment together. Now that my only job was driving the C.O. around, most of my time was spent running my bus line and bartering U.S. goods or American greenbacks with the locals.

After a few months, the war hysteria centered around these offshore islands died down and life settled into a monotonous routine in our tent cities. Rumors started that we would be heading to Korea where there were problems between the north and south. To keep the Communist Koreans at bay apparently called for a show of force by the U.S.

Charmaine was pressuring me to make an honest woman out of her. I was thrown because even though I loved her I hadn't given marriage a thought. I couldn't conceive of the responsibility of marriage, especially on private-first-class pay. Before we could begin to argue about our personal future together, the air wing was instructed to pack up everything and head to the nearest port. We were off to Korea.

This was the first time I had been forced to part from a girl I was in love with. What a traumatic experience. Charmaine and I had vowed everlasting love to each other. She promised to wait for me and I, in turn, promised to come back to Taiwan no matter what I had to do to make it happen. As I climbed aboard the ship in Kowshung, Charmaine was there waving goodbye. The realization that we were parting, and that it might be forever, felt like a punch in the stomach. These uncontrollable feelings welled up inside of me. It was the first time, but not the last time, a girl would have such an effect on me.

As we shipped out to Korea I was on another one of those slow-moving WW II landing crafts. The front of the ship had two large doors that opened to disgorge the cargo. I was with the motor transport troop again, and it hadn't changed any; it was still an army of misfits. Being the colonel's fair-haired boy had no effect on my living quarters: I was stuck in the hole of that ship with hundreds of other Marines. We spent about two weeks getting to the Korean peninsula. Too bad the laundry facilities weren't a little better; we were a smelly bunch by the time we arrived. Still, it was a relief to awaken one morning to "Land Ho" off the starboard bow. I stared out at the ominous-looking terrain of the Korean coast. The mountains were bleak and it took me awhile to realize what was missing: there were no trees. The whole country was like that. All the trees had been chopped down for fuel during the war a few years earlier.

We accomplished an amphibious landing on the coast, and it was quite an experience. We had to climb over the side of the ship on to a large rope ladder leading down to a small landing craft bobbing around a hundred feet below. There was a trick to boarding the small landing craft which swayed away from the mother ship. If you weren't careful, you could get caught between the boats. Once ashore I helped set up the command post and waited around for the C.O. He never showed up so I freelanced and served as a driver for whoever needed transportation. Not bad duty.

I mentioned earlier that my sense of direction wasn't my strong point. One day it almost got me and a whole column of Marines killed. I had been told to drive my jeep at the head of an armored column consisting of troop trucks, huge Sherman tanks, and various supply trucks. We were driving along a dusty, dried-up river bed in the summer heat. You had to wear a bandana over your face because a quarter inch of dust enveloped everything. As I led the tank column down the dusty makeshift road between North and South Korea in the middle of the much publicized demilitarized zone, I misread the map and took a right when I should have taken a left. We were headed right into Communist-held North Korea. As we rolled along, my mistake became apparent and we halted fast. Unfortunately, since we were in a narrow ravine on a dusty river bed, the trucks and tanks couldn't turn around. After much consternation, expressed in yelling, screaming, and flinging of epithets, we backed out of there with weapons at the ready. Thank God they didn't shoot. I was never asked to lead a column again. In fact, I was given the job of driving a Marine gunny sergeant and a Republic of Korea (ROK) army sergeant who had been given the job of paying for damages to the Korean countryside by our U.S. forces. The Marine sergeant and the Korean sergeant would estimate damage to roads, bridges, or rice paddies and pay cash money on the spot.

The Koreans I came in contact with were the toughest bunch of people I've ever seen. They all spoke Japanese because they had been invaded early in the century by Japan. The Samurai military leaders, it seems, decreed that all Koreans learn Japanese in one year. After the year was up, they summarily lopped off the head of anyone caught speaking Korean. At least that's the way I heard it.

Driving the Korean sergeant around to areas our troops had passed through gave me a chance to see how Korean politics worked. It was gunpoint diplomacy. We would go into a village and the Korean Army sergeant with his pistol very much in evidence would go up to a local and demand water to wash up; then he would more or less interrogate the village head man and, finally, the American and Korean sergeants would pay for crop or road damage caused by our forces.

When there was free time, I set to work establishing my trading business. My first big coup came when I found out that the Korean country folk loved our military "C" rations, especially the cans of fruit cocktail. I immediately requisitioned all the fruit cocktail in the area and set out for the nearest village. I found the local bordello and made a deal with the best-looking lady I could find. We had been warned of the phenomenal VD rate amongst these folks so I took the proper precautions. I became somewhat of a celebrity among my Marine buddies for my fruit cocktail exploits.

Once again, war fears died down and our fighter squadrons were ordered to a former Japanese island, Okinawa. Okinawa is a large fortress in the Pacific with a multitude of American military bases for army parachute divisions, air bases, naval installations, you name it. I still can't believe it, but I was chosen to be flown in to Okinawa to reopen an old military base and make sure it was habitable for the 1,500 Marines that made up our air wing. I was given two privates to assist me. I didn't even know where Okinawa was, but orders were orders.

We got on a flight to Kadina Air Base on Okinawa and then hitched a ride to the defunct base we had been assigned to spruce up. It was a mess. There were hundreds of WW II Quonset huts that had to be made habitable. First, we had to scrounge all over the island for bunks, mattresses, blankets, etc. and then we had to clean the years of accumulated dirt out of these living spaces. The Army, Navy, and "fly boys," of course, got fancy brick barracks; we got the dregs. Again, when our guys showed up we were ready for them.

The Okinawan gals were kimono-clad and were the closest I had yet gotten to Japan. The women were much more reserved than the women I had met in the Philippines or Taiwan.

Okinawa was truly a tiny island; you could drive a jeep around the entire island in one day. It gave new meaning to the term "rock fever." During my stay on this tomb of an island (thousands of American Marines died to claim it, and over a hundred thousand Okinawans and Japanese died defending it), I managed to wrangle a leave at a time when the colonel was away. Charmaine and I had been corresponding, but soon her letters had stopped coming. I was afraid she was not faring well. I didn't know what was happening but I was determined to see her. I got a military flight to Taipei and hitched a ride to Ping Tong.

Ping Tong was now a ghost town and the next closest town was completely changed without "the white devils," as we were referred to by the Chinese. I hit all the hangouts, going from place to place, asking about Charmaine. Finally I found an old woman who knew her and she gave me the bad news that Charmaine was living with some Navy swabby. She had found a man prepared to marry her. When I heard about it, I was consumed with jealousy and rage. All those months of longing, then traveling thousands of miles to see her, only to find out that I had been replaced by a swabby! It was a low blow.

I got blind drunk, wallowing in my first experience of lost love with maudlin and romantic self-pity. Drunk as a skunk, I stumbled to the old neighborhood where she lived. It was near some train tracks; the mournful whistles of those antiquated steam engines will always be a part of my perception of Taiwan. For a moment, I thought I caught sight of her— maybe she saw me, maybe she didn't. It was the first time I had been dumped, and the rejection was the most hurtful event in my life up to that time.

6

Japan at Last!

After that painful interval in Taiwan, we were finally shipped out to the destination I had hungered for since the beginning—the legendary and mystical Empire of Japan.

We were stationed at Atsugi Naval Air Base about thirty miles from Tokyo. In the morning, I would wake up to see Mount Fuji, Japan's national symbol, in the near distance. It was a spectacular sight. By now it was early spring of 1961. I had been overseas about a year and a half, and I had celebrated both my eighteenth and nineteenth birthdays, and Christmas, on foreign shores. My dad was right about serving in the Marines: I can't think of a better way for any kid to turn into a man. Sometimes I wonder what would have happened to me if I had remained in Brownsville and stayed on the shrimp boats.

In Japan, as at all the other bases, I still served as Colonel Andrew's driver. By now, Andrews was so fond of me he treated me like a son. He even wrote a personal letter to my mother over Christmastime and told her how well I was adjusting to military life and that she had done a good job raising me.

The colonel seemed especially proud of my boxing prowess. He had been a boxer as a young man and enjoyed reliving that part of his youth through me. He was a big supporter of all Marine boxers and promoted our interservice matches with the Navy and Army.

A welterweight, weighing in at about 143 pounds and just an inch under six feet, I trained for months. My greatest asset was a really long reach. I was blessed with 36-inch arms, something many of my opponents didn't figure out until it was too late.

A lot of guys hung around the military gym. Many of them came from rough backgrounds; some of them had been raised on the mean streets of Chicago and Detroit and had become skilled boxers. Others didn't want to climb into the ring themselves but liked being around the sport. A couple of them agreed to help train me.

The first time I climbed into the ring in Atsugi for a sparring match, I started to show off a little, getting in some good licks on my sparring partner. The boxing coach concluded that I hadn't told him the truth about my novice status and he decided to help the other guy. He went over and whispered a few words in my opponent's ear. (I later learned it had something to do with an upper cut.)

We started to get more aggressive and I threw a right with the intent to do damage. Unfortunately, my would-be victim was a quick study; he took the advice of the coach, dropped down and came straight up with an upper cut. I woke up on a pool table in the rec area with someone passing smelling salts under my nose. It was the first and last time I was knocked out. This humbling experience made me want to master this martial art.

From then on, whenever there was a "Saturday Nite Smoker," a series of boxing matches at the base, I was always one of the featured attractions and just about everyone on the base, Navy and Marines both, would attend.

A lot of my success and crowd appeal came from the fact that I didn't look mean or aggressive. Quite the opposite. I had the clean-cut look of a preacher's son. That and my charming smile deceived most of my opponents, who underestimated my ability and my will to win. Beyond that, not wanting to be beaten to a pulp and not wanting Colonel Andrews to be disappointed with me contributed significantly to my success in the ring. Still taking my models from Hollywood movies, I imagined myself as Errol Flynn in *Gentleman Jim Corbett*. As a boxer he smiled and moved about the ring like a dancer, splattering his challenger all over the canvas. This was the demeanor I wanted to emulate.

It added greatly to the general excitement that most of these fights were waged between the Marine Corps and the

Navy boxing teams, because practically nobody expected a baby-faced Marine to clobber some burly-looking swabby. It was great theater and the audience loved it. The rules were rather lax: if the Navy didn't have a welterweight to match me up with, they would sometimes put me in with a larger and heavier fighter. This didn't bother me because I soon learned that it wasn't size, but determination and quick thinking that counted.

Meanwhile, as Colonel Andrews' right-hand man, I was living well and, because of my free time, I was getting actively acquainted with the perks of making money on the black market. Working for the C.O. at headquarters, I knew most of the Marine officers on the base. Whenever they got themselves in trouble in town, the colonel would choose me to move in for the rescue. I made so many rescue missions (some unknown to the colonel) that quite a few of these guys began to owe me favors.

During this time, I also began to realize that a lot of Marines I had gone through boot camp with were stationed on Atsugi. Some had positions of power in supply or in motor transport, and all of these connections began to pay off. The colonel's top administrative officer, known as adjutant, was usually three sheets to the wind and consequently turned many of his duties over to me.

The adjutant held the rank of captain; he had come up from the enlisted ranks and had received a battlefield commission to officer status. Maybe he had seen too much war or maybe he was bored by our peacetime duties in Japan, but he stayed inebriated most of the time. He was one of the main ones I would go to town to round up, especially when he didn't show up for duty in the morning.

So, life was good. Through my good deeds and street smarts, I had managed to become indispensable to the people around the "throne" and I finally got promoted to lance corporal. It came about in an oddball way. I asked the adjutant one day when I could count on a promotion. He asked, "What rank are you?" (He didn't know because I had fallen into a bad habit of not wearing my rank insignia.)

When he found out that I had been a PFC for so long, he got out a form and typed up my promotion on the spot.

After a few months of duty in Japan I started selling contraband merchandise to the underworld. The Japanese especially liked Scotch whisky, which I could buy through my supply connections and double or triple my price on each bottle. Although the war had been over for fourteen or fifteen years, Japan was still in the process of rebuilding and westernizing. The average person in Japan was just beginning to become consumer-oriented. Taxi drivers, for example, had to pay a small fortune for a license, but they jumped into the fray with a vengeance. Every time I took a "Kamikaze" cab ride, I would brace myself, hang on, and pray. Accidents involving taxis were frequent.

Even though I hadn't started operating in the big cities of Tokyo, Yokohama, and Kyoto, I was chalking up fast profits selling coffee, American cigarettes, liquor, and golf balls. The Japanese were nuts about golf. There was a time when I had a lock on all the golf balls coming into the country. It was a very lucrative business. I was walking around carrying briefcases filled with money.

In my boxing career, I had gained an undefeated record of TKOs and knockouts. I even entertained visions of turning pro, probably because I loved the treatment I was getting; it seemed like everyone wanted to be my friend. I had put myself on a harsh regimen of no smoking, no drinking, and daily long runs.

One night at an interservice title fight my pugilistic career came to a grinding halt—make that a "bloody" halt. I was paired up with a Navy guy, a professional boxer whose only job was to fight for the Navy on aircraft carriers. The auditorium was full and, as usual, my colonel was there to root for our Marine detachment. There were men and women from every branch of the service. It was quite a festive atmosphere. I was first on the agenda, which I preferred. I hated to sit through the carnage as boxer after boxer was carried or helped out of the ring. Until this big-time event, I had usually worn 16-ounce gloves so the contenders couldn't get hurt too badly. However, because this was the interservice title fight, both of us were given 10-ounce gloves to wear. I was about to learn that getting hit with anything that had virtually no padding could offer a one-way trip to intensive care.

A second after the bell rang, this pro (who, incidentally, could have been my twin; he looked just like me and had long arms) hit me when I wasn't prepared. He broke my nose. There was blood everywhere. I stayed on my feet but that surprise shot to the head set the mood for the whole contest. From that first moment, whenever he hit me my knees would wobble. I got in a few revenge licks and raised a welt on his nose, but about a minute and forty seconds into the second round my manager stopped the fight. It was my first loss in the ring. I couldn't believe it.

Along with the broken nose, I had a dislocated jaw and gashes on my forehead. I spent the night in the emergency ward with ice on my face and lots of souped-up painkillers racing through my bloodstream. As I watched my face turn black and blue, it dawned on me that my dreams of a career as a professional boxer might have been off base. When a doctor told me that I was never going to take an unobstructed breath through my right nostril and that it would probably need surgery at some future date, I decided to give up boxing for good.

Colonel Andrews seemed a little disappointed when I threw in the towel, but I had already proved my worth with him and I could tell from the way he acted that I wasn't going to lose favor because I was no longer his gladiator.

Meanwhile, during my stay in Japan, I had become close buddies with a guy by the name of Jerry McCall, a brilliant, and debonair kid from a well-heeled family in Santa Barbara, California, and Hal Weston, an East Coast Yankee with a broad New England accent. Hal was in charge of dispatching vehicles in our motor transport. A dispatcher could control what kind of vehicle was available and could authorize and give valid off-base transportation passes. Jerry was the clerk/bookkeeper for motor transport. Between Jerry, Hal, and me, we could control the rolling stock—trucks, jeeps, etc.—on the base. We could also make off-base transport passes disappear. I began to realize that, as corporals, we were strategically placed throughout the air wing organization—in supply, motor transport, and command headquarters. It turned out we could pretty well run the whole base on our own, and we practically did.

My friend Jerry was a big handsome Irish super-achiever with a great sense of humor and an irrepressible appetite for mischief. Jerry was as aggressive as he was smart. I eventually learned that he wasn't as formally educated as he led Hal and me to believe. He did have a high school education, which put him ahead of me, but he had not gone to college as he alleged. Seems that Jerry's education had been put on hold when he eloped with a hometown beauty whose father, extremely wealthy and not happy with his new son-in-law, had the marriage annulled. He then made it clear that Jerry needed a change of scenery.

When I first met Jerry, he had all the polish of his Santa Barbara Country Club upbringing and he was incredibly well read. Even when I found out that he didn't have the college credentials I thought he had, he continued to be a great influence on me. Jerry was constantly reading about politics, philosophy, religion, history, and current events, and asking challenging questions. He introduced me to twentieth-century French philosophers and beat poets from the Village in New York, and gave me a larger world view than I had imagined possible. He had me reading books like *Mein Kampf, Das Kapital* and the Bible, and he asked me questions about the universe that I couldn't answer. Jerry had such an impact on me that for the first time in my life, at age nineteen, I got interested in higher education.

It became apparent that I had been unaware of a larger world out there. When I began to compare my educational background with that of some of my Oriental girlfriends, I saw that things were a little out of whack. I enrolled in a government-sponsored correspondence school and took courses in math, history, and English. I even took and passed the GED test for a high school equivalency diploma. But the GED didn't help me when it came to getting into the Naval Academy. Colonel Andrews had nominated me but I was rejected because I hadn't finished regular high school.

It was a bitter pill at the time but it was a wake-up call as to the importance of education, or rather, organized state-sponsored education.

Besides being in awe of Jerry for his mind and his worldliness, hanging out with the guy was certainly entertaining. One night Jerry and I were on liberty and he showed me his fake I.D. It looked like a standard green, military I.D. card with his photo, big as life, and "First Lieutenant" typed in with an officer's service number. What a coup! I promptly dug up the few hundred bucks of squeeze money it cost to get my own officer's I.D. and I became the youngest (albeit bogus) second lieutenant in the Marine Corps.

After I got my new I.D., I began looking forward even more to our weekend liberty. Jerry and I would have Hal Weston arrange for a limo from the Navy motor pool, which was staffed by Japanese civilians. The drivers made great interpreters and guides. We always dressed in civilian clothes for those excursions and the Japanese drivers never revealed our activities; they were just glad for the work and overtime.

Breaking the rules and living on the edge had strong appeal to both of us. Once, we decided to stay overnight in officer bachelor quarters at one of the military bases in and around Tokyo, a caper for a faux lieutenant. The BOQs were also staffed by Japanese civil servant types who just checked our I.D.s and had us sign the registry. I made the mistake of putting down my enlisted I.D. number instead of the officer number. The clerk pointed out the error and I quickly scratched the offending number out and put in the acceptable digits. He gave me a suspicious squint but let it drop.

This hobnobbing in officer clubs and staying in fancy officer living quarters was a far cry from my existence in the tent cities of Subic Bay, Okinawa, Korea and Taiwan. In fact, I was beginning to feel right at home in the cosmopolitan life of Tokyo.

My first exposure to Tokyo on a 72-hour pass was very different from the experiences I had with Jerry. He coached me on what to say and how to act in my impersonation of a second lieutenant. Our masquerade had a price tag, too.

For one thing, my new-found sophistication called for a better wardrobe. At this time in post-war Japan, Chinese tailors were on every corner catering to American servicemen. I got a tailor to outfit me in silk and wool suits. A white cashmere dinner jacket was *de rigeur* and camel hair coats were the overcoat of preference.

In addition, the practice in the nightclubs we frequented was to allow a hostess to visit your table; you would buy her drinks and basically pay for her company. The higher class the bar, the higher price the girl, of course. All of this fueled my plan to make it big in the black market.

Jerry and I had started out small in our black market operation, selling mainly American coffee and cigarettes. But in these first deals we established trusted trade routes and connections in various large Japanese cities and whetted our appetite for more. Yokohama and Yakusuka were near Tokyo and were chock-full of U.S. military bases. Jerry and I built up our business to a point where we were selling whole truckloads of contraband merchandise.

By this time, I had rented an apartment in the town next to Atsugi Air Station, and I had my own full-time houseboy. My hired hand was allowed to go on the military base. He cleaned the living quarters that I shared with some other Marines. He polished my dress shoes and boots and even made up my bunk, military style. His goal in working for me was to learn English. He was a college student and felt that speaking English would help him in the future. I also used him as an interpreter and as a go-between with my black market connections.

I always look back on this time in my life with a smile. Nineteen is an age when you think everything is possible. You're not afraid of anybody. But I found I was a bit naive, still, when it came to drinking saki, the Japanese wine made from rice with a fairly low alcoholic content.

It happened one day when I drove the colonel to Yamato, a town outside the base, to attend a "Yankee Stay Here" ceremony thrown by some local officials who wanted to show solidarity and friendship to Americans. I drove him to a Shinto Temple in town and the colonel had nodded his approval of my joining the festivities. Everyone had to take off their shoes before entering the shrine; then we were seated en masse in a great hall. A ceremonial sash with Japanese characters was placed around our necks. We listened to speeches while tiny grandmotherly ladies, barely as tall as the giant saki bottles they were wielding, served us. They would glide by unobtrusively saying *doso* (which means please and thank you at the same time) every time they filled my cup, which was frequent.

Colonel Andrews gave a speech and finally, the festivities over, the colonel gave the signal that it was time to go. I smiled, tried to get up, and found I couldn't move. Much to my surprise, I could not feel my legs much less uncross them. The colonel and someone else had to grab an arm and carry me back to the staff car. The colonel, veteran of foreign wars and highest ranking person on our Marine base, had to put me back in the car and drive me back to the base. He was a good sport about it. He even hauled me into the barracks and deposited me on my bunk. For the next few days I took a lot of ribbing from the headquarters' staff.

Overall, life was very good; everything was going along according to the plan I had envisioned while on the troop ship en route to the Orient. I met a wonderful girl at a U.S.O. Christmas party in Tokyo and I was making money by the bagful. The yen was 360 to the dollar so I had to carry around satchels of the stuff. Japan was recovering at a frenetic pace. Tokyo was surely the most exciting place on the planet. Jerry and I tried to keep up with the demand for Whitehorse Scotch, MJB Coffee, golf balls, American cigarettes and whatever else I could get my hands on. Naturally, this illegal trade was not without scrutiny from American and Japanese authorities. When I went to meet my Mafioso contacts in Yokohama or Tokyo, I felt the watchful eyes of unfriendly police types. I knew I was being followed. There were times when I would take five or six taxis to elude these spies. *Exhilarating* is the word that best describes how it felt to match wits with the military police.

When I dealt with underworld characters, associated with a Nipponese version of the Mafia, I began to realize that

I had to be very careful not to cross these hoods. One time I had a meeting with the big Mafia boss in the port city of Yokohama and I took special precautions to make sure I wasn't being followed. I took a train to Yokohama and ran through back alleys, caught cab after cab, and backtracked through some rough-looking areas of the city. I finally kept my rendezvous.

The head guy was a hardened old man. The war had left him with only one leg. I'll never forget this meeting because after we finished talking business we started talking about the war and the Japanese people's feeling about America. He believed he represented a large percentage of Japanese who would never forget that America dropped the bomb on Orientals and not Caucasians. He vowed to get even.

About this point in time I noticed that some C.I.D.-type guys (Civilian Intelligence Division) were following me around the base. I was at the enlisted man's club one night when this flatfoot with a crew cut and military-issue eyeglasses came over and sat down next to me. He was too old to be hanging around enlisted men in my age group. This nerd started asking seemingly harmless questions about how people could make a few dishonest bucks in the black market. He kept sticking his arm out toward me. On his wrist he wore a clunky fake watch that was obviously a microphone device. At first, I was just amused at his lack of professionalism but later I saw it was an ominous sign that someone in the C.I.D. might be singling me out for special scrutiny.

I became a lot more cautious and started to spending more time with my big city girl, the one I met at the U.S.O. Christmas dance. She wasn't one of the bar girls from the nearby town; indeed, she had never been in a bar. She was a college student from the upper-class. Her parents were mortified that she was fraternizing with the *gaijen* (foreigners). She went to U.S.O. dances to meet Americans so that she could practice her English and find out more about our culture. We hit it off right away. Her last name was Kikuchi, which means chrysanthemum.

The more time I spent with her, the more I realized that there was something coming between us and it wasn't just cultural differences; it was education. I was smitten with her beauty, her refined manners, and her girlish giggle characteristic of Japanese women. She was a big romantic and followed Hollywood gossip. The major media event of the moment was the breakup between Marilyn Monroe and Joe DiMaggio. She was devastated.

After dating for some months, she invited me to dinner at her parents' home. Her father was a university professor. Her parents were interested in me and where I came from. They wanted to know what my plans were when I was mustered out of the Marines. Once again, it dawned on me that I didn't have a plan and this Southern boy better start thinking about the future.

As this affair continued to take up more of my time, I began to perceive some resentment from my buddies. Jerry and Hal made it clear that I should choose their company over mere female companionship. The only thing that saved our friendship is that Jerry's overseas duty came to an end and he was rotated out of the air wing and sent home. We corresponded and I promised to look him up in Santa Barbara, where he planned to go to college after his hitch was up.

My own tour of duty was coming to an end but, because of my high-flying lifestyle, my black market activities, and my big-city girl friend in Tokyo, I put in for an extension. My plan was to finish out my enlistment (less than two years). Thanks to my ever-expanding business contracts, I even thought about reenlisting in the Corps if I could be guaranteed to be left in Atsugi for the entire four-year hitch. It was a real possibility; I had met clerical staff at headquarters who had been stationed overseas with the air wing for eight or more years. I figured that if I could pull that off, I would be worth a fortune. In my travels in and around Japan, I met a number of expatriate Americans who had decided to stay in the Orient after mustering out of the service.

As I would soon discover, this prospect was about to be nipped in the bud. There is a Japanese saying: "In the moment of victory, tighten your helmet straps." Anyone in a shady business venture over a long period of time, especially a successful one, eventually gets noticed—and the long arm of the law can't be far behind. I knew that, but, like many before and after me, I kept hoping I would be the exception and escape paying the piper.

This situation reached an unexpected but brutal climax when the Japanese military police seized my houseboy, threw him into a dungeon, and beat him unmercifully with rubber hoses. I will never forget that morning. This young man came running into my barracks, all battered and bloody, and in hysterics. While the other guys looked on open-mouthed, the student got down on his knees before me and begged my forgiveness. "For what?" I asked, horrified at the sight of him.

"They kept beating me until I finally told them what they wanted to know. I . . . I'm sorry, but I gave them the names of your contacts . . . told them what you were selling and the prices you've been getting . . ."

"You did what?" I glared down at him, watching his face turn red.

"Don't you see? I had to do this or they would have killed me. Oh, please please, Jack-san, forgive me, forgive me."

"Forgive you? You ——," and then I lost control.

As the full realization of what the kid was saying swept over me, I went into full panic. My whole life flashed before my eyes. Without another word I grabbed him and started strangling him. Black rage swept over me. It took a whole gang of guys to pry my hands off of him. All I could think of was that this rat fink was a traitor, and I wondered how my mom was going to react when she found out that her son was going to be spending the rest of his life in the brig, probably Leavenworth Federal Penitentiary.

After being forcefully removed from my faithful houseboy, I turned away from everyone's accusing stares. I sprinted to the nearest toilet and vomited up my breakfast. As I knelt there, sick and disgusted with myself, I had a distinct feeling that the fool's paradise I had enjoyed in Japan was about to come to a screeching halt.

The next day I was called into Colonel Andrews' office for a heart-to-heart chat. He let me know that he was continuing his father-figure relationship with me and was steadfast behind me, no matter what I had done. "I hate to tell you this, Jack, but your name is now on the 'most wanted' list with the C.I.D." I nodded glumly, ready for the worst.

"When is my court-martial to begin, sir?"

"Now come on son, let's not jump to unnecessary conclusions. It's my opinion you've just been overseas a little too long. The temptations have gotten to be too much for you, to the extent where they've led you into moral turpitude."

I didn't know what turpitude meant but I said, "You really think so, sir?"

"I'm sure of it; therefore, in order to preserve what's left of your sense of right and wrong, I've decided to send you home on the next troop ship. The sooner the better."

In short, Colonel Andrews, mercifully, was moving in to rescue his prized protégé before the military police or Japanese civilian police could begin prosecution.

"Now go pack your gear, Corporal Swanson, and on the double."

"Yes, sir!" I said, saluting and executing an about-face.

That was the last time I saw the colonel. The next morning I was delivered, sea bag in hand, to the port in Tokyo and deposited on a troop transport ship back to the States. I didn't get a chance to say good-bye to most of my buddies or to my lovely girlfriend. But I called her before shipping out. There was that familiar emotional upheaval that I had felt with my Taiwanese Charmaine. Again, we promised to write, to stay in touch, but we never followed up on this well-meant promise. The memories of my first Japanese lover lingered a long time until finally, years later, I managed to find one just like her much closer to home.

The troop ship that was my magic carpet ride back to the States was a World War II rustbucket that could stuff four or five thousand bodies into its stifling underbelly. The enlisted ranks were below deck and the officers and their dependents were topside in staterooms. There were only about 100 Marines to the three or four thousand Army personnel being shipped home from their tour of duty in Korea.

As far as interservice rivalry goes, these "bow wows" were our natural enemies. For us, the Army lacked the esprit de corps the Marine Corps stood for. In the Marines one had to earn one's stripes. Outside battlefield promotion, it took a few hitches (three or four years per hitch) to attain the rank of sergeant, especially staff sergeant or gunnery sergeant. In the Army, a trooper barely halfway through his three-year enlistment would quite regularly be sporting staff sergeant stripes—and with them, a lot more pay.

On the first day or so on board I was singled out to guard some prisoners being transported to a federal lock-up in the States. As I solemnly pulled my guard duty shift, rifle at the ready, I asked these guys what they had done to earn prison stripes. It turns out they had been caught selling U.S.-issue blankets on the black market. There but for the grace of God go I. It sure gave me pause.

Naturally, not being fond of guard duty and other "shit details" designed to keep us busy, I was casting about for a niche that would suit me. A great opportunity seemed to surface on cue. Some authoritative-looking old gunny sergeant came into the lounge area and asked if anyone had barbering experience. My hand shot up. "Yes," I told him. I was his man. (I had never cut a single head of hair.) There was a ship barber but he worked only on officers. The barber filled me in on the use and care of his tools of the trade. He said to charge a buck a head and to split my earnings with him. What a gold mine. After massacring countless "doggies" (Army personnel), I started getting the hang of it.

My bankroll started to swell as the Army guys realized that their obligatory haircuts didn't have to be the famous Marine Corps whitewall style. For only one extra dollar, I would give them a modified, more aesthetically-pleasing trim. Those dollars added up. By the time our troop ship hit port thirteen days later, I was rich.

7

To the Halls of Academe

I'll never forget our entry into the Port of San Francisco. It had been a couple of years since I had touched United States soil and seen American-born women. Five thousand troops were up on deck as we cruised under the fabled Golden Gate Bridge into San Francisco Bay on a beautiful, clear morning. The men let out a yell long and hard that traveled up toward the bridge's suspension, along with our hats. I never found my hat again, but that hardly mattered.

Our ship berthed on Treasure Island, the naval military base beautifully situated in the bay, between Oakland and San Francisco. I'll never forget my first sight of the San Francisco hillsides dotted with white houses that glistened in the brilliant morning sunlight. Back home in South Texas everything was flat and monotonous, but in this town every neighborhood had a special atmosphere all its own. It was the early sixties and San Francisco was the happening spot, even though it seemed a bit small to me after Tokyo. Beat poets, crowded cafes, and all-night jazz clubs were familiar city sights. Market Street was the main thoroughfare, and it stretched from Twin Peaks all way to the ferry building on the bay. In the downtown area, the ladies were all well dressed, many in hats and gloves, and the men wore dapper business suits and felt hats.

I hit the city running. I had plenty of money; I was padded with thousands of one-dollar bills from my days as a barber. In the couple of years I had been gone everything had changed. My boots and Western-style shirt no longer fit in and neither did my service uniform. Thanks to some locals I met who steered me right, I began wearing bulky sweaters and other cool threads of the day.

Music had gone through a revolution as well. I was shocked to find that the Beatles had beat out Elvis for top star status. At first, I wasn't sure I liked all the changes that had taken place. But as I explored the nooks and crannies of San Francisco, I was soon smitten. I decided that someday I would come back to live in this city by the bay. Even though I felt it would be many years in the future, the idea was solidly implanted in my mind. I took endless walking tours over the city's countless hills, and I found new, spectacular panoramas revealing themselves at every corner. Even though it was mid-February of '62, the weather was bright and surprisingly balmy.

Although many didn't realize it at the time, this was an era of sociological transition, the tail end of the Beat generation and just before the hippies. The jazzy area was North Beach, which still reflected Beatnik influences. As I went nightclubing through Chinatown and toured North Beach, I caught such performers as Miles Davis and comics like Mort Sahl, Phyllis Diller and Bill Cosby, who appeared routinely at the Hungry I and the Purple Onion.

I was finally processed out of Treasure Island and given a three-week furlough. After finishing my time in San Francisco, I decided to take the Santa Fe Flyer across the mountains down into Texas and visit my folks before reporting to my new duty station, Camp Pendleton.

After coming from the Orient and San Francisco, the provincial nature of the small towns I knew in the hinterlands of Texas was a shock. After three days in Kilgore visiting my dad, I was more than ready to leave and never return. A similar experience in Brownsville told me that I could not go home again. My future was definitely in California. It made me feel both sad and happy. I think my mom and dad were getting the distinct feeling that I wasn't going to settle down in Texas after my military hitch was over.

When my leave was up, I left Brownsville on a Greyhound bus. It was a horrendous and sleepless trip from the lower Rio Grande Valley to Los Angeles, I checked into Camp Pendleton. Pendleton is an enormous military base right on the ocean not far from the town of Oceanside. It's the size of some states, if you compare it to Delaware or Maine.

Pendleton is a beautiful area, but it was my misfortune to be stationed in a particularly remote area of the base, way out in the boondocks and uncomfortably similar to the scene I thought I had just escaped down in Texas. Once again I was assigned to a motor transport unit. But this time I was working cheek-to-jowl with a bunch of jarheads who had hailed either from Appalachia or the mudflats of Mississippi.

At this stage, I had recognized that I much preferred to be around people I could admire, people from whom I could learn something. And socially speaking, I was no longer as comfortable as I had been among the high school dropouts that constituted the majority of my fellow Marines. Here, it appeared that the guys had spent their entire enlistment at this one post whereas I had been shifted all over the Orient.

It worried me, too, that I looked so tailored and squared away. I was all spit and polish, with a regulation "white-wall" haircut and all my uniforms had been either custom-made or at least were tailored to fit me. As the colonel's driver, I had to look the part. When I saw that my new buddies wore poorly laundered uniforms with holes in them, I knew for sure I didn't belong out here in the boonies. In this unit, even the officers were a bunch of zeroes. I had to maneuver my way out of this hell hole.

Naturally, with my dapper appearance I stuck out like a sore thumb, and right away I felt bad vibes toward me, both from the brass hats and the enlisted folk. I feared if I stayed in this unit very long, I could be in for some bodily harm. One of the problems was that Colonel Andrews had given me high marks on my service record, a 4.0. The C.O. in my new unit didn't believe there was a Marine alive who deserved that kind of evaluation. The colonel, obviously well-meaning, might as well have painted a target on my back.

After I was there about a week, one of the sergeants in my barracks happened to mention that Camp Pendleton's top general, a General Leek by name, needed a new driver. It seemed his regular driver had been caught driving the general's staff car in the town of Oceanside without a proper pass. To top that off, he had also gotten a speeding ticket. So the general needed a replacement—fast.

I immediately saw my way out. But I knew there was no way to actually apply for such a job. Unless your commanding officer personally recommends you for an assignment, or puts in a good word for you, your hands are tied. I decided on the unheard of: I would apply in person.

Early one morning, wearing my best tailored uniform, I hitched a ride to the main headquarters about twenty miles away. I carried no official documents authorizing this trip. When I reached the First Marine Division Headquarters building, I marched up to a sergeant major on duty and, after exchanging greetings, I said assertively, "I am here to apply for the job as General Leek's driver. I drove for Colonel Andrews for nearly two years in the Orient. You can verify that by pulling my service records, which are on file here at headquarters."

My tone was firm, and persuasive enough, evidently, that the sergeant major asked someone to pull my record. When he saw they bore out my claims, he sent me to the next official in the chain of command. I repeated my story and was sent straight through to the general's office. After passing muster with the general's (male) secretary, I was led in to see the general's aide who, as luck would have it, was from Houston, Texas.

This young lieutenant by the name of Howard Russell was a great big gangly guy. He had freckles all over his face and an "aw shucks" personality. He looked like he would trip on his own shadow, but academically he was brilliant, as I later learned. Lieutenant Russell had graduated top of his class at Annapolis and chosen to enter the Marine Corps instead of the Navy. He was quite an accomplished golfer. But he was also about the dullest son of a bitch who ever drew breath, either in the military or out of it. For starters, he had no innate perceptiveness or sensitivity, nor did he know the first thing about relating to people, let alone dealing with power. To illustrate how slow-witted he was, every time he played golf with the general he would cheerfully beat him, never thinking beyond his own little victory.

Because the general's aide liked the idea of having another good ol' Southern boy working around the office, he got me in to see the general very quickly. Even before I met General Leek, all Marine generals in my estimation were gods. When I met this man face-to-face, I was really blown away. He couldn't have looked more like the ideal general if he'd been sent there by central casting. Pushing fifty, Leek was a tall, broad-shouldered, handsome guy with salt and pepper hair. He looked a little like Clark Gable.

I marched right up to his desk, presented myself, then gave him the same persuasive spiel I had given his office staff. After listening to my every word, he eyed me carefully up and down before he spoke. Then he said, "Tell me, Swanson," he said, "can you answer an important question for me?"

"Yes, sir! Ask away."

"Why would anyone in his right mind *want* this kind of pogey bait job?"

I was ready for this question. I knew the Marine Corps dogma about our mission as soldiers: every Marine should aspire to be an expert rifleman and remain combat-ready so you could get down in the trenches and kill, maim, and destroy the bad guys. I realized this was no time to bullshit, and that the only way to impress this guy would be to level with him. "Sir, the reason I want this job is because at present I'm stationed about twenty miles from nowhere, which means I'll probably be going on bivouacs for the next year and a half and get nothing accomplished."

"I see," Leek said, a slight grin on his face. "You have anything to add to that?"

"Well, sir, what I really want to do is work for you and use my free time to better myself—maybe go to night school and complete the courses I need to qualify for my high school diploma." Weirdly enough, I hadn't known that was what I really wanted until I heard my own words.

"Okay, Swanson," Leek said. "That's just about the only legitimate reason I could imagine anyone wanting this job for. You're hired. But first, I'd advise you not to go back to your outfit to get your gear. Because you obviously weren't sent here by your immediate superiors, you might be court-martialed. I'll have Sergeant Fegley, my secretary, arrange to have your gear shipped over to the service battalion here at headquarters."

"Sir, all I can say is you won't regret this. I'll be the best driver you ever had."

General Leek was the only one to figure out that I had not gone through proper channels. That explained at once why he was the general. As the general would soon learn, however, my promise "to be the best driver he ever had" was a bit broad in its claim. When I drove for the colonel in Tokyo I realized what a lousy sense of direction I had. But on a base as enormous as Pendleton, I quickly saw that this problem was about to mushroom a hundred times.

Like Colonel Andrews, General Leek had been an aviator. Not just any old aviator. He had shot down at least four Japanese planes in World War II to become an Ace. This much-decorated and obviously lucky pilot had climbed in rank from lieutenant to colonel during the Second World War. He also served in Korea and was the first air wing aviator to command the First Marine Division, "a division of grunts."

Lucky for me, he had the same knack for navigation that Colonel Andrews had—all they had to do was look up in the heavens to figure out where they were. Moreover, Leek had been stationed at Pendleton many times and knew the area like the back of his hand. I, on the other hand, knew I was in trouble the very next morning after I drove him from his house on the hill to headquarters. After depositing him at headquarters, I waited for our next excursion. Word came down for me to ready the shiny black staff car. I ran down the stairs, opened the general's door, and snapped my salute. I ran around to the driver's seat, got in and smiled brightly, saying, "Where to, sir?"

"Rattlesnake Canyon."

Oh boy, I thought. I'm dead. I turned around and, with a sly, self-deprecating smile on my face, said, "Sir, if you could just point me in the right direction I would appreciate it."

The general laughed. "You mean you've never heard of Rattlesnake Canyon?"

"Affirmative, sir."

The general then patiently gave me directions for the next year and a half. Thank God he didn't cancel my ticket then and there. He knew I owed him. I made up my mind never to cross him or misuse my power as part of the palace guard. I didn't want any more of the type of problems I had run into in Japan.

Meanwhile, life was looking up. I bought an old Chevy to tool around in within Oceanside and I enrolled at Oceanside-Carlsbad Junior College. With the general's permission I went to night school four nights a week, taking all the required subjects I needed to get my long-delayed diploma. I was a lance corporal looking to be promoted to full corporal. I went out and bought a Marine Corps blues uniform. I had many occasions to wear my "blues" now that I worked for the commanding general.

The general went out of his way for me time and again. There were times when I needed to go down the hill to Oceanside to take a test or flunk the class, and on those occasions the general would drive himself and his wife to whatever social function was scheduled. If he had gotten into an accident, it could have ruined his career, so by doing this for me, he was really putting himself out.

Meanwhile, the classes I was taking in English, Psychology, History and Political Science were really opening my eyes. They were college-level courses that I could apply to my high school diploma and an Associate of Arts degree. I studied like a demon and did my homework like someone possessed. (I had to do it in the laundry room, the only place where you could have the lights on after 10:00 P.M.) Eventually I completed eighteen units of college courses to go toward my university degree.

I began to see how formal education was slowly producing a marked change in my former "go-to-hell" way of living. I suddenly saw how much could be done once I had all this learning tucked away inside of me. For the first time in my life I was serious about school and not interested in conning my teachers by playing the angles. It was also the first time in my military career that I was too busy to be wheeling and dealing and trying to pull off some sort of something-for-nothing deal.

The general took a studied interest in my education. Often, when I had to wait around for him or some other bigwigs, he would give me reading material or quiz me on my classes. Although he was a pretty trusting person, he did let me know that he called the J.C. from time to time to make sure I was attending and applying myself. After a few months on the job I figured I must be doing something right because he promoted me to full corporal. Somehow "lance corporal" just doesn't sound as solid as "corporal." In fact, to preserve the good impression I had made on the general, I put my life of crime behind me, vowing from now on to dwell in the halls of academia.

Even though I had tried to do my job perfectly, I made my mistakes and faux pas. When I first began to work for General Leek, I once failed to complete an assignment and tried to charm my way out of it. This is when he gave me a pamphlet-size book entitled *Message to Garcia* by Elbert Hubbard. He told me that every WW I soldier had been given a copy before being shipped to Europe. When I read it, I realized why.

The story was about a young army lieutenant in the Spanish-American War. The lieutenant was called into President McKinley's office and, as he snapped to attention in front of the president's desk, he was given a leather pouch and told to take the packet with a "secret message" to General Garcia. The lieutenant took the packet, said, "Aye, aye, sir!" did an about face and marched out of the office. He then proceeded to research pertinent facts he would need to know, such as who General Garcia was and where he could be found etc.—questions he had not asked when given the assignment.

He promptly arranged for transportation to take him to Cuba where he learned General Garcia was based, and he rowed ashore, hacked his way through the jungle, found Garcia, and handed over the packet. He saluted Garcia, did an about face, and returned to his base in America.

I took this "message" to heart. Anytime thereafter, when I was given the responsibility to get something done, I did whatever it took, even if it meant employing unorthodox methods. Sometimes General Leek would wince when he found out about the questionable maneuvering I would employ to get something accomplished. He never came down hard on me, or yelled at me, but on more than one occasion he would smile (or grimace) and repeat his warning, "Swanson, you had better not stay in the Marine Corps."

The year and a half I spent with the general was no "walk in the park." It may have been peacetime, but the Cold War was the driving force of the military in those years. As I drove the general around to the various detachments and battalions, I would be privy to what the top brass were saying about threats to our national security. They hated the young president from Harvard, for example, and all the Ivy League types he surrounded himself with.

For myself, all I wanted then was a nice 9 to 5 job and enough time to do my homework, but the First Marine Division was a busy place to be in '62 and '63. There were incessant war games in the various detachments of the First Marine Division and periodically we were put on troop ships to participate in amphibious landings. All this time in the field disrupted my studies and kept me on edge.

I still had no long-term plan of what I would do after my enlistment was up. But an incident that happened to me one night as I drove the general and his lady down to San Diego for an Admiral's Ball was about to change my life.

One Saturday night I drove General Leek and his wife to a glamorous Admiral's Ball that was being held at the Naval installation on Coronado Island, a few miles outside of San Diego. It was a lucky night for my boss, as I later learned. He and his wife won the door prize—a brand new car. Why couldn't I have that kind of luck? The general, however, didn't feel so lucky; in fact, he cursed his fate. He had been planning on giving his wife a new car for Christmas, which was just a few months away, and winning the car had ruined his plan.

After I dropped the two of them off at the ball, I had the whole evening to myself. I was dressed to the hilt in my Marine Corps blues—a dark navy blue jacket with red piping, light blue trousers with vertical red stripes, white gloves, and spit-shined leather shoes. The outfit was topped off with a white military hat. When I was preening in front of the mirror earlier that evening I admitted to myself, in all humility of course, that I looked pretty damned good. I couldn't wait to step out in my full dress uniform and hit some local watering holes.

Once off-duty, I drove around until I found a really elegant restaurant on the island. I ordered a steak, which I proceeded to wolf down, when I was suddenly interrupted by a middle-aged couple who asked if I would like to join them. They explained that one of their two sons was in the service in Texas and they would like to treat me to dinner. It sounded good to me, so I picked up my platter and moved to their table.

Mal and Julie Gianni turned out to be great people. I didn't realize how alienated I had been feeling since my tour of duty in the Orient. Almost my whole Marine Corps experience had been overseas and I had almost no contact with the civilian world in American life. Mal and Julie were the first "regular" people I had met since joining the Corps. I had become accustomed to the local population being indifferent or downright hostile toward the military, and so it was nice to have someone single me out for company.

I learned a lot about the Giannis over dinner. Mal was a successful architect. He had designed the home his family shared on top of a hill in Glendale, California, a suburb of Los Angeles. After dinner, Mal handed me his card with their home address and phone number and told me that if I ever needed a home-cooked meal to look them up. I took the card thinking what a nice couple they were but doubting that our paths would ever cross again.

A few weeks later it was Thanksgiving weekend and I was carousing around Los Angeles' Sunset Strip on a 72-hour pass. I ate Thanksgiving dinner at a U.S.O. in downtown Hollywood where the table setting was picnic style complete with paper plates and napkins. It was basic fare but I was used to it and it filled me up. I proceeded to run around to all the girlie shows, strip joints and seedy bars, enjoying Southern California's demimonde. At the end of the evening I hit the night spots on La Cienaga, and realized then that I was running out of cash. All I had left for the rest of the weekend was gas money for the drive back to base. I spent the night in my '54 Chevy on the Sunset Strip and got run off in the morning by a cop on patrol.

With Saturday night to kill before my leave was up, I pulled out Mal Gianni's card from my wallet and gave him a call. He and his wife eagerly offered me directions to their Glendale home. When I rang their doorbell on that gorgeous November day, they received me like long-lost family, warmly introducing me to their youngest son, Jim, and to Julie's father, Grandpa Bennadetti, who was eighty years young.

Jim and I were the same age, and we both shared December birthdays. We hit it off immediately. Mal's oldest son was away in the service and they soon offered me his room for the night. A warm bed sure sounded good to me so I quickly accepted and settled in for the evening.

Dinner with this Italian-American family meant an authentic and delicious meal of polenta, homemade ravioli, and spaghetti covered with great sauces that Grandpa Bennadetti spent all day preparing. After dinner Jim suggested we go to Hollywood to see a movie at Graumann's Chinese Theater. He was taking his girlfriend, a cute little blond gal. Mal even thought to slip me a few bucks.

We went in Jim's red Porsche Sportster 1600 with a turbo charger. It was the first time I had seen a Porsche up close. It was Jim's prized possession; he called it his "baby," and it was definitely the light of his life. Over the next several years that I saw Jim, I can hardly remember a time when he wasn't washing and waxing that car to perfection.

The next day I headed back to Pendleton to my day job with the general and my night job attending school. I had left the Giannis with an open invitation to enjoy their hospitality whenever I was around. And I did. For the rest of my enlistment period, I headed to Glendale every chance

I got. I became the adopted "number three" son of Mal and Julie and, importantly, I began learning firsthand how to fit into civilized society.

My friendship with Jim also blossomed. He introduced me to his circle of friends and I started dropping by every weekend to hang out around the pool with his buddies and their girlfriends. There was always an abundance of food, beer and wine. Jim and all his guy friends drove expensive sports cars. We formed an impressive convoy as we headed off for spur-of-the-moment drives to Malibu, Laguna Beach and Hollywood. This was definitely a lifestyle I wanted to get used to.

Naturally I was flattered that the Giannis took me in so readily. I figured some of my mother's inbred Back Bay Boston social graces must have rubbed off on me. It was my first exposure to the upscale California lifestyle and a far cry from the flatlands of the Rio Grande Valley and the rough-and-ready shrimpers I had known in Texas. I felt so quickly at ease in their world and covetous of it that I knew I had to get educated without delay. No way was I was going back to Brownsville.

After getting to know Jim and a few of his best buddies, I began to realize that most of these kids were living so well off their parents' wealth that they did not appreciate their good fortune, including their free schooling. They attended college piecemeal, not one of them serious enough about his studies to earn a degree. And so, even though I envied them their easy financial advantages, it was hard to see how easily they threw away their chances at a college education. (My mother should have heard me say that!)

It was through Jim Gianni that I met a beautiful young girl named Bonnie. A friend of Jim was getting married and he insisted that I join their party of guests for the nuptials and lavish outdoor reception. It was a beautiful affair filled with the kind of society people I would never have rubbed elbows with if it hadn't been for the Giannis. I felt a little uncomfortable out of my Marine element, but enjoyed spying on how the moneyed class lived. I was looking around, drinking my champagne, when I spotted her. Her dark hair was up in a bun. She wore high heels and affected a sophisticated demeanor, but I suspected that she probably worked as a secretary somewhere. I was right on that count. She worked for IBM. We hit it off immediately. I made a date with her on the spot, and even managed to convey my thoughts about wanting an exclusive relationship with her, starting then.

As I would later confirm, weddings were great places to meet girls. An idyllic setting, a solemn ceremony, being all dressed up, and eating cake and drinking champagne seems to put people in a mating mood. It sure worked for Bonnie and me—our first meeting that night touched off a truly intense love affair.

Bonnie marked my first serious relationship with a California girl. Her parents owned a real estate company in Glendale and were well-to-do. She had graduated from high school and moved out on her own, living a prim and proper life at an all girls' residence club. I was soon to learn that the state of American morals, even in the sixties, wasn't nearly as loose as the permissiveness I had found in the Far East.

With an eighteen-year-old girl raised in a germ-free community like Glendale, I soon learned you had to take a circuitous route to arrive at what I considered a "normal" relationship. After feverish necking in my old Chevy, I found it extremely difficult to leave her on Sunday night and drive back to Camp Pendleton. I damned near fell asleep at the wheel more than once over the ensuing months.

Bonnie became another adoptee at the Gianni household. Grandpa Bennadetti loved to cook and we were always fed well when we visited. The old man would make ravioli by hand. He'd use a water glass as a dough cutter, fold in his special concoction of meat and cheese, and then press a fork around the folded dough to seal it tight. I could single-handedly knock off a hundred or so of his homemade marvels. Once a food salesman, Grandpa warned us not to eat anything Italian out of a can.

Sometimes Bonnie would rendezvous with me at Camp Pendleton for some social event, such as the Marine Corps Ball held in honor of the founding of the Marine Corps. On those occasions, we would stay at a motel in Oceanside, sometimes arriving late, sometimes not at all. Looking back I can't believe anybody could be that young.

I had been going with Bonnie for quite awhile when problems with Cuba started to take on an ominous tone in the media. It was 1962 and Cuba was now the main topic of conversation among the military brass I drove around. These high-ranking officers predicted American body counts in the millions if a nuclear war broke out between America and the U.S.S.R. Up to tens of millions were numbers being tossed around as sustainable losses. For them, it was critical to settle this undeclared war once and for all before the Soviets gained parity or superiority in nuclear warheads.

At home, the paranoia of a possible war reached such heights that the city fathers began to hold air raid drills in downtown Glendale. I went so far as to bring gas masks to Bonnie and our friends and to stock up on emergency supplies. We made plans to meet in the hills above Los Angeles in case we survived an attack. I don't think there has been another time in our history where the whole populace felt such an imminent threat of destruction. The fear of intercontinental missiles raining down atomic bombs was palpable everywhere you went. The First Marine Division at Camp Pendleton had been placed on war alert. Within hours one October morning the entire base, all 50,000 of us, was packed up on trucks and put aboard ships in San Diego headed for Cuba. It was a huge armada equal to some World War II convoys. The instructions were to assume an attack-ready position. President Kennedy had issued an ultimatum to Russian leader Kruschev to either remove atomic-laden Soviet missiles aimed at the U.S. or face armed conflict.

Here I was, at the end of my four-year enlistment, facing what looked like certain death. I kept looking up toward the heavens watching for the sign of a rocket falling to earth right in the middle of the hundreds of ships that comprised the invasion force. Up until this time I had wanted to earn my battlefield commission, perhaps even a medal or two. Hadn't I always wanted to be a warrior and make my mother proud? Well, my feelings had changed. Now that I had almost finished my requirements for a high school diploma, had started planning for college, and had met a wonderful girl I wasn't so sure about all this "gung ho" stuff.

At this juncture, I was on a different ship from that of the general, so I was out of the loop regarding what was going on in the minds of the senior military staff. Everything was at fever pitch when the news came over the radio that Kennedy and Kruschev were eyeball to eyeball, each with a finger on the trigger. A stillness hung in the air. Then the next thing we troops heard was that the Russians had blinked and were turning their supply ships around mid-ocean. They agreed to remove their weapons of destruction from Cuba, which, remember, is a close ninety miles from the Florida coastline.

Back we went to San Diego. I was elated and had a better grip on what I wanted out of life after this brush with the prospect of mass annihilation. When we first boarded the ship, everyone with less than a year to go on his enlistment was automatically reenlisted for another year, but with the crisis over, this extension was dropped. I began to develop the attitude of what they called the "short-timer." I was scheduled to get out of the service in the first part of 1963, so I needed to start making plans.

A lot of my civilian friends in Glendale had attended a junior college in town that was a good size school and a feeder college for UCLA. It dawned on me that I could probably get into Glendale College and live the life I had envisioned.

When I told my father of my plans to attend college in Glendale and hinted at his helping me out, he said that if I lived with him and went into dentistry he would give me a hand. Otherwise, forget it. He was in a bad place financially. It seems that the little town of Kilgore had its economic health tied to the 10,000 oil wells that pumped furiously to bring up the black gold that had been selling for a few dollars on the barrel. Then the oil ran out and the fabled east Texas oil bonanza was over, which meant ruin to the local economy. My father had everything he owned wrapped up in his dental practice and his home in Kilgore, and now no one was paying their bills. He had to give up everything and relocate to Houston, which turned out to be a successful move, but it was hard at the time.

I envisioned living in an apartment by myself in Glendale, keeping my relationship with Bonnie, and just hitting the books. I didn't count on the burden of supporting myself and it didn't occur to me that Bonnie and I might be at cross-purposes regarding our relationship. Bonnie assumed that, once I was free of the military, the next step for us was a short engagement and then marriage. Before either of us thought of exploring what the other was thinking, our affair went on as before—heavy on passion and light on conversation, let alone any real meeting of the minds. By now I was now an "A" student and loved taking my junior college night classes.

As 1963 came into view I started to wind down my military career. I had given some thought to staying in the service and was given the opportunity to go to a Marine Aviation Academy, but I chickened out. I didn't really like flying, and the four to six years of additional service just didn't feel right. About six weeks before I was to be discharged from the Marine Corps my boss and benefactor, General Leek, was suddenly transferred to Vietnam. The general was shrewd enough to project what was about to happen, and advised me to turn my back on the Marine Corps when my time came to leave. I heeded his advice.

I was really a "short-timer" now. I got a deck of cards and, for each of my last 52 days, I dropped a card on one of my fellow Marines, saving the joker to give to the guard at the front gate the day I drove out for my last good-bye.

Without the general I had no fixed work duty and, worse, without his protection I was vulnerable to the other Marines, who had taken umbrage at my favored position as his right hand. Among my detractors were some high-ranking officers who had particularly resented the influence I had with the commanding general, especially in view of my ridiculously low rank and short time in the service.

They did boycott me socially during those last few weeks, and that I could tolerate. As I ran into some of them around the base, however, I began to feel something menacing and hostile in the looks these guys gave me. I began to wonder if one of them might try to stage a convenient accident before I gained my freedom. More than ever, I wanted to finish up my last days and get off that base in one piece.

When the magical last day did arrive, I was in such a hurry to "get out of Dodge" that I got a speeding ticket as I headed for the main gate. I was so rattled that I even forgot my plan to drop the joker card on the guardhouse M.P. But that was just as well—I am glad to have that card as a memento of those days.

Everything was dovetailing nicely. This day of liberty also coincided with my finals at night school. If I passed the two final exams and completed these last courses, I would qualify for my high school diploma from Oceanside-Carlsbad Junior College. When I left the J.C. campus, I knew I had done exceptionally well on my exams. I was so impressed with my accomplishment that as I walked to my parked car, I really thought something extraordinary would happen: the skies and heavens would part, the archangel would appear, bands would play a resounding march. The anticlimax of the moment was overwhelming. Tears filled my eyes. I learned then and there that more than any approbation or acceptance you get from others for your accomplishments, it is really what you are worth to yourself, alone and standing still, that counts.

After the archangel's no-show in the parking lot, I drove the two hours north to Los Angeles and spent my first night in the apartment I had rented in downtown Glendale. I had applied to Glendale College and been accepted. Academia beckoned.

8

Revolutionary Times

Reality finally struck. I realized that the government wasn't going to be handing over a paycheck every two weeks, and that I needed a job—fast. Looking through the want ads for jobs compatible with my continuing in school was a daunting experience. When the opportunity came my way to drive one of those behemoth yellow school buses, I jumped at it. Driving for the local school district would let me work in the early hours of the day and late in the afternoon. I should have been thrilled but what a letdown after I had been driving the general around for a year and a half. My hunger for education would have to sustain me.

The job and my new college were both in Glendale, a conservative, white-collar suburb of Los Angeles, with a population of around 100,000 people in 1963. Luckily I had saved enough money to rent a small bachelor apartment downtown in an old house with a porch and small yard. I got a break on the rent for mowing the lawn and taking out the trash. This place bore no resemblance to the Giannis' Taj Mahal on the hill, but it was a start.

When I was discharged I had a fantasy of going on a bender. But I had to report to work immediately and start classes at Glendale Junior College, so I had no time for debauchery.

This first college semester placed an unexpected strain on me. I had done so well at night school that I viewed myself as pretty damned smart and certainly ready to breeze through J.C. But once face-to-face with higher education, I found it wasn't that easy. An added hurdle was being age twenty-one in a population of students right out of high school. They looked like children to me, yet when it came to book learning they were a lot quicker on the draw, especially in chemistry, biology and math. To fill in my learning gaps there were times when I had to hire a few seventeen-year-old prodigy types to tutor me. It was pretty damned embarrassing, but necessary. I envied these kids their book smarts, but, as I got to know them better, I found they envied my war stories and experiences away from home.

In time I would conclude that the challenges I encountered in college also contributed to building my character. This experience was one more reminder that not everything was going to fall into my lap so easily. Until then I had been able to successfully manipulate my way into the good graces of the top military brass in one situation after another. But in college I found that only very hard work would get me what I wanted. For the time being, my winning personality was incidental.

One of my English professors, an older lady who was a caricature of the traditional "schoolmarm" with her thick coke-bottle glasses, told me to see her after class to discuss my spelling and punctuation. She made it crystal clear that the "buck" stopped with her and that my college career wasn't going anywhere until I learned grammar and instilled discipline in my work. It became very clear that my days of smiling my way out of tough situations were over. I made the wise decision to capitulate and comply.

During my initiation into everyday civilian life, I slowly lost touch with the Gianni family. It was also during this period that I realized things were not working out with Bonnie. In my new college life, I soon realized how little we had in common. Bonnie had no interest in higher education. She had started working for some large company right out of high school and was more interested in a paycheck. She saw my studying and cramming for tests only as something that took me away from her. It was true that school and work now consumed most of my time and we weren't having much fun together. I could barely support myself on what I earned driving school buses. Gone were the carefree days when I would blow a month's wages on one hot date.

Bonnie wanted to get married; I wanted to hang out at the student union and ponder higher philosophical and theological questions. Unfortunately she thought marriage was a foregone conclusion. Her dad was even making a place for me in his firm. Bonnie soon issued the "marry me or lose me" ultimatum. I, in turn, started back-pedaling as fast as I could. After many agonizing late-night phone marathons, Bonnie and I decided to date other people. Breaking up is tough on everyone. You get used to a warm body, easy familiarity and companionship. We tried to reconcile a few times, mainly so we could deal with physical needs, but it was no use. My first California romance ended.

No matter how I rationalized it, this was a stressful time for me. Money was in short supply—budgeting had never been a strong suit of mine. If I had run out of money when I was in the service I could lay low on the base for a week or two, or borrow until the eagle laid another golden egg. In civilian life, there was no mess hall serving up free chow and I had to pay rent for housing. Furthermore, there was no one to turn to for monetary help. I was too proud to ask my friends for money and my family couldn't be tapped in any way. My mom had just retired from nursing. She had two small trust funds from the Sutton and Bull sides of her family. These stipends barely covered her normal living expenses. I knew I was extremely lucky that she had no real health problems that would require financial help from me. That left me free to pursue my dreams.

I was having a few problems in school. I might have been overambitious signing up for a full load the first semester. At any rate, it soon became apparent that the straight A's I had envisioned were going to be harder to come by than I had expected. I was getting good at studying into the wee hours of the morning.

One of my school counselors projected it would take me three years or so to attain my two-year A.A. degree. For a young man in a hurry, even knowing I had to work full-time, that sounded outrageous. I told the counselor I'd finish in a year and a half—"just watch me"—and I geared up to take more than a regular course load. I decided that my breakup with Bonnie was probably a good thing for it allowed me to transmute all my energy into dedicated study. Only a few short months later I found myself filing that powerful resolution under the heading of "famous last words."

I started becoming extremely interested in history. I was very lucky to get a fabulous teacher for an American History course. This eloquent professor was a mover and a shaker. He told such great tales and had such a forceful way of making events of the past come to life that I was always disappointed when the bell rang and his class was over. I hadn't chosen a major yet but, after being exposed to this phenomenal professor, the study of human history and a career in teaching fired my imagination.

It was in this American History class that I met a good-looking redhead who would later become my first wife. Joanna was a young, gorgeous intellectual with a Garbo-Dietrich haughtiness to her manner. Her aura was that of a very strong woman who seemed to fit better in the '30s or '40s than she did in the '60s. A very accomplished dancer, she, like just about everyone in L.A., had been bitten by the showbiz bug. As a sideline to help her out financially, Joanna got odd jobs as a professional Scottish folk dancer, entertaining in various night spots around L.A.

In many ways my involvement with Joanna was tied in with my new appreciation for higher education. She was the first attractive young woman I had met with whom I could share academic pursuits; she was a stimulating classmate and a stimulating lover. She was also on hand when I took my first course in Art History with a very accomplished professor who inspired me enough that I decided unequivocally to major in history. I also decided that I wanted a career in the art world—not as an artist, for I had absolutely no drawing skills and no ambition in that direction, but in some capacity that would allow me to express the deep wells of appreciation for art I only then discovered within myself.

Because Joanna was an integral part of these momentous discoveries of mine, I began to identify her with everything new and enriching that was going on in my life. As a result, I failed to see anything about her except that which made me happy. Admittedly, it was her spectacular looks that first caught my attention. I was so swept away by the purely physical impact she made on me, it was awhile before I realized how extraordinarily brainy she was. Joanna had the body of a model—dramatically defined calves, skin like white porcelain, sparkling green eyes, fiery red hair (and a temperament to match). She was Scottish through and through.

In the beginning, our paths crossed often; we were in the same classes and we'd run into each other at student hangouts. I wanted to take her out, but I wasn't making very good time with her. She already had a few boyfriends and, having been raised in Glendale, she had many friends. After she rebuffed me a few times, I signaled my frustration and proceeded to give her the cold shoulder. I was amazed at the impact it made on her. I could sense her fear of losing communication with me, and I then knew she actually cared somewhat for me, this former Marine with a southern drawl. The hair on the back of my neck nearly stood up when I realized it *was* possible to date Joanna. In almost no time at all, we became a campus item.

Although I had been close to some brainy Oriental ladies, Joanna was the first girl with whom I could carry on a real adult conversation. Despite her talents as a dancer, performing was only a part-time interest for her. Her most pressing ambition was to complete her education and perhaps become a grade school teacher.

We saw each other steadily and exclusively during the year and a half we remained at Glendale Junior College. Joanna lived at home with her recently divorced mother. She had been raised in a secure, middle-class family. We got together on weekends and one or two nights each week, meeting in my cramped studio apartment. Every time I looked at Joanna sans clothes, I couldn't believe my luck. I began to fantasize about what it would be like to be married to a woman with Joanna's insatiable sexual appetite.

When I discovered she also shared my new interests in art, that—plus the erotic fantasy she fulfilled when she finally spent the night at my apartment—convinced me that I couldn't live without her. I began to get these strong acquisitive feelings. Today I'd be considered a chauvinist for wanting to totally possess a woman, but all I knew then was that if we were married we could make love all the time. As I look back on this now I realize I gave almost no thought as to how I was going to support a wife or how both of us could be students at the same time.

Those first months we spent together were like being on a swirling, breathtaking carousel ride made up of equal parts intellect and passion. I visualized Joanna as some kind of mythical and glamorous creature. I realize now that I never truly viewed her in any realistic sense.

After a bumpy ride, my first semester drew to an end and I was launched. My grades weren't what I had hoped but I'd gotten over some hurdles and felt lucky to have discovered that I wanted to major in history.

I didn't sign up for the summer school session and my driving job ended with the school year. Anyway, I'd had it with driving buses, even though there were certainly some good aspects to the job. I'd learned a lot about the surrounding area and the local people. And I was very involved with some of the handicapped children I drove on the "home-school" bus where I would pick the children up right at their homes and help them into their classrooms.

I looked forward to finding a summer job working full-time in a new endeavor. I decided to try my luck at sales. People had been telling me for years that with my inherent gift of gab and my ease around strangers I would be a natural as a salesman. So during the summer of 1963 I decided to put those flattering predictions to the test. I answered an ad for a sales position for a water softener franchise and was hired. I went to work selling water softeners door to door.

I had visions of immense prosperity. My plan for the summer was to work hard and make thousands of dollars. My want list included a new car, new wardrobe for the fall semester, and enough money to buy my school books in advance of the school term. My employer, a square-jawed young guy in his late twenties, had just moved to L.A. and bought the Pasadena franchise. Bud didn't know much more about the area than I did. All he wanted was to support his attractive wife and small children. Bud was a good guy. He gave me some pointers on what he knew about selling water softeners, along with a map of Pasadena, and told me to jump in my car and start hitting doors. What he didn't know was that the Pasadena area had a problem with electrolysis in the ground soil. If a soft water tank was installed to water pipes in this electrically charged soil, the joining of different types of metal would eventually erode the hapless homeowner's pipes. As I started my new job I was not aware of these problems; however, most homeowners that I ran into were not "hapless"—they were well aware of this deal-killing monster.

In my enthusiasm to start my sales career, I had signed up for a straight commission job where I even had to provide transportation. I hit the streets all dressed up in my Sunday best, wearing slacks with creases reminiscent of my Marine Corps days, shoes shined to a satisfying gloss, and even a tie. But each day as I knocked on suburbia's doors, people were not reacting as I had expected. Not only did they have informed objections about water-softener equipment, but people didn't seem to trust someone all dressed up. They looked at me like I was some sort of slick flim-flam artist.

Undaunted, I read all the sales manuals I could get. I drove all over Pasadena working my rear-end off, but still had very few sales. Bud had told me that if I knocked on 120 doors a day that just from sheer numbers I would succeed in making sales. Well, no deal. Here I was wearing holes in my "Sunday-go-to-meeting" shoes, my old Chevy was eating gas and oil, my tires were wearing thin, and I wasn't even covering expenses.

After six weeks of on-the-job experience in sales, I had made $190 in commissions. I couldn't make my rent. My dreams of glory were fading fast. In desperation I quit. I had come to care a tremendous amount for Bud and his family and I was devastated. Bud was from a wealthy family and I don't think he really understood what it meant to work to support yourself. I could see that he was shaken when I gave notice.

Angry at myself for not succeeding at this first try, and refusing to be defeated, I applied for a sales job with another franchise selling water softeners. It was a Glendale-based franchise in an area that, I made sure, didn't have these electrolysis problems. This new franchise encompassed some brand new towns north of Glendale where they were building tract homes faster than I could bang on the newly installed doors. Millions of people were flooding into the L.A. basin, making it a lucrative time to be in the construction business.

With the summer almost over, I needed to sell my little heart out. Joanna thought I was screwing up big time and the last time I had seen my landlord I had to ask him to carry me on his past due account. I had a new plan. First, I decided that the straight-laced business attire had to go. I needed to make a more casual impression on the predominantly female clientele. I decided to dress more like our route men, the guys who lifted the soft-water tanks and drove the trucks. My jeans had a couple of holes and the faded look that would become a fashion statement years later. I bought some blue short-sleeved workshirts and had "Jack" emblazoned across the front, finishing the look with my rugged-looking Marine Corps combat boots.

I hit the bricks and diligently knocked on 120 doors a day. Things began to look up. I identified myself as the soft-water route man and told them I was trying to expand my route. All of a sudden I was being asked in for coffee or tea. I had a brochure made up with a photo of a water softener that I would deftly hand out to each housewife who opened her door. "Are you familiar with this product?" I'd ask. If they said they already had one, it saved me a lot of time.

I began to chalk up a phenomenal sales record. In one housing development of 300 homes, I wound up selling a water softener to virtually every single house. Within the next year and a half I had built up a large enough customer base that the franchise needed only enough new customers to replace those lost through normal attrition.

As summer drew to a close I was current on my rent and traded in my old 1954 Chevy for a two-year-old Ford Falcon. I had also earned myself a great job that I could continue during the school year. As the school term rolled around, I was able to work afternoons, evenings and weekends selling door to door. I did so well I worked only an hour or two a day, or sometimes just on Saturday, but I still earned the equivalent of a full-time salary while going to college.

My boss was thrilled. He agreed to pay me a base salary plus commission on my sales, and to pay me extra to train salespeople for other soft-water franchises all over the state. It got so he wouldn't let a prospective client purchase a franchise unless they were trained in the art of door-to-door sales by me.

Things were looking up when I went back to school. I knew a little more about how to give the teachers what they wanted. The 1950s seemed like ancient history, and the '60s decade seemed to promise unlimited expansion. There were some powerful hammer blows to the national psyche in November of '63. Everyone who was alive at that time will remember where they were and when they learned that President John F. Kennedy was shot. I remember I was leaving a hamburger joint across from Glendale College on my way to class when someone gave me the news of the catastrophe.

This national tragedy brought me even closer to my girlfriend, Joanna. My first thoughts about the killing were that the military had done in Kennedy. I knew that the military had been highly frustrated at Kennedy because of the Bay of Pigs fiasco, the Cuban missile crisis, and his letting the Russians put up the Berlin Wall.

Joanna and I followed the events after Dallas closely and didn't agree with the official version of what happened— that there had been a lone gunman. I do not claim to know or have any special knowledge about who did what nor do I have proof of a conspiracy of governmental agencies working together or alone, but the overwhelming feeling I had about Kennedy's assassination was that there was a cover-up and it was incumbent on the students to get involved in helping America steer through what looked like perilous times.

The assassination sparked a lot of changes in our society. It seemed to give us all a sense of relatedness. In the case of Joanna and me, it got us more involved in politics, starting with an awareness of the generation gap between ourselves as students and our parents. I had never been at odds with my elders or parents before regarding political issues.

As we students began to question authority and started taking politics very seriously, changes began to take place in our dress, music, and mores. Longer hair on men was *de rigeur*, young women abandoned their bras, and the first flower children or hippies started to appear. Overnight, plastic beads were hung in doorways and psychedelic posters decorated formerly blank walls. Fresh green plants flourished, the music shifted to political folk songs and hard rock, and our more conservative 1950s' clothing style was replaced with wild, colorful tie-dye prints and a more bohemian look. Experimentation with marijuana was endemic to the new '60s' culture.

Having been so recently discharged from the service, I was more resistant to the fashion change than most of my new friends. But dress aside, I was caught up in the rebellion against the status quo like most college students of the time.

I settled into a routine over the next year or so, in order to complete the required curriculum and graduate in the year and a half I had given myself to earn an A.A. degree. I also wanted to synchronize my graduation from Glendale College with Joanna's. We had spoken about going on to UC, either in Los Angeles or Santa Barbara after graduation. I visited UCLA in Westwood and witnessed firsthand the pandemonium that occurred when the bell sounded to signal the end of a class period: about 30,000 people spilled onto the campus grounds. I didn't like it at all; after all, I had been raised in a small town. UCLA had three times as many people as Kilgore, Texas.

Another thing that made me think I should take a look at Santa Barbara was the smog in L.A., quite bad even then. Quite often when I was driving down the freeway, the smog would be so bad my eyes would start watering, often forcing me to pull off the road. On high "smog alert" days some people actually dropped dead. City officials finally started passing air pollution laws around this time.

After that experience, I went to visit the UC Santa Barbara campus. Notably, it was 15 to 20 miles outside of town but there were only about 6,000 students. Most of the classes were held in WW II buildings left over from the Marine Corps air base. After the war, the base airstrip was made into the Santa Barbara Municipal Airport and the rest of the base became the UC campus at Santa Barbara.

I talked to the dean of admissions, who received me personally when I walked into the Quonset hut that housed his offices. He put his hand on my shoulder and let me know I had been accepted. He offered to help me get set up with classes and counseling when I finally moved there. Few students today can expect the dean of admissions to take a personal interest in them and offer to help them fill out the necessary forms. Nowadays, there are huge lines and computer printouts—a dehumanizing ordeal where the aspiring student usually doesn't get to talk to a live person, much less the dean of admissions.

While we were finishing up at Glendale, I started toying with the notion that it was time for Joanna and me to get married. Well, the thought didn't come out of thin air: Joanna had been giving out hints and signals as graduation approached. She, too, had been applying to different colleges and she finally gave me an ultimatum: either propose or she would go off to a different school and become some other guy's woman. Tired of my own cooking and fantasizing that marriage would mean wild, abandoned lovemaking every night, I jumped in without much thought about how I would support both of us in college. In my defense, I will say that I thought I was in love with her. Who could resist this titian-tressed dancing girl who looked like a Degas figurine come to life?

The plan was to marry as soon as we graduated and then go to UCSB where we would live in married students' housing. I had just found out that I was eligible for the GI bill, so with a $120-a-month check from the government and my job working for a soft-water franchise in Santa Barbara, I figured I could support the two of us.

For my graduation, my mother came out to visit and to watch me don cap and gown. Of course, she got to meet Joanna and her family. In true parental fashion, she told her some embarrassing stories from my childhood, and she also brought up the name of my ex-girlfriend, Bonnie, a few times. While we were having dinner with my future mother-in-law, Joanna and I set a wedding date in late August and planned the move to Santa Barbara to take place right after the nuptials.

I should have known things weren't going to work out too well when we had a huge fight in the elevator at Glendale City Hall on our way to plunk down the few dollars for our marriage license. I don't remember what we were fighting about, but I remember that Joanna had a very sharp tongue; it cut like a broad ax. Some people just have a knack for that sort of thing, and she had it.

We had a traditional wedding celebration and we definitely looked the part of the radiant young couple just starting out on the threshold of a promising and meaningful life together. We picked a beautiful old Episcopal church for our ceremony. Our wedding day was bright and summery. Joanna looked stunning in her white satin bridal gown, and both families, hers and mine, were well represented.

Mal and Julie Gianni and their son Jim were in attendance. (Jim Gianni had gotten married before me and he and his wife were expecting a baby in the coming months.) My boss at the soft-water franchise also attended. He had helped arrange my future employment with his brother in Santa Barbara and had given me a generous bonus to help launch our married life. My mother again flew out from Texas and brought a few of my relatives with her. It came as no surprise that my father didn't show up. He hadn't come to my graduation either. I'm sure he had his reasons, but these no-shows did not pass by unnoticed.

Joanna looked the perfect blushing bride. Nobody present, including me, would have suspected the incredible change that would come over her as soon as she could identify herself as "Mrs. Jack Swanson."

After the festivities came to an end, we jumped in my trusty light blue Ford Falcon and headed down to Rosarita Beach in Ensenada, Mexico. It was a bargain-basement honeymoon, the only kind we could afford. I had been dreaming about this vacation honeymoon for a while. I hadn't taken a break from work or the books since I got out of the service. Never having been to Baja, California before, I looked forward to sand and surf and quiet time with this long-legged wife of mine. What I did not expect was the immediate marked change in what had earlier been my bride's sparkling party personality. Thinking back on it, I compared it to the feeling I got when the gong sounded at the start of a prizefight.

We didn't reach our motel in Rosarita Beach until later in the evening after a four- to five-hour drive. Since we only had a fleeting three or four days before we needed to report to class in Santa Barbara, I was in a hurry to consummate the marriage, especially since I had not been allowed to see the bride-to-be the day before the wedding.

Once we were settled and unpacked in our beach cabaña, I got the shock of my life. Joanna pulled away from me and let it be known that she was not interested in any physical contact—and she wasn't talking about this particular moment. I was ready to understand fatigue after the ceremony, or being worn out by our car trip, but what she said very plainly was that she would no longer put up with what she considered a gross invasion of her person. I was pushed out of shape, to say the least, to think that while I was having visions of nonstop marital bliss, she was "enduring" our lovemaking just waiting to get that wedding ring.

I didn't get much sleep that night, especially since I was directed toward the couch. My alarms were going off but I didn't know how to deal with this ill-favored turn of events. I just hoped that it was not as serious as it appeared to be and that she would come to her senses. No luck. Our wedding night set the tone for our whole marriage. Since we had just wed, I couldn't entertain the idea of divorce or annulment, so for the sake of appearances, I decided to give it the old college try and see if we could work things out. Nothing can prepare a person for this kind of eventuality. Getting married at twenty-three began to look like a very dumb idea. As I looked back I realized that there had been warning signs

I should have heeded. If my friends could see me now, I thought to myself.

Once we settled into married student housing next to the UCSB campus, Joanna and I signed up for almost all the same classes. (At least we had the same interests academically.) We found a cat with no tail wandering around lost so we took him in.

I started working for the soft-water outfit and made some unsettling discoveries: Santa Barbara is a small city compared to some of the 100 or so suburbs that make up L.A., and there was very little building going on in this sleepy Spanish-style town. On top of this, I found that the big cheese who operated this so-called model franchise had left hundreds of tanks attached to homes of nonpaying customers, simply to make his business look more prosperous than it really was. Finally, in Glendale I had been a valued employee, but here I was the new guy with too many smart ideas.

I found myself working harder for less money, all the while trying to cope with my unresponsive wife and school work. Joanna was intransigent when I mentioned her helping out by getting a job of some sort. She embraced the feminism of the early '60s that said we should share housecleaning responsibilities, but she refused to get a job to share financial responsibilities. It became obvious that we had wanted to marry each other for grossly conflicting reasons. I had wanted to own her beautiful, long legs and she had wanted to use me both as a meal ticket and a target for indoor torture.

9

Finding My True Calling

The university environment at UC Santa Barbara was so stimulating that I put my problems with Joanna on hold and threw myself into my role as a serious student of the history of man and art. I found professors there who truly deserved being defined as "intellectuals." One history professor so impressed me that I decided to major in Middle Eastern History. Originally from Syria, he had mastered ten different languages, and served as an active consultant to President Johnson regarding the Muslim countries bordering the Soviet Union. For me, he made ancient civilizations in the Middle East come to life. He opened my eyes to the great civilizations of Rome, Byzantium, the Eastern Roman Empire, and the Caliphates of the Arabic empire that once almost circled the globe. The Arab empire in the Middle Ages had been larger than the Roman empire had been at its peak.

The study of the Holy Lands and its various religions and cultures, especially those of the Greco-Roman, Jewish, Muslim and Christian groups, helped me understand the ascent of mankind. Through my studies I became aware of the tenets and dogma of various religions, how they differed and where they were similar.

I also became fascinated with the art works and artifacts associated with these powerful Mediterranean cultures. The art history courses I chose covered all known civilizations and I was soon able to compare ancient cultures and become knowledgeable about the artifacts and structures that had been preserved over the centuries.

At the same time, it was hard to study in this laid-back beach community. When Joanna and I walked to class, we would walk a block or so from our house to the beach and follow the beach around to the campus. Our apartment was just north of the campus in an area known as Isla Vista. Hundreds and hundreds of apartment houses, large and small, were being built to accommodate the influx of students to this expanding university. In the three years Joanna and I were going to UCSB, the student population went from 6,000 to over 15,000. The population of Isla Vista doubled and doubled again. There was an unprecedented building program on campus. Hundreds of millions of dollars worth of buildings were being erected, from huge student centers to nine-story libraries only partially filled with books. Everything was new. The Marine Corps buildings were swept away to allow the children of America's returning WW II heroes to attend a tuition-free university.

These were tumultuous times. It was the beginning of the jet age, civil rights struggles, and the longest running war in American history, Vietnam. Post-war Europe and Asia were still trying to rebuild their bombed-out cities and manufacturing plants, but here there was no talk of recession.

My love affair with Joanna was definitely winding down. I certainly cared for her but we fought constantly. Our arguments were explosive and I threw away my wedding ring quite a few times. There was always tension in the air. Any intimacy between the two of us was either a furtive encounter when her defenses were low or when, in sheer frustration, I would damned near take her by force.

I'd stomp out and not return for days. I began to develop new, single friends. It was appalling to see how the young, unsupervised college students lived and partied with no thought of the future. I loved it! I established crash pads all over Isla Vista, mostly grungy couches with stuffing spilling out of crumbling cushions.

On one of my excursions, I ran into my old Marine Corps buddy, Jerry McCall. He lived in a guest house on his parents' private estate in the hills above Santa Barbara. Jerry was the epitome of the proverbial playboy. He had every toy imaginable, including a red two-seater Jaguar. He wore driving gloves and even a neck scarf that flew catchingly in the wind. Although he was a bit affected for my taste,

I had to hand it to him. He pulled it off with élan and the girls ate it up. It did kind of bother me that wherever we went he just had to sign his name and charge it to his old man. On the other hand, the kind of lush life Jerry lived served as a welcome respite for me when I wanted to escape my war-torn marriage.

I had great fun with Jerry. My only reservation about his lifestyle was that I was afraid he would take the route of some of my Glendale friends and not finish college, despite his avowed plan to continue on to law school. A year or so after our reacquaintance, he dropped out of school and became a full-fledged, long-haired hippie. I lost track of him for a year or so, and then ran into him one night at a student hangout. He had just come from the Haight scene. I no longer recognized the former Marine or rich kid I had once known. I was glad he hadn't done himself in. From what I learned about his later life, I know he paid for his mind-altering experiences.

Years later I found his name still listed in the Santa Barbara phone directory. I dialed the number and asked if this was the Jerry from Marine Corps days gone by. It was. I got together with him and found that he was a respected businessman with a growing family. When I met him for lunch after a twenty-year gap, he said, "Funny thing, I was just thinking about you." He said his young son was growing up and the thought crossed his mind about how he wished he had boxed in the Corps like his old friend, Jack, because he would like to be able to help train his son in martial arts.

When I look back on my college years, I always think in terms of work. It seems that I was a worker first and foremost and a student second. Soon after I started at UCSB, UC went from a semester to a quarter system, which squeezed even more into a shorter period of time and made it harder on students who had to work.

I was eking out a living as a door-to-door salesman, but I found myself more and more a sales trainer for the parent corporation. After about a year at my new job in Santa Barbara, I was still something of a celebrity in the company because of my sales record in L.A. When the parent corporation had its franchise convention, I was held up as an example. I was planning to hang in with this service business for the foreseeable future, thinking a vice presidency was in the offing after I graduated. Don, president and owner of the corporation and someone I had come to admire, had other ideas. He was getting flack from some of his young, aspiring executive types about my earning a regular wage when I was not a full-time employee. Having become a friend of the family, I had easy access to Don, and that also drove some people nuts.

Don called me aside one day and surprised my by saying: "Jack, you have a great future here—might even take my place someday. But if you want to stay with us you're going to have to quit school and work full-time." What a blow. I knew that Don hadn't finished college and was somewhat touchy on the subject. Yet here was my mentor and semi-hero telling me to give up school now, when I could finally see the finish line.

The ramifications of losing my job in this college town that had so few opportunities to earn decent money were enormous. Student wages and typical student jobs didn't appeal to me, nor would they feed my wife and our burgeoning menagerie of pets. (By now we had four dogs, a tailless cat, and a couple of well-occupied fish tanks. I always seemed to be a couple of hundred dollars in debt to the local veterinarian.)

After thinking overnight about Don's ultimatum, I decided to turn in my badge. When I quit I could tell that Don was aware that he had crossed the line and withdrawn the support that he and his family had previously given me. When I turned in my resignation, I wrote him a 19-page letter in which I itemized everything I felt was wrong with the company and enumerated the changes I thought he should make if he wanted to stay in business. I saw myself as Martin Luther nailing his 95-point protest to the Catholic Church on the Wittenburg Palace cathedral door. (I later heard that Don had implemented all the changes I had suggested.)

After quitting my job selling water softeners, I held down several part-time jobs. I drove trucks and buses, and worked as a food checker. One of my part-time jobs was driving a bus on Saturday mornings. I had to get up between 4 and 5 A.M., go down to the transit yard, pick out a school bus and drive all over Santa Barbara picking up migrant workers and taking them to various lemon orchards. The pay was good because it was a union job, although it always bothered me that the Teamster guys would come around once a month collecting our due—cash only, no checks.

One Saturday morning I overslept and was late picking up the Sunkist lemon pickers. I was told that if I was late again I was going to lose both my bus-driving job and my job as bus washer on Sundays. Perhaps it was God's way of telling me I couldn't keep up with the pace, because damned if I didn't sleep in the following Saturday. This meant curtains for my job.

If I hadn't been getting a monthly check from the G.I. bill, I wouldn't have been able to keep going. Joanna and I were down to rolling pennies as I looked around desperately for help. My folks wouldn't help—something about making your bed and now lying in it.

One of my best friends at this time was Stan Pedroncelli, my French professor. He was a young Italian guy in his early thirties. He was going through his own trials and tribulations at this point in his life. His second child, a beautiful young girl of eighteen months, had just come down with spinal meningitis and had to have brain surgery. It would leave the baby alive but destined to a life of invalidism. To top it off, Stan didn't have sufficient health insurance and he was $60,000 in debt.

Stan was one of the only people I felt I could talk to at that time. Even with all of his own problems, he was always sympathetic to others. I told him about my immediate hardships and he did something I will never forget. He took a ten dollar bill from his wallet and offered me a loan. I took the ten dollars and vowed to repay him. His act of kindness had quite an effect on me. That afternoon, I felt motivated to climb out of the hole I had fallen into and to get a job that very day.

I put on my most presentable pair of slacks and a clean shirt and started walking down the main street of downtown Santa Barbara, going from door to door, asking each business establishment I entered if they could give me a job. I was working my way down a secondary street, not the main drag, and wandered into an office not even knowing what type of business it was. I heard some radio sounds and static and asked if someone there needed a willing and able-bodied man. The guy in the office smiled up at me and asked if I had a valid driver's license. I said, "Yes, I do." He pointed at a cab outside in the parking lot and told me to jump in that car, head down to the bus station, and get to work.

With no hesitation—I'm not even sure the dispatcher checked to see if I had a valid license—I hopped in to this Green Cab company vehicle and pulled up in front of the bus depot. It was in the middle of the afternoon. My first fare opened the rear door, jumped in, and told me where he wanted to go. I smiled cheerfully, turned the ignition key, and nothing happened; the car wouldn't start. I didn't know it, but the back seat was wired in such a way that if you had a fare sitting down, the cab wouldn't start unless you turned the fare meter on. One of the local cabbies saw my predicament, sauntered over to my cab, reached his arm through the front window and bent the meter arm back. It then flipped forward and started ticking off its "time is money" message.

I was launched. I made enough money on tips that first shift to buy groceries and give my friend Stan back his ten dollar bill, which I never had to use. I drove the cab for a few months. It was actually fun, and taught me a lot about the citizens of Santa Barbara, especially the group that emerged from the bars around 2 A.M. It was good money but the late hours were hard on my study time. So after a couple of eye-opening months observing the demimonde in this quiet little city, I found more conventional employment at a men's clothing store.

Despite the nagging struggles with my marriage and the constant problem of keeping my head above water financially, I was developing a genuine love of learning. I was never going to be a Sanskrit scholar but I was fulfilling my goal of getting a formal education. Around this time I was feeling good about my personal achievements, so when a fellow employee at the men's store asked me, "What are you going to be when you finish college?" I was taken aback. I looked the "grand inquisitor" in the eye and said, "I already am."

I was quietly becoming integrated into the culture of my adopted city. I was part of the university community, a wage earner in a local store, and, driving buses, trucks and cabs, I certainly had learned my way around. Besides the garden ambiance of Santa Barbara and its offshore Channel Islands, I loved the old sections of town, which were exclusively adobe style with characteristic Spanish architecture. I would hang around El Paseo where there were many quaint shops and art galleries. The local galleries displayed rather conservative art works, mostly regional paintings of the California coast or paintings of Spanish-style haciendas of days gone by, but still, I was drawn to them and, at that time, only vaguely aware of the mercantile opportunities.

Something about the smell of fresh paint and the gentility of the people who purchased these decorative paintings piqued my interest. Many were more like vanity galleries than serious businesses, frequently owned by a well-to-do doctor's wife or socialite who merely wanted to dabble in art or busy themselves with a job.

I was around enough that eventually I'd watch over the galleries for the proprietors while they ran errands or went out to eat. Slowly, I got more familiar with what went into buying and selling art work. I then discovered some outdoor shows along the beachfront in downtown Santa Barbara where many local artists displayed their works and sold them to the public. I was very impressed with some of the young artists' work I saw displayed along the beaches and, pretty soon, I would show up at these art shows on the waterfront every Sunday.

The great changes taking place in so many areas encompassed arts as well as politics. There was a wellspring of activity coming from newly evolving artists, especially in the visual arts. And because the country had been on a kind of economic roll since the end of the Second WW, people were generally more affluent. Having acquired all the basic labor-saving machines, televisions, and cars they needed or wanted, many turned their attention to cultural pursuits and decorative arts.

The sixties also ushered in an era of increased public tolerance about the arts in general, as well as a lot more permissiveness in literature and films. Many of the fledgling artists I observed in Santa Barbara were just ordinary people who had been inspired to experiment. Some of them had former careers as commercial artists or architects and now had the time and money to drop out of the traditional working world and discover their own artistic possibilities. In general, free self-expression was the order of the day and nowhere was this more apparent than in California's newly evolving art world.

This new art scene was not being subsidized by some noblesse oblige European aristocracy. It was fueled by an outcropping of creative energy within artistically inclined people. My sense was that the experimental artists I met on the beaches of Santa Barbara were all linked to the revolutionary climate of the times. Direct contact between the artists and the general public was a new phenomenon and a far cry from the old-world system where, right up to the nineteenth century, the majority of artists and artisans were commissioned by the aristocracy or merchant princes. Many of these twentieth-century American artists were still in their teens and were painting from the gut. They were living from hand to mouth. The profit motive hadn't entered the picture for most of them. This new era was so exciting, the desultory life of drifting from one pad to another didn't faze them. Unlike many of the psychedelic hedonists of the later sixties, most of these young experimenters were productive and creative. They were on a political mission to make art accessible to everyone.

I made friends with some of the artists I met on the beach. I watched in awe as they worked on their paintings and sculptures. I remember a radiantly beautiful young woman named Vijali Clark, who was the most talented sculptor I had ever seen. She did bas relief portraits in stone that captured something I felt pointed directly to a divine force. This artist also painted some of the most dramatic and moving portraits of Mahatma Gandhi and other spiritual leaders that I have ever seen. As I got to know Vijali, I found out she had been a nun, and later, rejecting that lifestyle, she had walked barefoot across India. The last time I heard about her she was wandering around isolated desert areas in the American southwest carving sculptures in random acts of beauty.

I was as involved with the 1960s' art renaissance as anyone could be without actually grabbing some tools and creating a work of art on my own. The thought that these talented newcomers needed some cohesive support and encouragement was taking seed, even then, before I left college and moved to San Francisco. When I finally entered into this career a few years later, it wasn't quite the "overnight" phenomenon it must have seemed to family and friends.

It was in late '65 and early '66 that Joanna and I got involved in serious anti-war protest demonstrations. We participated in local student peace marches, and staged walk-outs and sit-ins in our college classes. We held silent vigils outside the building where the university's governing Board of Regents met. Everything had become polarized. Amid many free speech rallies, the Black Panther activists were alerting the students to the rage felt by disenfranchised people in America. The war in Southeast Asia was heating up, and more and more American service people were being sent overseas. The students constituted a main voice of dissent against the politics of the government, or what was now derisively referred to as "the establishment."

I was still working full-time, studying full-time, and trying to hold my marriage together. But there was energy in the times and in the community we shared as student activists. I had turned into a typical '60s' rebel, though having been a Marine I drew the line at wearing my hair flowing down my back or growing a scraggly beard.

I instigated at least two anti-war demonstrations, organizing bus trips to the State Capitol building for 5,000 protesting students who marched down the capital's streets. These were peaceful protests; we actually went inside the offices of our state legislators and spoke person-to-person. Ironically, these were issues that my wife and I agreed on, so quite often we marched shoulder to shoulder even when our home life was still an on-again off-again disaster. We had the same meeting of the minds about the war as we had about our studies. But, my personal life took a back seat to the anti-war fever that seemed to permeate every aspect of our lives.

As I studied the history of Southeast Asia and Vietnam, I learned about French colonization of that land and America's involvement in helping the French reestablish themselves in Indochina after their defeat by the Japanese in WW II. After the Second World War, the French were given back their former colony by the Western powers, America being the primary player. The French were summarily thrown out for the second time in 1954. American leaders felt our military forces should secure South Vietnam as a free "democratic" haven for those Vietnamese who were aligned with the west and supposedly anti-Communist.

The more I researched our role in Vietnam, the more it looked to me like we were, in effect, being neo-colonialist. With the Geneva Accord of 1954 signed by the French and so-called Communist Vietnamese, the U.S. had brokered a deal that would help extricate the French from a losing situation. The Vietnamese were led by Ho Chi Minh, a charismatic leader whom America had befriended and helped arm so that he could drive the Japanese out of his home-land during WW II. After the war, Ho Chi Minh thought he had vanquished the bad guys and now his country would finally be independent. That's when the Western powers forced the French on this small nation. Vietnam had some seaports and harbors that seemed perfect for strategic defense of Southeast Asia. The country was also rich in oil and prior to the devastation of war with the U.S., had been the "rice basket" of Asia.

The Geneva Accord stated that the Communists would pull their troops back and control the northern half of Vietnam, that the French would withdraw their troops, and that America would support the pro-West Vietnamese in the south. The agreement called for free elections in two years' time, letting the Vietnamese people decide by vote who would control a unified nation.

The so-called free election never took place. The leaders of America became worried about the possibility of a Communist world takeover and abandoned the idea of a free election. As Ho Chi Minh continued to try to liberate his country, we found ourselves between two sides in its civil war.

I felt that we had no business in this war, and I was surprised that the American people allowed President Johnson to escalate us into a full-fledged war. When Johnson announced our Navy had been "sneak attacked" in the Gulf of Tonkin off South Vietnam, I felt it was a ruse. Years later I found out I was right.

I could have been called back into the military at any time, but since I had served my country already I didn't have to worry about being drafted. I don't know what I would have done if I had been called back. I'm glad I never had to make the choice between relocating to Canada or staying to fight in what I considered a civil war that America should stay out of.

The stand I took was not too popular either with my family or Joanna's, whose mother demanded to know how a wholesome young girl like her daughter could turn into a Communist in a town like Santa Barbara. When I got involved with the Peace and Freedom Party, and made the mistake of trying to explain to my father what I thought a new political party could accomplish, my dad wrote back that I should support the powers that be, right or wrong.

I soon became disillusioned with the Peace and Freedom Party. As the presidential election of '68 began to take shape, the well-meaning national leaders of this fledgling movement decided they wanted Dr. Spock and ex-convict and Black Panther, Eldridge Cleaver, to be their presidential and vice-presidential candidates, respectively. I could see these liberal leaders of the peace and freedom movement were not serious about winning a national election. They wanted recognition but were not doing what was necessary to win, or even come close to winning.

I soon felt I had made a strategic error in judgment, easy to do in this time of panic and overreaction, when mobs of kids were making dramatic pronouncements just to get their faces on the 11 o'clock news. The original ideals got eaten up by violence and hostility, and we accomplished very little except to create bad press for all those involved.

In the midst of all the jockeying for power within these newly formed organizations, I got quite an education about the inner workings of politics. I started to worry that a civil war was in the offing in our own nation if the national government didn't show some flexibility. I heard people from every walk of life—matrons, clergy, professors, students—talking about challenging government policy.

It had reached a feverish pitch when, unexpectedly, President Johnson announced he would not seek another term as "your president." This was a major event and meant that someone else would soon be at the helm and, we hoped, end the war.

Even though the war in Vietnam was to continue and there were years of turmoil ahead, Johnson's act of withdrawal somehow defused a powder keg that was about to go off. This subtle but real change in the body politic had its effect on the activities of the people I was working with to bring about change. Our fund-raising efforts were decimated, for example; many past supporters thought the war would soon be over and, therefore, the sense of urgency no longer existed.

The Peace and Freedom Party lost momentum and seemed headed for extinction. On a personal level, I felt that my part in the anti-war movement had played itself out. As I backed out of political activities, I was confronted with the fact that my graduation from U.C. Santa Barbara was imminent. Finally, in June 1967, both Joanna and I donned cap and gown and received our diplomas with B.A. degrees in History. Again my mother flew out for the festivities and Joanna's family attended the graduation and reception. My dad was nowhere in sight, but this time he sent me a hundred dollars as a present.

Joanna and I were civil to one another in front of our families but we were at sword's point whenever we were alone together. I had been hoping that once we were out of school and both working things would be better between us. Instead, Joanna announced that she wanted to continue on to get her master's degree and teaching credential. I was disappointed but agreed, and we signed up for more debt.

Just before graduation, I had seen a new shopping mall being built in Santa Barbara. I was very much taken with the largest building in the complex, an impressive structure with Spanish architectural motifs. It may seem strange, but it was the look of that building, a soon-to-be Robinson's department store, that made me decide to work there.

As soon as the store started accepting applications, I was one of the first in line. I got a job managing the men's clothing department and the luggage department. I wasn't making a lot of money, but, once again, I was learning about managing people, this time in a retail organization, and I was living in Santa Barbara. Joanna and I rented a house on a hill with a view of the Santa Barbara Mission. We still had the four dogs, the cat, and our aquariums.

Even though Joanna and I didn't see much of each other during that time, we managed to have some memorable squabbles. She beaned me with an Old Spice bottle during one of these spats, and I seem to remember a large bowl of spaghetti being unceremoniously dumped on my head during our last year of wedded bliss. I can't remember for sure, but it's possible that I may have behaved inappropriately a few times myself.

At some point, Joanna told me that she didn't intend to teach school—that she was too sophisticated for teaching elementary grades. Her plan was to be a housewife; she had decided not to enter the workforce anytime soon.

Once out of school, we no longer had anything in common, and our relationship went steadily downhill. When I mentioned personal dreams, she poked holes in them. When I talked about moving to San Francisco to pursue different business opportunities, she made it clear that she would never leave Santa Barbara.

One afternoon I dragged out my suitcases and started packing. Joanna looked on and, strangely enough, seemed totally astonished that I would actually take this "final" step. As I headed for the door with my luggage, she said, "But Jack, what am I going to do? What about the dogs?" I turned and blurted out Clark Gable's famous line in *Gone with the Wind*: "Frankly, my dear, I don't give a damn."

After the histrionics of breaking up with Joanna, I went to bunk with some buddies of mine who were still in college in Isla Vista. Isla Vista was growing in population, but it was a unique community because it was all students—no "civilian folk" lived in its environs, no workaday adults to speak of, just 20,000 college kids all packed in together. The gals outnumbered the guys. My pals and I rented a huge house with five bedrooms where we happily crashed together and shared expenses. We were all bachelors, or at least I would be as soon as I could get around to legalizing my new status. I had now come to the conclusion that the marital state should be as extinct as the dinosaur.

One of my roommates was an Arab guy from Iraq with a high squeaky voice. Ali and I had met in one of my Middle Eastern History classes. He was "R.O.B."—right off the boat, when we first met, naive and thoroughly convinced all Westerners were corrupt and that the Koran was the absolute word of God. Over the next few years he became more American than I was. He had the best and largest record collection I had ever seen, and what a great time to be into music! Every week there were new albums coming out—the Beatles, the Doors, the Stones, the Byrds, Otis Redding, Janis Joplin, the Jefferson Airplane, even an occasional Elvis hit. Folk singers like Bob Dylan and Joan Baez were perpetually playing gigs on our campus or on other UC campuses in Los Angeles or San Francisco.

What a great time we all had in the spring and summer of '68. I was the only one holding down a full-time job, which meant I had some money to throw around. Most of the other guys were still being amply subsidized by well-to-do parents. Nevertheless, on the weekends I was free and I hung out with these guys at the beach, ogling the gals. I was doing really well at Robinson's, and, since I had become great friends with the personnel manager, he let me recruit most of the new salesgirls they needed. I would walk down the beach tiptoeing through gorgeous suntanned bodies, periodically stopping to ask prospective candidates if they wanted to work in various departments in our four-story store. I pointed out our flexible work hours and the 33-1/3% discount employees were given on ready-to-wear merchandise. I had that store stocked with UCSB students and recent graduates in no time. I even got Ali a job as a janitor.

I also encouraged Ali to be more persistent and demanding when he wanted dates. My prompting worked a little too well. He went for the numbers and found himself swamped with girlfriends. He went a little sex crazy, turning into a Lothario of sorts. He ended up dropping out of school to pursue his new, all-consuming addiction. Ali just let it all hang out. He had signed a deal with his government that he would serve five years in the Iraqi army for each year they paid for his schooling in America. He felt now that he couldn't go back; he no longer was a "true believer" and returning home would be his downfall, as he saw it. He could no longer contemplate serving twenty years in the army. His conclusion was to party it up for the foreseeable future until our government found out he wasn't in school. Then, when the jig was up, he planned to head to Canada and ask for political asylum.

I found myself leading a normal life for the first time in years—no more night classes, no more working two jobs, no more wife. But I did wrestle with the fact that I had failed in my marriage; it was something I never thought I would do. It messed with one of my "core values." And it was hard to write home and inform the folks.

One night as I was out hitting the night spots, I went into a popular college kids' bar on the beach called "The Strap." It was a favorite hangout for the jocks. There was a volleyball court out in back and a couple of pool tables, usually taken over by the local bikers. A good friend of mine was the bouncer so I always got preferential treatment and occasional free beers. I hadn't been there long when I saw an apparition before me. She was dressed in a strapless white cotton summer dress. She was dancing with some guy, probably her date for the night. I was dazzled—struck dumb on the spot. She was around nineteen, quite tall, and a brunette with extremely sensual facial features. She had enormous brown eyes and a hell of a body. Her most provocative feature by far was her unusually large and sensuously full, sexy lips. Without a doubt, she was the most "far out" lady I had ever seen.

I gaped like a tongue-tied school kid as I watched her dance. I couldn't stand on ceremony any longer. I walked onto the dance floor and cut in on her and her date after the first dance, a rock and roll hit, "Ride Sally Ride." I inhaled the intimate feminine scent of her and her perfume and I knew I wanted her in my life.

"Hi, my name is Jack," I said, smiling at her. "You're so beautiful it's about to give me a heart attack."

She laughed. "I must say you're holding up very nicely for someone in that condition."

"What's your name and when can I see you?"

"My name is Pam and you can't. The man I'm with tonight happens to be my fiancé."

"Oh, God," I said, "Tell me you're kidding!"

"I'm serious. And here he comes now."

That was the sum and substance of our first meeting. She continued to dance only with her escort for the remainder of that night. I couldn't believe a girl that special was about to throw her life away and marry such a straight-arrow type; the guy looked like an engineer or tax accountant.

I couldn't get Pam out of my mind. The next weekend I was strolling along the Isla Vista beach and, lo and behold, she and her boyfriend walked past me. She was in a bikini.

Holy shit! I thought. Look at that. Never had I seen a woman look so voluptuous. I was in love, again.

Because her boyfriend was with her, I just smiled and nodded at her in passing. She smiled briefly as well. This young girl with the short pixie haircut was what was known at the time as a "stone fox."

Serendipitously, a few days later, I saw her shopping in Robinson's while I was on duty. Thank God for small towns. Without even glancing my way, she strolled past me and out of the building. Although it was against the rules to leave my post during working hours, I threw caution to the wind and ran after her. When I caught up to her, I smiled and said, "Pam, please don't try to pretend you don't remember who I am."

"Oh, I remember you," she said, returning my smile. "I met you at The Strap last week, and your name is—let's see—."

"My name is Jack, Jack Swanson. And I also saw you at the beach a couple of days ago. Do you remember that?"

"Oh yes, I saw you."

"Hey, listen. I don't have much time so could you please give me a few vital statistics? You know, like your name, address, phone number?"

She laughed out loud at that. "I'm sorry, Jack, you're really very nice. And though I hate to repeat myself, I'm still engaged."

"Okay, okay," I said. "So nobody's perfect. I still want to know you and talk to you."

She gave me a look and, shaking her head, she quickly jotted down her phone number and gave it to me. We started dating from then on and after our first week of seeing each other nightly, Pam never again mentioned her now-former fiancé.

From our first date I knew I had never known a woman as generous and giving. Just to know she was pleasing me appeared to be her greatest turn-on. We were soon spending all our free time together. Surprise of surprises, I even got her a job part-time at Robinson's.

One of the amazing things about Pam was that she seemed totally unaware of her looks. She told me she had been an ugly duckling growing up and had an eye patch at one time to correct a vision problem. Now with contact lenses she had turned out to be a rare beauty with the sensitivity of someone who had had to cope with a disability. In fact, she was the first gorgeous girl I had ever met who didn't seem to know or care about her physical beauty. In her own blithe way she was simply letting the world "take me as I am." My buddies loved her. She fit right into our pad, and in those innocent collegiate days, we sometimes shared the same room with another couple, thinking nothing of it. We hung a sheet to provide some privacy. This was the era of "free love," but as I contemplate my experiences with the opposite sex, I will have to say that free love has never been and is never free.

Pam and I continued seeing each other steadily all through that summer and fall of '68. Meanwhile, Joanna and I had already signed the necessary documents to get our divorce under way. Though I hadn't lied to Pam about being married, I must have led her to believe my divorce was already final and that I was free to marry whenever I chose. Of course, the key phrase was "whenever I chose."

No matter how much in love I was with Pam, I was not ready to jump right into another marriage. Before initiating divorce proceedings or getting close to Pam, I had wanted to move to San Francisco. I was hot to start some kind of business of my own. I was nearing twenty-seven now and felt I no longer fit in with the university crowd. When I walked around campus I felt out of place, a little long of tooth. I noticed Pam even told her father, Dr. Lang, that I was younger than I was. I don't know if she meant to lie, but it gave me pause to think that my age was a factor to be reckoned with.

It was time I moved on. I knew that I wasn't going to climb the corporate ladder at Robinson's. I didn't own any stock in the company and only members of the Robinson family held executive positions. And Santa Barbara, the serene beach city, I had enjoyed so much, was clearly not an environment in which I could make my first million, something I was determined to do by the time I was thirty.

As fall rolled around, my trial date for divorce court was coming up. I knew it wasn't going to be pretty. My lawyer had warned me that Joanna meant to go after me financially and, with the help of one of her rich uncles, had hired a high-priced attorney. To obtain a divorce in the '60s, one of the parties to the legal procedure had to be found guilty of some unacceptable behavior or action.

On my day of judgment, I appeared with my counsel. I was more wrought up about appearing in court than I thought I would be. On this particular morning we were first on the docket. The courtroom was filled with other litigants. My wife was there with her lawyer. She looked stunning; she was wearing a new outfit and her red hair was beautifully coifed. Joanna stood up for the presiding judge as he entered the courtroom and I saw that she was wearing a mini-skirt. She leaned over and put her hand on her lawyer's shoulder and I was jolted at the realization that they were close, very close.

After I was sworn in to tell the truth and nothing but the truth, I found that I was being charged with desertion, mental cruelty, and a host of other wrongdoings. When Joanna took the stand, she was such a good actress she had the judge believing I was an all-around cad. I didn't like the look in the judge's eye. The judge granted the divorce, then proceeded to make a shambles out of my future finances. He awarded Joanna alimony and handed me all our bills and joint debts, including our school loans.

I left the courtroom in a haze wondering whether I would be paying alimony to that man-hating redhead for the rest of her life. I was patted on the back a few times on the way out of the courtroom by sympathetic onlookers who thought I had gotten the shaft.

Thank God my sweet Pam was around and remained a welcome comfort through these trying times. She was making me a thousand times happier than Joanna ever had. What a contrast. But there was a catch to our idyllic affair. Despite the sexual revolution that was sweeping the country, Pam was already thinking of me as her future husband. Now I was torn in two directions: determined to stay single and equally determined to keep Pam in my life. There were telltale signs that Pam wanted more of a commitment than I was willing to give.

During the summer, I took a vacation and drove all by my lonesome to Texas to see my folks. I hadn't seen my dad for years and I was beginning to be homesick for the border towns I had been raised in. I had a really good visit with my dad and found out I liked the old codger. When I was in Houston hanging around his office, he asked me not to tell some of his associates that I was adopted. I asked why and he said that he wanted to appear younger than he was. He was sixty-five and hoped to keep on yanking teeth for quite a few more years.

When I was down Mexico way saying hello to my mom and catching up on what was happening with some of my buddies, I learned that my old bodyguard Willie had married and was the father of four young children, all girls. A few of my high school chums were working on shrimp boats. One was a captain of his own boat and another owned a whole fleet. My buddy Willie had moved back to Brownsville after his second hitch in the Marines. He came out a staff sergeant, had spent a tour in Vietnam, and had gotten a job with the border patrol. My mother was chagrined about my marital failure but, as usual, she was a fountain of strength and support.

The drive from Texas back to California gave me a lot of time to consider where I had been in life and where I wanted to go. When I got back home and saw Pam, I wanted to consume her. But Pam had been doing some serious thinking on her own while I was gone. I was a bit nonplussed when I felt her put a barrier between us. As I feared but didn't want to acknowledge, she wanted something I couldn't give her—marriage.

I was aware that she might make me an ideal wife, but my destiny was drawing me to San Francisco to start out in a new place with a new job, and new experiences. This city, famous for its Barbary Coast, cable cars, Chinatown, and Italian North Beach section, was calling to me. I knew intuitively that San Francisco was where I would find fame, fortune and my place in the world. Years later I would regret that the timing had been so wrong for us. As much as I wanted to have my cake and eat it too, I felt that building a career for myself came first and to do that I knew I would have to focus all my concentration on nothing but that one primary goal.

I had lined up a job in San Francisco selling insurance and I knew we had to have a heart-to-heart talk. I told her I was leaving in three days. When she realized I was not offering marriage, it was as if someone had punched her in the stomach. She started weeping hysterically. I had said we could live together, but that was unacceptable to her. When she recovered, she said she would apply to graduate school in the state of Washington.

We proceeded to say "so long" to each other by spending the next three long days and nights in bed. It was the most fun-filled, poignant, nonstop passion I had ever experienced. If she did that to make sure I would never forget her, she truly got her wish.

After these three near crippling days and nights, I packed my new aquamarine '67 Mustang with my books and clothes and turned my back on Isla Vista, Santa Barbara and Pam. I was never to see her face-to-face again. I had lined up an apartment on Stanyan Street near the Haight-Ashbury in San Francisco. Here, I hoped to find all the wonders of the hippie counterculture, as well as get plugged into that historical city, well-known for opening its heart to all newcomers.

10

Art Fever and the Dalí Scandal

It was October of '68, a few months before I would turn twenty-seven. I was in a hurry to make my mark. I moved to San Francisco and jumped into the fray with both feet. I couldn't believe I was actually living on Stanyan Street, for me that heretofore mythical street right in the middle of the infamous Haight-Ashbury. When Pam and I first got together, I gave her a poetry book by one of our favorite pop poets, Rod McKuen, a raspy-voiced troubadour. It was entitled, *Stanyan Street and Other Sorrows*. The title poem had quite an effect on me. I told myself then that if the opportunity ever came my way I would move to that fabled street. I'm sure Rod McKuen was the pied piper to many of my generation.

My first stroll down Stanyan Street to the carnival-like Haight Street told me that the reality was even more far-out than the advance publicity. Everybody knew that history was in the making. On that street between Stanyan and Masonic, it looked like the land of perpetual Halloween. Everyone was in costume. Wherever I looked I saw vari-colored ponchos, serapes, love beads, sandals, and headbands—and hair, a flowing tidal wave of the stuff, either hanging straight to the tailbone or puffed out in an Afro.

I had loosened up from my Marine Corps crew-cut days, but since I had "corporate ambitions" I kept my hair collar length, but I did sport the obligatory sideburns. I was all for flower power and admit I got swept away in the "Summer of Love" excitement. It was the high point of the Beat and hippie revolutions. Everyone was descending on San Francisco in wildly decorated Volkswagen vans and old school buses. I quickly recognized, however, that what I was seeing was as much a drug culture as a youth revolution. Everywhere I looked, I saw disquieting scenes of kids not even old enough for a driver's license dropping LSD or popping amphetamines as if they were gumdrops.

The Haight and the area around Golden Gate Park had changed from a quiet, middle-class, blue-collar community to a veritable riot of psychedelic "head shops," leather boutiques, and coffee houses, all reeking of pot fumes and incense. The music scene was actually centered in San Francisco. All the hit names leading the musical revolution were using Bill Graham's Fillmore Auditorium as a launching pad to stardom. It appeared that the whole world revolved around San Francisco and that this new world order was going to last forever. Although nothing like the squeaky clean experience of my Santa Barbara college life, still, there was a purity about these flower children at the beginning of their crusade—at first blush, anyway.

It didn't take long for me to realize that there was something horribly wrong with this counterculture. It was an exciting time in history, but there was an underlying feeling that things were going to get ugly. As more and more rock idols overdosed on drugs and liquor, and scores of young people completely destroyed their minds on drugs, I decided to be an observer and not a participant.

Luckily, the pressures of my new job left me no time for experimenting with this drug epidemic. Of course, all of my college friends, myself included, had used marijuana, and even my professors, at least the younger ones, talked freely about drug use. We often discussed what we thought the pros and cons were regarding this wave of experimentation. Basically we thought it was pretty harmless and considered it a lark. We thought "grass" was the greatest thing ever invented: you could get high and not worry about getting sick. Few of us foresaw the massive use of cocaine and crack cocaine and hard drugs that would surface in the coming decades.

I decided to throw all my energy into business and get started on the fame and fortune part of my career. No sooner had I made that decision when I realized how very isolated and alone I was. I didn't have any close friends in this town; I had yet to find someone I could really talk to. Some of my old college buddies, like my old roommate, Ali, visited me in San Francisco. We hung out in Berkeley and he told me about his role in burning down the Bank of America branch located in my old haunt, Isla Vista. He was disgusted with me when I chose to toddle off to work every day. The last time I saw him he was heading up to Canada and he called me a "capitalist tool" or some such epithet.

Now that I had some time to myself, I realized how much I missed Pam. I couldn't stop thinking about her. I called her in Washington and asked her to come spend Christmas with me. After a significant silence, she asked, "What would be the use?" She stated matter of factly that if I couldn't make some sort of commitment, there just wasn't any point. I wish I had never made the call. I just felt more cut off and knew it would be a futile effort to try and get in touch with her again.

For someone living in the Haight, it seemed a bit ironic to me that I went to work every day in the heart of the uptight financial district. I had to dress to the hilt—blue blazer and tie—and save my hippie threads for the weekends.

Admittedly, my first few weeks on the job at Pacific Mutual Life Insurance were rough and made me wonder if I was in for a repeat of my water softener selling days. My first sales training, if you could call it that, was being handed a city telephone directory and told, "Here are your leads and potential clients. Start calling people." I don't know what I had envisioned regarding sales training, but this wasn't it. I grabbed the proffered phone book and promptly started calling all the men's clothing stores in San Francisco. I would use my door-to-door sales pitch about how I was going to be in their neighborhood and thought I would drop by.

A few of the owners or bosses of businesses in the garment district took to me right off. They probably saw themselves twenty or thirty years earlier in my fledgling attempts to get started in the city. A couple of these seasoned businessmen informed me they were in need of much more sophisticated financial planning or estate planning than I could provide, but they wanted to help me out so they introduced me to their employees. Using the old statistics trick or "bean theory," as I called it, I would put ten beans in my left pocket and every time I would talk to a "real prospect" I would transfer a bean to my right pocket. The idea was that by the time I had transferred all the beans from one pocket to the other I would make a sale.

By following the carefully crafted, almost canned, speeches and sales programs organized by the insurance company, I began to sell policy after policy. I met a nice bunch of salespeople at work. Most were extremely helpful, both in terms of finding my way around and with sales tips. I pushed myself to the limit those first months on the job. I would go into work early and attend meetings and then hit the bricks. I made most of my appointments in the evening, which was the best time to talk to a wife and husband together.

I found out that it rained a lot in northern California and it was colder than Santa Barbara. As I ran from place to place on my appointed rounds, I was rained on incessantly. Damned if I didn't come down with pneumonia. Between the illness, my car being towed away for illegal parking, and just the high cost of working downtown, I realized that a great deal of perseverance was going to be needed to make it in this big city.

As I cranked out sale after sale in the "sink or swim" program the company was using, I finally came to the attention of the firm's general manager, a rather conservative-looking guy I pegged as being pretty old. Actually, he was thirty-six or so. He had the habit of wearing felt hats and pinstripe suits reminiscent of the '30s or '40s. He had the gift of gab and liked to teach peripatetically. He often asked me to walk with him. After watching Mr. Fred Paxton in action, I saw that I could learn a lot from this guy. Thanks to Fred's careful tutoring, I learned to sell life insurance like a pro.

After six months of on-the-job training, I was becoming one of the seasoned veterans in the office. There was a phenomenal turnover in sales staff. One of Fred Paxton's running jokes was that when anybody asked him the number of salespeople he employed he had to look at his watch to estimate how many people had quit in the last few hours.

As I got to know the office staff, I noticed a new receptionist manning the front switchboard. She was just what I had been looking for. She was a young Japanese woman; her name was Sharon Yamamoto. She had just moved to the Bay Area from Hawaii. Sharon had a round face with rosy cheeks and a wholesome demeanor that radiated intelligence and kindness. She may not have been beautiful in a Western sense, but she was close to perfect for me. Sharon's beauty came from her upbeat personality and an abiding goodness. She was born and raised in Honolulu and was thoroughly Americanized. Never having been to Hawaii, I pictured the capital city of Honolulu as a small town with thatched huts. How wrong I was! Sharon's grandparents came to Hawaii from Japan and never learned English, but she was determined to embrace American customs and was annoyed when people asked her whether she spoke Japanese.

From the first, Sharon reminded me of the Japanese girl I had known in Tokyo, the one I didn't get a chance to say good-bye to properly as I hastily exited the Orient. In the back of my mind I had always had a romantic notion that I might find another Oriental girl with similar qualities. I knew, of course, that San Francisco had a large Asian population, so I had half-hoped this might be the place where I would find such a jewel. And here she was—a petite, five-foot-one Japanese dazzler. Now the question was how to get to know her.

One day I bumped my head on a low-hanging chandelier in a fancy restaurant. I wondered if I had incurred substantial injury. So back at the office, I used the incident to strike up a conversation with Sharon. Would she check for a bump on my head? She would. She seemed to think that no permanent damage had been done.

After breaking the ice with Sharon I started taking her out daily. Though she didn't suspect it, I was really interviewing her for a live-in position, hoping she would be amenable to living with me out of wedlock. When I learned she was

living in a residence club for women, I knew it was time
to move in for the rescue. Sharon had always wanted to live
in San Francisco and had saved her money to buy a one-
way ticket to the mainland. She had obtained her liberal
arts degree from the University of Hawaii and, upon arriving
in San Francisco, took the first job offer that came along.
She had been hired as the company's switchboard operator
and receptionist, but, fiercely ambitious, she wanted to rise
up in the ranks of a powerful corporation.

When we first met, she had been in the city only a few
days. So after a few dates, I convinced her to move in with
me. Although I was genuinely fond of her from the start,
this was mostly a relationship of companionship and comfort;
it certainly didn't compare with the fevered passion that had
consumed me during my Santa Barbara days with Pam.
Nevertheless, I ended up planting Sharon in my life for an
incredible *nine* years. When Sharon moved in, I was positive
I had it all—I was living in San Francisco with a beautiful
Japanese girl who had long, flowing black hair, and, to top
things off, I had finally managed to buy a fancy red sports
car.

Sharon and I settled into our relationship, moving from
Stanyan Street to a charming penthouse apartment on Telegraph
Hill, the center of North Beach. Our apartment had a 360-
degree view: in the distance was the Golden Gate Bridge
and the Oakland Bay Bridge. Closer in was a view of the
financial district and the cars slowly winding their way down
the foot of Lombard Street, the "crookedest street in the
world."

Work was going well. At this point, I was improvising
and inventing new ways to mass-merchandise life insurance.
As my income rose, I began to purchase art works from some
of the galleries around town. I bought them to display in
my office and apartment, but I also regarded them as
investments. I began touring the local art galleries, as I had
done in Santa Barbara, and ingratiating myself with the
dealers and personnel I met in the shops. The urge to build
some kind of career for myself in the art world was still with

me, and I began to sense that if I ever did start such a venture, this was the right city and the right time.

At the start I only bought things that moved me personally, with no thought of selling my newly found treasures. My exposure to the field of art history had left me in awe of the masters, but, as I wandered around galleries and museums on my time off from work, I started to become attached to some living artists. Some, such as the diminutive Benjamino Bufano, were regionally well-known. I had first noticed his sculpture and mosaics at Leo Hill's gallery on Sutter Street in downtown San Francisco. I wanted to own his work, but I also started thinking about moving it around from one appreciative collector to the next to somehow make people happy in the same way my own discovery of art had made me happy.

When I took note of the stratospheric price tags attached to some of these paintings and sculptures, I became intrigued with the business end of this world I had come to love. Until then, I hadn't fully realized what enormous sums of money were involved in buying and selling art. I thought how wonderful it would be to turn my admiration for art into a successful and remunerative career.

It was about this time in 1969 that I realized I had gone as far as I could go selling insurance. The recognition came about forcefully with an unsettling incident. My boss had me devoting a lot of time to an independent business venture within the insurance agency. The deal he made with me was that if I trained the salespeople and oversaw his "brainchild," I would be paid a percentage of sales. This new venture took off like a shot. I was overjoyed. But it seems my boss hadn't cleared this business arrangement with the home office. When the bean-counters at headquarters saw the windfall profits, they sent a confidential letter to him saying he had no right to offer me such a deal. Sharon saw this letter on his desk and told me about it. And so he reneged on our deal. Once again, I felt betrayed. First Don Carroll had threatened to fire me unless I dropped out of college, and now it was Fred Paxton backing out of our business venture.

In my mind, he should never have made a deal with me if he didn't have an iron-clad contract with the home office.

In resigning from Pacific Mutual Life, I left the insurance game behind me permanently. I was determined to enter the local art world. I landed a job as a salesman in an art gallery on Fisherman's Wharf. The owner, Lou, had two galleries at the time, one on Stockton Street near Union Square and the other one near Fisherman's Wharf. I took to selling art like a duck to water. In a few months, in what felt like no time at all, I and another high-powered salesman were selling about $70,000 worth of art a month. It wasn't long before I realized that Lou knew very little about art, and cared even less.

Lou was a P.T. Barnum type of guy who had spent most of his sixty or so years importing olive oil and other delicatessen foods from Europe and the Middle East and selling them to the burgeoning supermarket chains in America. While knocking around merchandise marts in Europe, he had bought some factory paintings done by literally starving artists in various European countries. He placed some of these paintings, usually landscapes, in a Safeway supermarket in San Francisco and found there was a market for inexpensive decorative art. On the strength of that experience, he opened his first gallery and added the works of some local California artists to his display. With his cash-and-carry background, he was successful in promoting, selling, and bartering art, albeit like a sideshow barker in a circus.

Lou was the first local merchant to start selling what I called "mass market art." He aimed his merchandising at people who had never bought a painting in their lives. He didn't tell people that most of his paintings were done by a factory assembly line set up by a group of artists. He bought most of these "original" sofa-size canvases for less than it would cost to reproduce them photomechanically as a poster. As the demand for this kind of decorative art grew in the sixties, he started buying better quality art, including those of local California artists, but he continued to rely on the factory paintings which he finished off with a fancy wood frame stamped "Hecho en Mexico" on the back. He soon

Lieutenant General F. E. Leek
U.S.M.C. (Ret) 1962

General Leek gave me a job as his driver. He was the Commanding General of the First Marine Division. He allowed me to attend night school to complete my high school education.

Harry Calvin

Harry Calvin, my uncle on my mother's side of the family. He gave me this WW I photo himself just before he passed away. He knew we wouldn't be seeing each other again ar wanted me to remember the special bond we had always shared. Uncle Harry and his v Aunt Sally, were extremely generous to my mother, Constance Swanson, over the years.

*Me as gun-toting wild west
lawman. We had just moved from
the Houston area to Brownsville,
a border town in tropical South
Texas. This is in 1950. A year later
I came down with polio.*

*Me with Dr. and Mrs. Swanson and
Ada Sutton Bull (using cane), my
new, very Victorian grandmother.*

*first photo taken of Sally and
with our adopted father, Doctor
nson, 1945.*

*Our new mom (Constance Bull Swanson)
with her Texas cowpunchers. We lived in
Clute, Texas, 50 miles south of Houston.*

My sister Sally and I, ages 6 and 4, respectively, taken right after we were adopted by the Swansons.

The way I looked the first time I drove across the river to Matamoros, Mexico, 1954. Flat-top haircut and braces (not shown). This is the only photo I have of myself as a teenager until I joined the Corps in 1959.

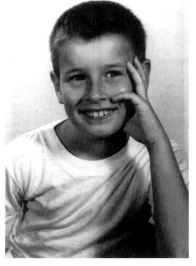

This is my favorite picture of myself, probably age 7.

Photo of my mother's parrot (Bill) taken in her backyard in Brownsville. Bill always mimicked my mother's protestations—"Jack! (squawk) Where are you going Jack?"

Pensive college graduation photo taken in 1967. Someone asked me what I was going to be. I told them I already am.

Promotion Ceremony, Atsugi, Japan, 1961, where I was advanced in rank to Lance Corporal. I had gone through boot camp with most of these fellow Marines. After a year or so we became strategically placed throughout this huge Navy and Marine air base.

Great Buddha statue in Kamakura, Japan. It was an awakening to learn of other cultures and their religious beliefs.

Old salt—Atsugi Air Base, Japan. I had always dreamed about being stationed in Japan; now it was a reality.

Poster boy Swanson. By now I am driving the commanding officer of the Marine Air Wing and have been promoted to Lance Corporal. This photo taken at Atsugi, Japan, 1961.

White huts, Cubi Point—Subic Bay Naval Base and air field, Philippines, 1960. These barracks were high on a mountain near a jungle overlooking Subic Bay and U.S. Seventh Fleet. Japanese soldiers were housed in these huts during WW II.

Recent boot camp graduate, 1959, on leave in Brownsville, Texas. Showing off my Marine Corps uniform that took me three tries at boot camp and six months to earn the right to wear.

Sent to Subic Bay Philippines right after boot camp. My first job was busting tires and eventually I was assigned to driving (and painting) 25-ton fuel trucks on the flight line, 1960.

Japanese village outside of Atsugi Air Base near Tokyo, Japan, 1961. Atsugi was about 30 miles from Tokyo and the city dwellers of Tokyo would always remark that Atsugi and the adjoining town of Yamato was out in the country.

Marine fighter squadron. I used to walk guard duty around these jets— usually graveyard shift, midnight to 4.00 A.M.

Me with my Chinese counter- parts (Republic of China, Taiwan) at Ping Tong Air Base where I was assigned a Chinese Marine Corps motor transport outfit to help ready the base and runway for arrival of our Marine Air Group.

Corporal J. H. Swanso in front of Division H.Q Camp Pendleton, California. I had cards made up with name an address and a saying printed on them , "Ha Seabag, Will Travel".

Graduation day at Santa Barbara, Jun 1967, with my moth Constance Swanso sent copies of my diploma to a few o high school teache who had befriende and had been supp ive of me when I he serious doubts tha would ever make i

December 1970. My first gallery in an open and drafty warehouse on Beach Street in San Francisco.

Beach Street gallery. We just kept building more rooms and peg-boarded all the walls. The place was huge—the buying public felt at home coming into an unpretentious space and viewing art work.

...cond gallery I opened on Beach ...reet—on the corner of Beach and ...rkin. This two-story building ...ve me 16,000 sq. ft. to display ...al artists' work. I moved to this ...rner location in 1977.

*My Sausalito gallery—second gallery location.
Opened first year I was in business (1971). It is
a beachfront location. The bay is on other side
of the road.*

*Photo taken at my Sutter Street gallery after a
successful show. I love the sign, and always
have it prominently displayed at each gallery.*

Wai Ming and his dealer, 1976. He brought me one painting a week for many years.

Boat full of sushi and food for an extrava-ganza one-person show for Jacquie Marie Vaux, 1978, at our new Beach Street gallery. Jacquie painted wildlife, especially large cats, so we brought in a 600 lb. tiger from Marine World Africa U.S.A. I upped my insurance for this special appearance. Luckily, nothing untoward happened.

Me and Dennis Debo, early 1970s at Sausalito gallery. Arthur Ashe bought one of Dennis Debo's paintings and Dennis was on a roll—his portraits rival those of Rembrandt.

*Ruby Lee, Jacquie Marie Vaux,
and proud gallery owner.*

*Jacquie Vaux's two children—Jennifer
and Stefanie, flower children, 1976.*

Late 1970s. I'm spending a lot of time traveling to my East Coast galleries.

The Schake's son Kurt at his 1984 graduation from the Air Force Academy.

Celia and Wayne Schake and their daughter Kristy (with hat) and Kory. We were sailing on San Francisco Bay. About this time, Wayne and I went to Greece so Wayne could participate (successfully) in the re-enacted original marathon.

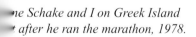

...ne Schake and I on Greek Island ...after he ran the marathon, 1978.

*Eileen and I on our
wedding day, May 1984.*

*Our honeymoon. Here we are on
the Orient-Express.*

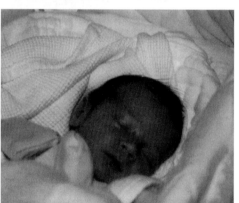

*Another happiest day of my life. Jack Jr.,
born January 1990.*

*My daughter Christina—hours ol
May 1985. One of the happiest dr
of my life.(Middle).On our way t
Father-Daughter Dinner Dance r
Francis Yacht Club, 1988.(Botton*

Eileen and Jack Jr. at my 50th birthday party, December 1992.

My Harley-Davidson on a "Redwood Run" to Northern California, 1989.

Tea party with Christina. Be careful of what you wish for—you might find yourself in cramped situations.

Eileen, Christina (age 4 1/2) and baby Jack, or "Buddy," as we nicknamed him.

After I sold my galleries in 1989, I traded in my sailboat "Marathon" for this motor yacht. I almost named it for Harris Shapiro, who bought me out!

Eileen and I at an art show after I sold my galleries in 1989.

started to place etchings, lithography, and reproductions by some well-known European artists into the mix to give the gallery more credence generally and to legitimize the local art work he was selling. Toward the end of the '60s, Lou had turned the public's desire for these florals and landscapes into a real business. I'm not saying that all of the factory art that Lou was selling was bad art or unsophisticated art. Some of the artists who supplied him did so only because of the devastated European economy. Many were competent artists with impressive educational and cultural backgrounds.

As Lou's retail art business grew, the demand for indigenous California artists grew with it. There were some real bonuses to selling the work of local artists: he could have more of a say on size and subject matter and didn't have to worry about his supply being cut off by unforeseen circumstances. He could also get some of the local artists to leave things with him on consignment. That way, he didn't have to pay for art work upfront.

After working at Lou's gallery for about six months, I knew that the only part of his business I wanted anything to do with was the local artist. Although he had amassed a large cadre of California artists, his best markup was on the European paintings and prints purported to be limited editions by famous artists. It was easier to sell the work of "name" artists, even a third-rate work of dubious origin, than a masterpiece by an unknown hometown artist. Through his New York City connections with some print publishers, Lou decided to expand on the "famous artist" theme.

Lou was one of the first to get involved with do-it-yourself print publishing. He was aware that Salvador Dalí had been commissioned by various print and book publishers to illustrate classic books. Working on a litho stone or etching on a plate, Dalí would execute the image, or even have an artisan do it for him, and the publisher would print it.

Lou hit on the idea of commissioning Dalí to do graphic images of San Francisco in Dalí's surreal style. Dalí was to send him the plates and then Lou would hire artisans to print them. Knowing that Dalí wasn't coming to San

Francisco anytime soon, Lou had Dalí send him *presigned* lithograph paper and paid him per signature. These presigned blank sheets of paper were not numbered, so people would have to trust Lou (now turned publisher) as to the real size of the edition—i.e., how many etching graphics were to be sold of each image.

I watched in amazement as Lou set up his own printing shop and started knocking off print after print. He had his lawyers create copy for his brochures and certificates of authenticity. These official-looking certificates stated that the Dalí prints created in Lou's printing shop were multiple-original etchings, signed by the artist. The public was given to believe that Dalí either did the printing, was involved in the process, or at least worked with the printers, and that all hand-coloring was done by Dalí. The public was also led to assume that Dalí signed the prints only after he personally approved the finished works.

The first few Dalí print editions sold like hotcakes to the unsuspecting public that walked into Lou's retail emporium—so well, in fact, that Lou started dealing almost exclusively with these questionable art prints. Lou knew full well that this invention could be used for almost any name artist willing to go along with the program—or else living so far away from San Francisco that neither the artist nor his agent would squawk about a few forged signatures. Lee Catterall's book entitled, *The Great Dalí Art Fraud and Other Deceptions* (Barricade Books Inc.) gives an in-depth account of these goings-on, and mentions just about every publisher that got involved in the manufacture of Dalí prints.

The more I observed Lou's shoddy tactics, especially the way he treated local artists, the more I wanted out. I started thinking about how I could open my own gallery selling *only* local artists, preferably live artists. I learned that it was almost standard practice for galleries not to pay artists whose work was left on consignment, or else to drag out payment in small increments. Even old-line galleries that served as clearinghouses for estates indulged in this practice. In this way, the amount due the artist became an alternative source of financing for the gallery. Most artists just accepted it as something that happened to "starving artists."

As I looked for a way to separate myself from Lou's gallery, I grew certain that I could round up a group of local San Francisco artists and convince them to lend me their works on consignment. I would work out a commission arrangement where they would get paid every two weeks for anything I sold and for which I had been paid in full. I also would agree not to sell anything on time without their approval. I was right on the mark in my thinking. These young and vulnerable artists were highly frustrated with every gallery they had ever dealt with.

Only by starting my own art gallery could I right some of the wrongs I had seen certain unethical dealers pull off. Surely if crass-minded dealers like Lou could be so successful without knowing a damned thing about art, there was no telling what a much more informed and educated person could accomplish.

Another problem artists faced was that there was no real outlet for the young and experimental among them. If they went to the established galleries, they invariably encountered a wall of resistance. "Old school" galleries in cities like San Francisco preferred artists that were long deceased or, if not, were very "hot" at the moment, having been recommended by recognized critics.

Their response was to band together in artists' guilds and have group shows in an artists' cooperative or outdoor shows in parks and shopping malls. Some would set up their pegboard partitions and paint as onlookers gathered around; others would simply display the works they had already finished. When I first viewed these outdoor showings, I had enough sense to know that this was a real innovation in the delicate business of making and selling art. It gave the artist a sense of freedom and control.

By the early '70s, there was an "art fever" raging. On a personal level, a plan was taking shape in my mind: If I could move these artists indoors and represent them from a business standpoint, I could develop my own stable of working artists and free them from the necessity of selling their own work. I saw my chance to develop a completely original concept of the art dealer, one for which I would have little or no competition. My plan was simple: invite them to show their work in my gallery, do all the sales and administrative detail for them, and then pay them fairly and punctually. Years later, I was able to say that not one of my checks ever bounced and that after twenty years in the art business I didn't owe a dime to any of the hundreds of suppliers and artists I dealt with.

With my dream charted out, I started looking for a gallery location. I knew it was going to be a shock to my manager at Lou's gallery; he had begun to rely on my sales ability, and my leadership. (My manager, an erudite old dude who loved to dress up and hit the bars in the gay section of town on Halloween, was always throwing around literary phrases. One saying that I picked up from him was: "Delay is the worst form of denial." It struck a chord with me and, when I opened my own gallery, I had a sign made up with that saying and hung it in plain sight.) When I told him that I was striking out on my own, he smiled malevolently, cigarette in hand, arms crossed over his chest, and said, "Jack, you bastard! I've always wanted to do what you're about to do, but I lack the courage."

His reaction was more positive than that of my girlfriend, Sharon. When I told Sharon I planned to quit Lou's and open my own gallery, she thought I had lost my marbles; the whole idea was beyond her comprehension. No one in her family had ever been in business for himself. Like most sensible, young, Japanese-American girls, especially those raised in the wholesome atmosphere of Honolulu, Sharon's idea was to keep on working for the same powerful corporation long enough to pile up as many fringe benefits, stock options, and salary raises as one could reasonably expect to earn over a lifetime. In her eyes, turning away from a regular paycheck to free-lance at *anything* seemed nothing short of suicidal. She was gentle enough to say: "I don't mean to sound discouraging, but don't you think you're taking a crazy risk?"

"Of course I am," I said, laughing. "But don't you see, honey, that's what's so wonderful about it: *all* risks are a little crazy. If they weren't, there'd be no sense of adventure."

She wasn't buying any of my ideas, however, and I saw that she feared our whole lifestyle was going to go down the tubes or, worse still, that she was going to have to become the breadwinner in the family. She damned near grew a mustache right then and there. She urged me to stick to sales work now that I was successful at it. When I assured her I could make more money working for myself than I ever could working for anyone else, she simply nodded her head in a condescending manner, obviously hoping the whole thing would go away.

11

Success Against All Odds

It was 1970. Nixon was in the White House and had promised to end the war in Vietnam—"peace with dignity" and all that. The business climate looked propitious: there hadn't been any economic downturns or recessions for a long time. America seemed to be on top of the heap.

I had my eye on a newly developed area close to Fisherman's Wharf, where two huge developments were just opening up. As more and more tourists were flocking to San Francisco— it was the "jet age"—I felt I should locate my gallery where there was a steady flow of walk-in traffic. The site I pinpointed was on Beach Street where there was an old lumberyard-warehouse between two brick buildings that had once housed the Ghirardelli Chocolate Factory and the old fish cannery. These old factory sites had fallen into disuse and developers realized they could make them into lucrative malls with shops and restaurants to attract tourists. With tourist traffic expanding in this once-neglected area, it would be a great location, I thought, for my future gallery.

I walked into that large, drafty barn of a warehouse and introduced myself to an old Norwegian guy who was running a Scandinavian furniture store out of this hangar-like structure. You could drive your car right inside and he would load knocked-down and crated furniture into your vehicle. This rather humorless fellow was obviously having problems; not only was his business down, but he certainly didn't have a retail personality.

I approached Erik Jorgensen and told him that I was interested in opening a gallery in his warehouse. I explained that I had a stock of merchandise and would like to begin my new venture by leasing just the wall space, which he wasn't using at the time. I emphasized how well I had been doing as a salesman and I offered him 10% of everything I sold. He said to bring by some of the paintings I would display and that he would think about it.

I immediately telephoned an artist friend of mine and got him to come by with the battered and bruised van he had purchased from a utility company. Together, we gathered up some of the art works I had been collecting, along with his, and headed back to Beach Street. Jorgensen and his wife approved of the art work and said I could move in ASAP on a month-to-month basis.

So I rented my first gallery space in December of 1970, a week before my twenty-ninth birthday. When Eric Jorgensen said, "You got yourself a deal," I felt I was embarking on a dream I'd held almost my entire life—to be master of my fate. In my mind, you just had to set a date and do it. I still didn't know how I was going to pull everything off, but as far as I was concerned, those were petty details. My artist buddy, Victor, was jazzed. He had been looking for a gallery outlet and was 100% behind me. We set a date to start moving in our stock. I called Sharon and told her that we were going to celebrate with Victor and his girlfriend that night at the Trident, an "in" restaurant perched on stilts and overlooking the water in the artsy town of Sausalito. The Trident was owned by the manager of the Kingston Trio and was the hangout of every rock group that hit San Francisco.

We partied hard that evening as we planned our fantastic futures. If dreams were currency, I didn't have a thing to worry about. That's how it began. We moved into the warehouse on December 15 and, with hammer and nails, began to hang our paltry store of art work. I'm glad I had Victor to help. He was framing and hanging, and you name it, Victor did it. I was lucky to have him, not only because he had a van, but because he was an accomplished and prolific painter and very effective in finding other talented artists for me. He would eventually be my first star artist and would later serve as my first vice president.

I had no overhead to worry about, which was fortunate because I had just enough money to carry my personal expenses for a while. Sharon wasn't thrilled that I had burned my bridges and quit my job at Lou's.

As excited as I was, it was still a very scary experience when I opened my gallery. Even the weather was damp, chilly, and foggy. In fact, the fog actually drifted right into the gallery that first day. I found it less than romantic to have a bank of fog obscure my paintings. On opening day, we also discovered there were no heating facilities in the warehouse, not even an electric heater, and that the lighting was completely inadequate. I wrote "floodlights" on the growing list of things I needed to buy if this barn was to look like an art gallery.

During those first two weeks, I displayed only Victor's work and some pieces from my personal collection. But business was discouraging. It became clear that people didn't buy art work as Christmas presents. We sold only $2,000 worth of art work during those first two weeks. I stared at those figures and said to myself, "I'm in deep shit." To say that I had projected much higher sales and profits would be an understatement.

When I told Sharon of this initial disappointment, she looked like she was ready to bite her tongue in half to keep from saying, "I told you so, you idiot!" During those weeks she did make some veiled threats about leaving me. At the time I wouldn't have blamed her. Just as I was beginning to think I had made a very serious mistake in judgment, it all began to take off—very slowly but very surely.

During January, the gallery took in $4,000. It still wasn't exactly fantastic, but it meant I could afford to put in a few flood lights and buy a couple of space heaters so I would no longer have to be wrapped in three or four sweaters when I greeted the public. During February, my third month in business, the gallery took in $8,000. In March that figure doubled to $16,000. In April, we made a grand total of $30,000. The business was gathering momentum with such a fast snowballing effect I felt like I was riding the tail end of a comet.

As it turned out, the new year of 1971 was to be the luckiest year of my life. By the end of the year I accomplished what I had set out to do—earn my first million by the time I turned thirty. I was staggered by this swift success. I felt like a little kid on Christmas morning who was suddenly having all his wildest, most fantastic dreams come true. Much of this phenomenon, I concluded later, was due to my lucky sense of timing. When I opened my gallery, it was the only one in the neighborhood. At the start, of course, this also made me the target for a lot of local ridicule. Most of my detractors stopped laughing in May '71 when the Beach Street Gallery took in $60,000 and doubled again in June to $120,000. Against all odds, I was on my way to fame and fortune.

I hadn't been in business for more than three months when my old boss, Lou, dropped in on me and, to my amazement, offered to merge our two businesses. He saw that most of his local artists were leaving his gallery for mine and that his Dalí wave, however prosperous, could not have a long-term future. I thanked him for thinking that highly of my endeavor but answered, "No thanks."

With this success, I started hiring more salespeople and persuaded a lot of local artists I had my eye on to join our "new wave." Victor and I rounded up more and more undiscovered, young painters. As we added artists, we built more walls, and we built more rooms. The warehouse was huge—about 16,000 square feet, if you included the loft.

I seem to have been graced with an incredibly good "eye" for art. I have always been able to look at a painting and recognize a real artist. Very much like handwriting analysis, quite often I glean a tremendous amount of personal information about the artist just from his brush stroke. I also have a talent for assessing what the art work is worth, at least in market terms. These skills, innate and acquired, gave me an edge when it came to my competitors. Without these talents, you are almost obliged to sell only those art works that have been already documented and critically accepted. Because I could make correct decisions about whose art had a future, I turned out to be one of the few art dealers in town selling original paintings by live artists.

But it was my revolutionary policy of paying my artists what they were worth that turned out to be the cornerstone of my success. Until Swanson Art Galleries, Ltd. burst upon the local scene, no artists in town had met any dealer who actually paid them, paid them on time, and paid them regularly every two weeks. If I truly believed in some new artist, I would offer some sort of steady income. And, since the concept of "financial security" had heretofore been out of reach for most of them, this strategy turned out to be the warmest welcome they had yet seen. Quite often I would agree to purchase a percentage of an artist's work and take the rest on consignment. Then, guaranteeing that they would be paid two weeks from the time I sold each painting netted the artist quick payment. I never failed to keep my word on this arrangement, and it wasn't long before I became a much-talked about hero among the city's newly emerging artists. And of course I was being deluged by artists from every quarter of the art world, many of whom never expected to be selling their work to the legions of tourists passing through Ghirardelli Square. (I have to point out that tourists were usually the wealthiest, best-educated professionals in their hometowns.)

In the beginning I had to deal with a lot of artistic temperaments; it was a part of the business I thoroughly enjoyed. I liked being surrounded by creative, talented people, and since they knew I wasn't competing with them as an artist, I assumed there would be none of the petty rivalry I had experienced with coworkers in the conventional business world.

I had a lot of notions about forming a cadre or mastermind group that would march into the sunset together. One for all and all for one. I envisioned that my first business associates in this "pegboard revolution" would be lifelong friends and that we would all be "rich uncles" to our children and families. That alone, of course, proved how young and naive I still was at twenty-nine. For, in time, some of the warm personal relationships I had with my artists would backfire in ways more vicious than I could have anticipated.

But I was in love with my new career. If I needed more money, I would just write the required sum on my hand or palm and work the floor. Sometimes I would still be chasing my goal late into the night. The immense walk-by tourist traffic made it feasible to stay open seven days a week from ten in the morning to eleven or twelve o'clock in the evening.

One day I needed $12,000 in sales to fulfill certain business obligations. I had never sold $12,000 worth of art in one day before, but after an exhaustive day I whittled that $12,000 down some. At the end of the night one of my employees had to physically push me toward the last customer. I ended up selling him the only expensive piece in the gallery and it completed my dollar goal. It was this way of working that I taught my salespeople, and the results showed in the incredible profits I chalked up during that first million-dollar year in business.

After the gallery's initial success, I incorporated and made Victor vice president. We used the British term "Ltd." instead of "Inc." in our company name to add a touch of sophistication to our sign out front. Among Victor's many assets, invaluable to me was his background in architecture. He helped me select the four buildings and locations for the gallery's expansion in that first year of business. Victor also knew how we could fix up a space without spending a lot of money. I relied on my vice president a great deal that year.

I opened my second gallery in Sausalito, just across the Golden Gate Bridge. Like San Francisco's Fisherman's Wharf area, Sausalito was a popular tourist haven. One of Victor's young, hippie girlfriends worked at a gallery owned and run by the Keanes, the couple who became well known for their paintings of little children with huge, sad eyes. A controversy developed about who really did the paintings. The Keanes divorced around this time and it came out that Margaret Keane was the real artist. All the bad publicity surrounding the divorce forced them to close their gallery, and that's when I started negotiating with the Keanes to buy them out of this space. The husband, Walter, was difficult and unreasonable. Victor's girlfriend provided me with inside information about unpaid rent and gave me the name and number of the landlord of the building. I called the landlord and struck a deal, which saved me time and money but cost the Keanes a significant amount.

After opening up in Sausalito, I immediately opened another gallery at the opposite end of the wharf from my Beach Street location, and next, a fourth in downtown San Francisco on Sutter Street near Union Square. Sutter Street had quite a few established galleries, and when my sign went up, I wasn't welcomed with open arms. For my part, in my religious zeal for bringing art by living artists to the people, I looked at these old-line galleries as apostates and less than holy.

All of my galleries had several different showrooms with dimmer switches where I could take prospective collectors. I never volunteered the price of a painting; I waited to be asked. I wanted them to enjoy the painting without being immediately prejudiced by the price of it. I had already learned enough about selling in general to know that once you quote the price it's all over. You have nothing left to sell and no other means to whet the customers' appetites.

Once a customer expresses interest in a certain painting, I or one of the salespeople would take it off the wall and bring it into a separate viewing room. The customer would be seated, offered a glass of champagne and, in my case, be given a warm dose of Southern hospitality. A spotlight would be aimed directly at the painting as it was discussed, and, with the use of rheostat lighting, I could turn the spotlight up and down so they could view the painting in a variety of lighting situations. It was a form of show business that was very effective in selling art.

In most cases we let our customers know we were willing to negotiate the price. As experienced art dealers know, you cannot set a fixed price on a painting; many customers of art, in particular, enjoy haggling and making a good bargain. Some customers claim they are positively allergic to this sort of bartering; they will look you in the eye and say, "Give me your best price and if I like it, I'll buy it." And yet it's often those very same people who end up trying to get a

lower price anyway. I quickly learned to give all those asking
for my "best price" the regular retail price—not my "low,"
as we call it. Nine times out of ten they would maneuver
me into giving them a better price. With great reluctance
and sweat on my brow I would release the art work for the
"low" price, my real retail price all along.

During that first amazing year of success I was eager to
share these happy tidings with just about everybody who
knew me. I took it for granted that my friends and relatives
would be happy for anything good that happened to me.
My first disappointment came when, naturally, I assumed
Sharon would be proud of me, even overjoyed. Instead, she
seemed oddly disoriented and strangely threatened by it all.
Her reaction to my good fortune had me wondering if
perhaps my rarefied success would turn people away from
me. As it turned out, my mother was the only member of
my family who seemed truly proud and happy for me. As
for the others, the general consensus seemed to be that any
man who got rich so fast must be involved in something
shady. When I first started dreaming of making it big in
the art world, it never occurred to me that I would get such
reactions. It was even harder to take when I began having
similar problems with members of my staff. My first big
letdown came when Victor turned against me.

Obviously, I had been too busy to notice that Victor had
grown slowly envious of what some people in the business
had begun to call my "Midas touch." Victor refused to cosign
the bank loan I needed to expand, and that really hurt.
Besides making him a salaried vice president of the company,
I had given him 15% of the stock in my new venture as
a heartfelt thank you for all his help. And, since I was
incorporated, he would not be assuming any personal liability.

The whole thing unfolded one day when I took all my
profit and loss statements to the local Sausalito branch of
Wells Fargo. Without making an appointment, I walked over
to the assistant manager's desk. He was youngish, around
thirty, with unremarkable features except a mustache and
a few extra pounds around the middle. He asked, "What's
up, what can I do for you?" I gave him my spiel about my

newly established business and how well it was doing, then handed him my records and said I would like a business loan for $5,000 for starters. He reflected for a moment before saying no. I was shocked, and asked him, "Why not?" He looked me in the eye and mumbled something about money being tight. I waited for him to go to lunch and demanded to talk to the head man. I was in luck. I got an audience with Mr. Christiansen, a twenty-year veteran employee with Wells Fargo. I ranted and raved about Wells Fargo's announcing they wanted business and promoting themselves as the bank that helped settle the West. Mr. Christiansen calmed me down and then looked over my records. He said, "Jack, you should have come to me in the first place. You don't need $5,000, you need $10,000. Let me fill out this application for you and just have your vice president sign the form. Bring it back to me tomorrow and we'll lend you the money."

I was ecstatic. I got together with Victor that same afternoon and told him my story of rejection and redemption. He smiled at me and said, "That's great, Jack, but I'm not going to sign that loan application! It's only $10,000 now, but soon it will be $30,000 and then $200,000. I just don't want to be part of it." I was flabbergasted. I pointed out that I needed that loan and that it was going to look really bad for me to go back to the bank without his John Henry, considering what I had done to get the manager's ear. Victor stonewalled me and walked out.

The next day I returned to Mr. Christiansen's office with the unsigned application. I told him what Victor had said. Mr. Christiansen looked appropriately nonplussed, then smiled and said to give him the application. "We'll just scratch Victor's name off it. I'll give you the loan on your own recognizance." Then he said, "I never liked that Victor's paintings anyway!" With that, our long and prosperous relationship was launched. For the next decade or so he was my personal banker, even lending me money under the table a few times when the economy dipped. Branch managers of Wells Fargo no longer have the latitude to make those personal decisions.

Victor's arbitrary refusal created a serious rift in our friendship. I stopped selling his art work in all four galleries and removed him as vice president, although he held onto his 15% interest in the business for about nine years. It took me that long to talk him into selling his shares. The last time I saw him he was going to real estate investment seminars.

Unprepared for Victor's betrayal, I began to wonder how many more friends would turn away from me now that I had achieved success. It was not a comfortable feeling. In trying to understand it, I wondered whether he had grown jealous of the attention I was paying to the several other artists I had taken on. Their work was far superior to Victor's, and their sales were a lot higher than his. In my mind, that was just business; Victor was still an integral part of the gallery and would always have an honored position in the scheme of things. Being the only stockholder, he should know that, I thought.

With the rapid expansion of the business during that first year, maintaining competent personnel grew to be a problem. By the time I opened my second and third galleries, I was taking staff members out of my large Beach Street gallery and putting them to work in the new places. At the same time, I was constantly searching for new talent, new merchandise, and new financing.

In all of this hustle and bustle, I hired a guy named Frank, a smooth-talking ex-bartender, a bit flaky but congenial. I needed sales help immediately and just had no time to interview people, so I told Frank to put an ad in the newspaper and have new applicants ask for him. The next day he came in high on booze or drugs, and I had to let him go. All day long, applicants came in asking for Frank. To keep it simple I just said, "I'm Frank."

One of my first really great employees was Jeff Ingerson. He applied for the job one rainy day (I now kept a running ad in the paper) and ended up becoming a great manager and lifelong friend. Interestingly, when I saw him filling out his employment application, I didn't see him as a salesman. He seemed to me a very proper and conservative guy. In fact, he had graduated from an Ivy League school back east and had served in the Navy as a pilot before going to work for a big commercial airline. Even though I wasn't feeling the pinch at the time, there was a downturn in the economy in '70 and '71 and the labor pool was awash with stockbrokers and airline pilots. Jeff had been temporarily laid off because of an airline industry slowdown. He told me he wanted a job only for a year or so—he was not looking for a career. This was very honest of him, but not exactly the strongest selling point I had ever heard from a prospective employee.

I gave him a job anyway, mostly because of his engaging personality. I figured if he could make it as a pilot in the Navy and fly a commercial jet, he had to have something going for himself. Even though he had never held a traditional retail job before, he did extremely well in sales. I had him work in all four of my galleries that first year and then made him my right-hand man and manager of my largest gallery. Because he was married and had a family, I paid him more than I was paying myself.

Jeff helped immeasurably with the expansion of Swanson Galleries but, true to what he had told me, he wasn't interested in a career. As time went by, he started letting me down when I most needed him. He seemed never to be around during a crisis, even though he always had a damned good excuse. I don't know what it was, maybe he just couldn't stand being the number two man, but he became too unreliable to tolerate any longer. What Jeff really wanted was to move to Hawaii and start his own air freight business. Rather than simply saying so, he deliberately goofed up so that I would be obliged to fire him.

Jeff did go to Hawaii, where he got a job as a fish spotter. Eventually he built a very successful inter-island air freight business. At least he hadn't gone into competition with me. A few years later we were able to resume our friendship.

On the other hand, I cannot say I wound up friends with Erik Jorgensen, the sour-faced furniture dealer who was still earning 10% of everything I sold at the Beach Street Gallery. Jorgensen's personal life was all screwed up; he was going through a messy divorce. Besides that, his business was going down the tubes. Even though the rent I was paying him was his only stable source of income, he was soon taking in $10,000 a month as his share of my rent. He was so bitterly resentful of my swift success he seemed determined not just to get rid of me but to take over my business. The ensuing conflict I had with this self-destructive nut would turn out to be one of many feuds, fights and ill-conceived lawsuits I would later encounter in what I learned to call "the flip side of having it all."

Jorgensen was subleasing this space from a guy who had a master lease on the whole building, a man by the name of Gilbert Racine who also owned a popular restaurant in that same block on Beach Street. Unfortunately, I had a month-to-month agreement with Jorgensen, so when I began to see that he was covetous of my flourishing art business, that was when I decided to open a second gallery on Fisherman's Wharf. My fears proved to be well founded. Erik Jorgensen handed me an eviction notice after I had been open about a year. Not only was I attached to the location, I had spent a lot of money fixing up the building. I was appalled when Jorgensen told me, "I'll open my own gallery here and, what's more, I'll be an even greater success than you ever dreamed of being."

I moved out. In short order, his new business flopped miserably. He did not know anything about art, and his accumulated business debts and his divorce made it unlikely that he would be able to hang on for very long. I had been watching, and so when I saw him failing, I went to Gil Racine, Jorgensen's landlord, and offered to lease Jorgensen's space on Beach Street. "I know Erik can't last much longer in that location so Gil, with your cooperation, I'd like to move back in as soon as I can swing it."

"Jack, you're in luck," said Gil Racine, giving me an oily smile. "Considering what you were paying Erik, I'm surprised that he gave me three bum checks. Here they are, I'll show them to you. Anyway, when his lease runs out in a month or so, yes, I will lease the space to you."

I knew Racine owned a building next door to the Beach Street location and I pointed out that if I rented from him I didn't want a gallery to pop up in his building next door.

He said, "No problem." He was a man of action as well as a blatant opportunist. He demanded that we sit down then and there and type up a lease on the spot for me to sign. I was pleased that he wanted me as a tenant, but I was apprehensive about signing a commercial lease with all the addenda he was typing in. I asked, "You won't mind if I first take this to my lawyer, will you?"

"Yes, as a matter of fact, I would mind," said Racine. "If you want this lease, you sign it now or never."

I thought about it for a moment. "You will agree to make it a five-year lease with a five-year option?"

"Agreed."

"And once you get Jorgensen out of there I'd like your promise that you won't rent to any art gallery in that same block."

"Well, naturally that goes without saying," Racine said with a smile. "But yes, you have my word on it."

"Okay, now what kind of rent are we talking about?"

"$10,000 a month or 10% of your monthly sales, whichever is greater."

I nodded and said, "That'll make us partners of sorts, okay?"

"Great," said Racine.

Then he typed up the lease agreement while I waited in his office. When the document was ready, Racine said, "I'll expect the first and last month's rent in advance plus a $20,000 deposit, which comes to a total of $40,000. I trust you brought your checkbook with you?"

I signed the lease and I wrote him a couple of postdated checks, asking him to deposit them piecemeal to give me time to dig up the money. I knew that I would be writing a lot of big numbers on my hand, the sales goals I had to reach to cover those checks. I was still a novice then and bank loans were not something that entered my thinking. My plan was to follow my tried and true practice of selling my way out of the crunch that writing those checks put me in.

I didn't completely trust Gil Racine and hadn't from the first time I had laid eyes on this man. He refused vehemently to let me look at the master lease he had with the building owner. He did let me know that my lease with him for a possible ten years ran concurrently with the lease he had with the owners of the Beach Street property. Nevertheless, Racine and I had a deal, and I went about my business, lease in hand, telling only a few trusted people about it. A couple of my new managers refused to believe that I had pulled off such a coup.

We made preparations to move back in. Time flew as I chased the money I needed to cover the rent checks. Move-in day came and I went down to Beach Street. Erik had moved out of the space but, to my shock, he had moved next door in Racine's building. Knowing he probably wouldn't last long did little to assuage my anger with Racine. Some partner.

When I confronted Racine with this breach of trust, saying, "Why would you rent to this person who had given you bum checks and who would be in competition with me, your more or less partner?" Racine gave me his best Machiavellian smile and mumbled something about their being European immigrants who had to help each other out when they could. They had known each other in the war or something or other. I controlled myself, realizing I had leased a space from this guy even if I had not found a friend in him. I asked that in the likely event Erik's business bit the dust would he please not rent to another outfit selling art work. He assured me that he wouldn't. Somehow I didn't believe him.

After a few weeks I was able to get my Beach Street gallery up and running again and to repair the damage Jorgensen had done to the building when he moved out. I watched him try to emulate what I was doing. He picked up a few artists, but when he started paying them with bad checks, his troubles mounted fast. Eventually, most of the artists who had been stiffed by Jorgensen ended up seeking refuge with me. They knew I paid off in real money. Jorgensen was on the ropes and began to grope around for a life preserver. He took in a couple of partners, people I had known at Lou's gallery—one who had worked at Lou's in sales and the other who was in the print shop where Lou manufactured his Dalí prints.

Jorgensen had to drop out after a few months. He left his new partners with the lease, and they renamed the business. At first, they, too, emulated my gallery by trying to sell the work of local artists even before the paint was dry. They followed the same practices as Erik had, and, before long, I found that I was picking up some of their artists, just as I had with Erik.

I complained to Racine about his letting these people stay on, but he just smiled at me. As time went by, I saw them displaying Dalí prints à la Lou's gallery, and then prints purported to be done by Miró, Chagall, Picasso, and others. Their gallery took on an air of austerity and three-piece suits, but they kept the showroom lights and rheostat dimmer I had initiated. Soon, almost every street-level commercial gallery in the country stooped to selling questionable prints from internationally known artists.

I think a lot of people who wound up selling these prints were seeking social recognition. They wanted to have their names magically and instantly associated with artists who were famous in an art world that most of these dealers didn't understand. I don't think these purveyors of bogus prints were aware of how much the media explosion at the end of the nineteenth century and early twentieth century had contributed to the name recognition of the artists they were ripping off. In the 1970s a reasonably well-to-do person with some college education had heard of these now famous European artists and were familiar with the different art movements—Impressionism, Surrealism, Dadaism, Cubism, Abstract Expressionism, and every other kind of "ism," either through art appreciation courses in college, articles on art in the newspapers, or PBS documentaries on television.

These aging artists were now media darlings, their so-called original, signed prints showing up in hundreds of retail galleries. Besides believing that these prints were hand-done by the artists themselves and personally signed, the buying public was told that the number of prints was limited to what was indicated on the face of the print.

In this wholesale scam, many of the gallery salespeople were duped by their employers, i.e., not told that the prints had been manufactured through some sort of photomechanical process.

I kept asking myself why artists with the stature of Chagall, Miró, or Picasso would sign tens of thousands of these prints when they could sell one of their paintings for a million or more. It got a little ridiculous when these dealers started to use the imminent demise of one of the older artists in a sales pitch. "You had better buy now because Picasso is ninety years old," or "Miró is in his eighties," or "Chagall is on his deathbed." These artists were probably unaware that they were being victimized by these dealers making photomechanical prints of their work. Probably most of them had never been to the cities where their art was so much in evidence.

My warnings went unheeded and almost all the dealers I ran into began to deal with the publishers who mass-produced this stuff. All art works these dealers sold was not tainted, of course, but I think many prints by Dalí, Miró, Picasso or Chagall that were published in the late '60s or after 1970 are certainly suspect.

One rather macabre aside to this fraud was something I witnessed in 1983 on the day that Joan Miró passed away. An acquaintance of mine who had a gallery across from me on Sutter Street put a sign on his gallery door, "Due to the death of Miró, we are closed today." A few years later one of the partners of this gallery, Ted Robinson, was found guilty of art fraud. Thousands of fake prints by Miró and other modern artists were found in Robinson's warehouse in Santa Rosa, California where he had been running a telemarketing business to sell these signed Mirós, Dalís, Chagalls and Picassos. Robertson, in France at the time, was arrested and extradited to the U.S. to face counterfeiting-related charges.

Many of the would-be dealers who glommed on to this new retail art business started dressing the part of what the television and movie industry portrayed art dealers to be—and the image was less than complimentary. Every time there was mention in the media of illegal art dealing, the dealer would be dressed in a flashy suit and wearing a ponytail.

Years later when this whole Dalí debacle was over, these galleries obviously had to replace these modern-day masters with other artists. At that time, the only artists that had the name recognition to even begin to fill the bill were illustrators such as Norman Rockwell, Erté, or Leroy Neiman of *Playboy* magazine fame, whose work was known because it had found its way to magazine covers. As the contemporary greats passed from the scene, these eager retail merchants started advertising and promoting various illustrators who would let them reproduce their works of days gone by. Many of the illustrators agreed to sell or license their names and to let merchants and publishers either make reproductions of their work or have their prints done in their signature style. Once again, the dealers got them to sign blank sheets of paper or to have someone else forge their signature. I always smile when I see a nice crisp signature on a graphic, especially if I knew the artist was in his nineties, or even dead, when the edition in question was published.

I refused to sell any of these questionable graphics, including the latest round of illustrators. I am not saying my artists were all great artists, but they were usually the best at what they were doing and, for me, shared that indefinable spark that makes them a real artist.

While many of my fellow art dealers were zeroing in on the Dalí craze, I just kept adding room after room of accomplished live artists to my gallery at Beach Street. Things were going so well I had great big redwood sliding doors with shatterproof glass panels installed in the front of my old lumberyard building. I was taking in over a million dollars a year at this location alone, and, since I planned to be there for at least ten years it made sense to remodel.

I was having some trouble with Gil Racine, however, whom I would come to describe as "the mad landlord of Beach Street." I was always punctual with the rent and even rented an apartment from him to use as an office. I needed the apartment also so my troops, now numbering about fifteen, would have restrooms. My warehouse gallery had a huge fire alarm and sprinklers, but no indoor plumbing.

One of the stipulations that Racine had typed into my lease was that I had to pay him $10 a month for water use in addition to my $10,000 or more rent. Since there *was* no water—the only water I used was from the apartment turned office—I refused to pay the monthly charge. Each month, Racine would send me a separate bill for that amount. This went on for years and years, and the outstanding balance was finally factored into a future lawsuit.

Not being able to find the right people to work for me continued to be a major hassle during that first accelerated year in the business, more so than any problems I had with neighboring competitors. I got some firsthand knowledge of why people say that going into business for oneself is not for the faint of heart.

Toward the end of that first year I was lucky enough to engage a truly glamorous addition to my staff. Helga Mueller was an attractive and coolly sophisticated German woman in her late forties. When she applied for the job of head bookkeeper, she gave me a bewitching smile and said, "Now Mr. Swanson, I do hope the fact that I don't have much in the way of formal training will not stand in the way of my getting the job." From her very strong accent I knew she had spent most of her life in Germany, and from her age and beauty I suspected that she must have some interesting stories about the Second World War. "No, of course not," I said. I was extremely impressed with her lilting accent and her striking blond coloring. In those respects, she resembled Zsa Zsa Gabor, though Helga was taller and more beautiful.

She pulled out a stack of references from past employers, including some documents from Germany that looked suspiciously like they had Nazi stamps on them. I had heard that Germans are known to keep meticulous records, and Helga was no exception to the stereotype. I was sure that with her beauty and powerful presence she had probably lived well during the war. When I asked about her work experience, she told me she had done some bookkeeping for her second husband, an Englishman who owned a hotel in Jamaica.

It took only a few moments for me to come to a decision: I knew I had to hire her. I already figured out that I could hire a couple of assistant bookkeepers to help her out. Helga had such class that I was certain she would be a fabulous addition to my growing business. Not only did her bearing demand respect, Helga had studied philology in Heidelberg, and mastered ten or twelve languages. That alone would be a great asset to me, especially with the more snobbish customers.

Before long, I learned Helga's life story. She had always loved America and particularly San Francisco, which she had visited with her first husband, an American military officer she married after the war. She had always wanted to live in San Francisco and so, after divorcing her Englishman, she decided to relocate to Northern California, and buy a Dalmatian or two and a Ford Mustang. All she needed then was a job where she could prove to herself and the world that she could accomplish something on her own.

Her stories of what it was like growing up in Germany after the First World War were like something out of a novel. Her parents were part of the aristocracy, and, even after 1918, things were precarious for the well-to-do. During the '20s she had lived in a gated community where guards patrolled. Helga had been deeply affected by the disastrous war and the economic depression that gripped Germany in the '20s and '30s.

Quite young at the time, she had volunteered as a nurse when the Second World War broke out in 1936. At first things went well, but as the war escalated into world war, she decided to find a safer occupation. Her love of languages landed her back in the university. "First of all, you must realize that I have never been a political person," she went on. "And even now I have no politics to speak of except, perhaps, the politics of survival!"

She intimated that her German beaus during World War II had been leaders in the Nazi movement. As I had thought, her beauty had ensured that she would not lack for material things. She attended fancy schools during most of the war.

Toward the end of the war she fled to a little town in the Austrian Alps, hoping to stay out of harm's way. Her former lovers, one by one, had been captured or killed by Allied or Russian forces. As fate would have it, the American army came crashing through the small town she had chosen as her getaway place. The Americans were advancing on Berlin and the tank commander who captured Helga's little town needed an interpreter. Being the consummate survivor, she agreed to work for the dashing young tank commander, who was to save her once again: At the end of the war, she was in the Russian-controlled section of Germany when her American warrior came to her rescue. He later married her.

After the war he opted to stay in Europe and help relocate the survivors of the concentration camps and Helga, with her language skills, helped in this heartbreaking effort. After a few years, they returned to his home in the States. No sooner had she begun to get used to the gingham halter tops that went with the weather in the southern state where they were stationed than her soldier husband had to go off to war again, this time to Korea.

As her story unraveled, I had the feeling that I was watching an old MGM movie on the late show. "And then what happened?" I would say, and she would pick up the story again.

"Well, in the long run it got rather boring to be attached to another professional warrior, even if he was on the winning side. He was always off fighting in some undeclared war in some pesthole of a country clear across the world. Finally it all grew tiresome. I had an affair with a British nobleman. I divorced my American and married the Englishman. He owned a string of Jamaican hotels and he began to insist that we make a permanent home in that monotonously tropical climate. That was when I divorced him and decided to move where *I* wanted to live. I'm still close to both my ex-husbands. One of them has a condo in San Francisco so he can stay in touch. And now here I am, sitting in your office."

I told her she was now my new controller and that her first job was to go to Sausalito and rent an office. "I want you to organize my bookkeeping department and hire somebody to help you if you need to." She went out and found a great office with a view of the bay and San Francisco. Despite Helga's lack of formal experience as a bookkeeper, she turned out to be adroit with figures and a genius at organization. She eventually handled all my finances and ended up serving as the secretary-treasurer of my corporation and my right-hand assistant for five years. Beyond these skills, she had such effusive charm and such an open manner that none of the VIPs we had to work with—my banker, tax attorney, and accountant—could resist her. If she called the bank and asked for a favor, they would never say no.

Among the thirty or so staff members I had working for me after that first year, Helga and the two bookkeepers she hired were the only women. But that was a situation that would change dramatically a little later on. At this point my galleries on the wharf and in Sausalito were open fifteen hours a day, seven days a week. There seemed to be an endless stream of tourists to both areas; people would bang on the doors even after we had closed. I remember making sales at 2:00 A.M. It was an exciting time to be selling art. Everyone profited. The artists were creating something the public loved and the doctors, lawyers, businessmen, Indian chiefs, and assembled masses were eschewing the kind of modern art found in museums and art academies and buying art of the "I know what I like" school.

In the '70s the government gave large tax breaks to these professionals, letting them write off artwork as office furnishings and take art works home or donate them to a museum for an additional write-off. As an art dealer, I would fly back and forth over large metropolitan areas and dream damned near orgasmically about all the waiting walls represented in the millions of homes below us on terra firma.

My greatest excitement came from working with the many young "stars" I discovered. The high I experienced every time I gave these newcomers their first big chance made it clear to me, over and over, that I had found my true avocation. Finding one's career path is not that easy for many young people. I used to think it would be nice if some God-like figure would yell out from on high to those floundering about in search of a career, "Take a left!"

One of my first stars was a young artist I'll call Jim. Jim did spectacular seascapes. They had such enormous commercial appeal that in just a few years I sold something in the neighborhood of 3,000 of his paintings. Jim became quite wealthy in the process. He was my first hugely successful artist. Nobody is saying that his paintings represented high art, but those who saw them were transfixed. I've even seen tears and quivering lips on those who viewed his paintings in the magical glow of lights and dimmers. Over the years Jim's work was much copied. His seascapes may be looked down on by the benefactors of public taste who belong to the museum boards, but I have never seen anything like the response he got from his paintings in the early '70s.

Jim first came to me after he had been stiffed by a local gallery. He said he had, literally, a truckload of his paintings that he would bring me. He wanted me to agree to buy the lot and to pay him in cash. Then he wanted me to write him a check every week when he delivered more paintings.

I said, "No problem," trusting my luck that it would work itself out. Each week he would back up his van, unload the paintings, take my check for $4,000 or more, and drive off into the sunset. Fortunately, the frenetic pace he set was equal to the demand: we always sold enough of his paintings to cover the checks I gave him so confidently.

Sadly, like so many young artists in the free-swinging early seventies, Jim didn't hang on to his money. He had a beautiful, devoted wife, and they lived quite luxuriously, but he also had a heavy drinking problem. In time, he managed to drink away every cent he earned.

Knowing how gifted Jim was made it doubly sad to see how badly his personal life was going and what a self-destructive kick he was on with his growing addiction to alcohol. In a typical scenario, he had turned to liquor in the first place as a way to maintain that surge of creativity that was bringing him such success. But his illusions of heightened production turned out to be delusions. His spending soon exceeded what I was paying him. He kept demanding that I pay him a higher and higher amount for his paintings. As time went on he became more of a liability than an asset to me. It got so that I could no longer make a profit selling his art.

I was at my wit's end as to what I should do with him. Just as I was going to tell him that I had to stop selling his work, Jim called me and, in pretty slurred speech, said, "Look, Jack, I really hate to do this to you, old sport, but I'll soon be opening my own art gallery in San Francisco." As it happened, Jim would be the first of about a dozen of my star artists who attempted to go on their own as artist and dealer. None were successful.

When Jim left, he started another trend: taking one of my managers with him to help run the new venture. He also took a copy of my mailing list figuring that a manager, his wife, and that mailing list would be all he'd need to make a million running his own gallery. About six months later, Jim phoned me with a tale of woe. "Listen, Jack, old friend, I'm in big trouble. I've got about eighty paintings in the back room and I don't know what the hell to do with them. I'm in a real shitty bind and you're the only guy I know who can get me out of it." It came as no surprise that he had gone bankrupt in six months; in fact, I was amazed that he had lasted that long. Although I agreed to handle some of his paintings again, I refused to deal with him personally from then on. Jim continued his drinking. His wife remained loyal through all those bad times, even when he had all but quit painting.

This kind of self-induced tragedy was repeated by a staggering number of gifted young artists, many of whom seemed hellbent to burn themselves out while they were at their peak. In most cases, it was a process that backfired until, in the end, it destroyed what little talent they had left. Meanwhile I was discovering other potential stars but discovering, at the same time, that no matter how much I befriended them and made money for them, there seemed to be an unwritten law that the relationship between dealer and artist had to be adversarial.

One of the brightest of these new soon-to-be stars was David Meyers. I met him, as I had met so many other painters at the time, in one of the city's now flourishing artist cooperatives.

He painted in a colorful kind of cubist style, which was quite innovative at the time, and, as it would turn out, very salable. David was in his early twenties and very well-educated. He had been earning his living as a school teacher.

As I did with all my new discoveries, when I first saw his work I got excited and made expansive statements, saying, "Look, this is the greatest. You quit your job as a teacher and I'll agree to finance you and buy enough of your paintings to keep you afloat." I would later learn to curb some of this exuberance, for ultimately it seemed to work against the artists. Having learned how most of the city's art dealers had treated their artists, without realizing it I was going to the other extreme and leading my artists to expect too much too soon, and worse, to assume these glory days would go on forever.

In any case, I started doing very well with David's work. Later he became one of the first artists for whom I started to do reproductions. The complexity of his style made it impossible to produce very many paintings, so my decision was to make reproductions of his work in limited editions and have him sign each print—after it was printed! The plan was very successful, but our relationship suffered.

In my view, it is David who holds the distinction of being the first to try to turn my artists and salespeople against me. I found out that he was contacting my printer in secret and creating his own reproductions so that he wouldn't have to answer to me or pay me any commission. (I actually saw my artists' works one day when I was at the printers. He hadn't even bothered to find a different print shop.) He then signed up some of my other artists, promising to publish their works in the same way. He even got some of my most trusted salespeople and managers to work for him on a moonlighting basis. Together, using his work as the centerpiece to begin with, they started their own publishing company. In effect, he was in direct competition with what I was doing as Swanson Art Gallery, Ltd.

What really ticked me off is that he wanted me to keep selling and promoting his work at the same time. When I decided not to do business with him or his buddies anymore, he tried to persuade my artists to quit in protest if I stopped selling his paintings. None of this occurred, or could occur, of course, until after he had earned the phenomenal sum of money he did out of our relationship. When I started selling his paintings, they fetched a few hundred dollars. In just a year or so I was getting $5,000 to $10,000 for his large canvasses.

I was particularly pushed out of shape when David recruited a kid I had originally employed as a stockperson; he needed a job while he was going through college. After interviewing him and learning that his dad had just passed away, I called his mother for a reference. I then took him on and did what I could to help him make it through school. He took some time off to go to art school in Florence, Italy. When he came back to finish college here, I made a part-time job for him in sales where he could make better money. When I found out Steven was on the payroll of my ambitious and disloyal friend, David, I was hopping mad. David and Jim were just two among ten or more of my super-successful artists who ended up betraying me in the same way. In the long run, they lost, because their "independent enterprises" soon bit the dust.

Once I had been established for a few years, I was able to luck into some long-term employees, but during that first year or two when the pace was frenetic, California's art fever brought out the worst in many of my artists and sales staff.

By 1973 I was adding artists to our roster at a fast clip. The artists' co-op on Union Street was my best resource. Although it gave the artists autonomy and a sense of control, their by-laws limited the amount of work they could display and sell. By contrast, I offered these artists various locations where they could show almost as many works as they could produce. Jim's seascapes had been extremely popular, so when he opened his own gallery, I quickly found three or four seascape artists to replace him. During that period, I added some magnificent artists to my galleries. I found a Korean artist named Nong who painted Oriental masterpieces, and, when I opened my Sausalito gallery, I inherited a portrait artist by the name of Dennis Debo. Dennis' portraits were reminiscent of the work of Rembrandt. During the early '70s he got caught up in the Civil Rights movement and captured the struggle in his extraordinary renderings of African-American faces. He continued to bring me fabulous paintings for years.

More and more women were coming into the art world. Jean Kalisch was an artist I got through the artist co-op. She had already established her name in San Francisco having garnered critical acclaim from local art critics for her impressionist paintings. Unlike many others, Jean had participated in shows at the DeYoung Museum. She was in her late fifties when I began to represent her, and she was one of the few artists, in my experience, who just kept getting better and better, right up to her forced retirement twenty years later.

Another one of my early stars was Marsh Nelson, an all-American housewife. She had the 3.2 kids, stationwagon, dogs, conservative husband, and lived in the suburbs. She had missed the '60s revolution. Her paintings, in gouache, were hauntingly beautiful. She did nudes, wildlife, landscapes and dreamscapes that encapsulated the moods and preoccupations of the times. Her painting style, coupled with her ability to work hard, brought her tremendous success. I see that she is still doing some great work in the 1990s, a lifetime away from the early '70s.

Evelyn Embry was an artist who just walked into my gallery on Sutter Street one day. She did beautiful sepia tone paintings of the human form. I found them breathtaking. Her signature was indisputably that of a woman, and looking at it made me realize that the times, indeed, were changing. Women no longer felt they had to take a male nom de plume to make their art acceptable.

With all the wonderful art work finding its way to my galleries, my senses were constantly stimulated. Every day I was bombarded with art works of every imaginable style. I kept telling people that for me every day was like Christmas, that regardless of the stresses, I was extremely pleased with my life—not simply because I was making a lot of money but because I was doing what I wanted to do. I had found my niche.

Sharon stuck with me and lent me her considerable intellectual and moral support. I promised her I would buy a house in a year, and I made good on that promise. It was a great house in Sausalito that had been built by an older couple who owned an antique shop in San Francisco. They planned to take the money from the sale of their house and move north to start a farm raising tomatoes. I was aware of this business duo, as it turned out, and had been an admirer of their taste and personal style. When Sharon and I saw their unique home, we agreed we had to have it. I went to my new-found friend and banker, Mr. Christiansen, and he wrapped up the paperwork on a mortgage in a day or so.

One of the great things I found about living in the hills of Sausalito is the near absence of any street traffic. And from its windy, European-style narrow streets, it takes only twelve minutes to reach downtown San Francisco. You just glide over the bay via the beautiful art deco Golden Gate Bridge and you are there.

Another perk of my success meant that I could do some things for my mom while she was still alive. She was plagued by life-threatening medical crises, mostly from circulation problems, but I was grateful she was still around to witness my accomplishments in the art business.

Just before Sharon and I moved from our North Beach penthouse to Sausalito, I got a surprising letter from my ex-wife Joanna, telling me she had moved to San Francisco with the dogs and that she was in therapy. She said she had "changed," she was sorry for what she had done to me, and she wanted to talk about a reconciliation. I was flabbergasted! All I could think about were her wicked put-downs—that woman had a tongue like a cuisinart—and how happy I was that the only contact I had with her was to see her signature on the back of my alimony checks. I wrote back saying, "Thanks, but no thanks." Actually, that out-of-the-blue contact brought a sense of closure to our failed marriage. I was happy to hear a few years later that she had remarried. (I could also forget about sending any more alimony payments.)

I couldn't take any time off in the first year or so, but in my second year of business Sharon and I made what was my first trip to Hawaii. What a wonderful feeling to step barefoot onto the sands of Waikiki. I was dead wrong thinking Sharon had come from a thatched-hut village; of course, Honolulu was huge. To me it seemed bigger than San Francisco and things were booming. Jet travel was turning Honolulu into the hub of the Pacific. I was also aware of how lucky I was to have Sharon introduce me to the inner workings of this island culture. All I knew of it before was what I had gleaned from reading Michener's *Hawaii*.

Sharon was from the group of Japanese that had been the last wave of immigrants to the islands. Both Japanese and Chinese had been brought to Hawaii to work in the cane fields and, over the years, they gained economic parity with the American and European settlers. By the time I got there, the Asian and native Polynesians made up the majority of the population, and no one seemed to notice that Sharon and I were of different races. Her folks had not been thrilled at our living together and, although they treated me cordially, I knew they didn't approve of Sharon marrying a non-Japanese.

I never got much response from my mother or dad about Sharon being Asian, but they never said anything that would have me believe they disapproved. Neither one of my parents had known any Asians firsthand. My dad kept asking me over the years whether or not Sharon celebrated Christmas. He probably assumed she was a Buddhist or a follower of some esoteric religion. Once he met her in person she had him wrapped around her little finger in two seconds flat.

Sharon and I were busy with our lives, she with her business career and me with being a father figure to all my artists and employees, and we just never discussed marriage or starting a family. I assumed that when the timing was right, we would get around to it. She didn't push because of her family and because she knew I was still getting over my failed marriage to Joanna. Besides, in the early '70s nobody seemed to be getting married; those who did were a bit odd.

The "me" generation was just bursting into public consciousness. Sharon and I had moved to one of the most affluent suburbs in the world. Sausalito damned near had a "couples only" sign at the city limits. An older retired crowd lived in its hill houses and there was a sizable population of gay people, but mainly its populace was young couples, professional and business people on the way up. You seldom saw any children in the hills of Sausalito, just fancy cars and well-dressed two-income families. Sharon wasn't much for the cocktail party scene, but she had moved up in the company and had to socialize more than before. With my naturally outgoing way and need to cement business deals and scout new artists, we had a hectic social life.

Without family and the more traditional preoccupations of hearth and home, we began to think of the behavior of our singles' crowd as the norm. Once you get into a no kids/ and no family responsibilities mode, it's hard to give it up. Even though we had cut drugs out of our life, we had friends who were just beginning to experiment with drugs and who were carried away with the relaxed moral standards of the '70s. "The Pill" and the relative ease of getting an abortion were major markers that followed the social revolution of the '60s. More and more women were joining the workforce and becoming affluent on their own merits. Most of us thought that wonder drugs had all but eliminated venereal disease and, consequently, anything you did was okay as long as you didn't physically hurt someone else.

Those were years of wild sexual experimentation where no one gave a thought to the possibility of potentially fatal viruses as a result of sexual contact. Some of our friends, solid couples either married or living together, made overt propositions to Sharon and me to swap partners. As tempting as the idea was, I felt there must be some sense of emptiness they were trying to deal with, and that eventually their swinging ways would ruin their primary relationships. We were embarrassed a few times when friends mistakenly assumed we had joined their swinging scene and made us an offer we had to refuse.

When Sharon and I first got together in 1968, Sharon was twenty-two and still making her own clothes. We enjoyed smoking pot and listening to the Beatles' "White Album,"

Jefferson Airplane, Santana, and The Doors. But as Sharon pointed out, there is usually a flip side to everything. As my business pressures grew, I saw some negative effects of getting stoned. For one thing, there were lingering effects that seemed to hang on for days. We finally decided to stop any form of drug use. We knew that to live up to our responsibilities at work we would have to ban all hallucinogenic substances from our lives. Having seen the lives of so many friends and business associates ruined over the past twenty years through drug abuse, I thank God we did.

My plate was certainly full when it came to managing my galleries. We were taking in a couple of million dollars a year and my sales staff was turning over as fast as I could hire them. When I lost Jeff in 1973, in his place I hired a South Carolina boy, Harry Clark. Harry, who had been a supply officer in the Navy, had the damnedest way of sitting back with his mouth open, some mannerism that might have gone unnoticed in his laid-back southern climate, but didn't fit with big city life in the Bay Area. Harry was great with management but couldn't sell his way out of a paper bag. He worked for me for a couple of years and never made a sale over $3,000, whereas some of his new hires would make a $20,000 sale the first day.

I always looked into who made those big sales and found that in almost every case the salesman was driven by need, a pressure for immediate money. I also found that it usually was detrimental for a new person to make a big sale the first month of employment because disappointment inevitably came the following month if fewer sales were made, or because the pressure to meet the high standard they had set was too great.

Harry seemed to be constantly amazed at the galleries' success. He had no real affinity for the art business—to him it was just another job—but he was a good manager and rightly observed that if he kept the numbers up his position was secure.

One of the replacement artists I picked up when Jim left to open his own gallery was an artist who had been selling exceedingly well at national outdoor shows and art fairs.

These new outlets were helping to popularize arts and crafts throughout the country. His name was George Lee, a marine painter extraordinaire. When he joined our gallery group in '73, he was already making $100,000 a year. He brought in other artists who, like him, were also doing very well financially. I can't claim to have discovered guys like George Lee but I did provide them with a stable place to show and sell their work. I either bought all their paintings outright or took them on consignment, whatever was better for both of us.

After Jim opened a gallery on Union Street and took one of my managers and my mailing lists with him, you can understand how touchy I got when I saw any of my gallery personnel hanging around with any of my important artists. One day I saw Harry, who managed my biggest gallery, having an animated conversation with one of my ex-employees at the then very popular Buena Vista bar. This particular guy had gone with Jim to help him set up shop. I was shocked to see them. Harry knew that this ex-employee was persona non grata and that it didn't look good for him to be seen being buddy-buddy with this guy. There was an unpleasant moment when our eyes met. Harry was aware I was not overjoyed at this breach of protocol, especially taking place right down the street from our gallery. I said nothing but began to conclude that many of the people who worked for me, Helga being the exception, were not to be counted on.

The disappointment I felt in being unable to count on the loyalty of my employees was enormous. The pressures of playing surrogate father and personal banker to many of my artists, and the divisiveness among my sales staff, many of whom expected remuneration they had not earned, put me on notice that major changes were in order. Some of the people who were the biggest drain on me psychologically were very likely unaware of what they were doing. I made the decision that regardless of whether a member of my sales crew or one of my star artists accounted for a substantial portion of my gross sales, if their attitude or actions were bringing me down, I would discontinue working with them.

12

Women Enter the Art Gallery

I quit dealing with the few problem artists who had been a source of trouble to me and, one by one, I got rid of most of my sales force. I then hired a very debonair and impeccably dressed guy in his thirties to be my new vice president in charge of personnel. Jake Wigand had just come back from Southeast Asia where he had been a civilian claims adjuster for an airline. Jake was a free soul who was not averse to bending the rules. With his competence and charm, I felt he was the one to help me with my personnel problems. And he did just that! A very dapper dresser himself, he had an eye for a well-tailored suit of clothes.

He soon filled up my four galleries with new sales help, mostly women. For me, this was a new twist. Up until then, no women had ever applied for commissioned sales jobs. Now, all of a sudden, Jake started hiring women of all shapes, ages, and educational backgrounds. When I spoke to these applicants, I asked why they hadn't thought of working in these kinds of sales positions before. It seems that until this time most of them didn't see sales as something women did; they had been steered into more traditional jobs for women— nursing, teaching, bookkeeping—and, in general, jobs that paid a predictable hourly wage. A few of them told me the women's movement was under way with a vengeance, and it was the right time to branch out into new career paths.

It wasn't easy for a lot of them to get used to commissioned sales, but I had come up with a small base salary and various incentives and bonuses, and soon these women were doing as well as the men. Most of the saleswomen we hired were right out of college and had a teaching degree to fall back on in case they didn't make it in their new field of endeavor.

This shift in hiring spilled over to my stock help. We needed about eight people to take care of all the shipping, crating, intergallery transfers and framing. When we started hiring attractive young girls for these jobs I wasn't sure they could do the job, especially when it came to lifting and moving the heavy stuff, but they managed. Soon all my stock help were well-educated young women dressed in overalls and combat boots.

One of these young gals, Valerie, was a weightlifter. She proved to have strong leadership qualities and she soon rose in the ranks and became manager of the stock department and frame shop. Valerie also had a college degree, but she could have posed for a painting of a peasant woman working in the fields.

She and I developed a camaraderie that let us talk openly about people and events. Eventually it led to a surreptitious affair. Over a period of time, I discovered that she and I were interested in some of the same girls. I was surprised to learn that she was having an affair with a cute young blonde gal from Florida we had just hired in sales. Knowing that didn't hurt our friendship but it did open my eyes. Valerie stayed with the gallery for years; she finally left to take a management job with a delivery company.

Jake had started us out in this new direction by hiring women as staff help and, in the next few years, at least half the artists I represented were women. One clear advantage I found was that there was now little or no competition between me and my women artists or sales and administrative staff. Not only did the men I had hired compete with me, but a lot of these men, egged on by their girlfriends or wives, started to feel it was beneath them to be number two—they had to be number one.

I now made sure that all my Help Wanted ads said "Saleswomen/Salesmen." Over the next two decades I hired over two thousand people and the majority of them were women. I developed many close, supportive relationships with these women, who were very important to the success of my galleries, which had risen to seven in number by the late '70s.

I returned their support for me by helping them prove themselves in areas that had been exclusively male-dominated. They particularly liked succeeding in selling art on commission because it meant that they were being paid according to their ability under exactly the same pay structure as their male colleagues. How much their success affected their confidence and self-esteem was voiced clearly by Helga who, beaming with pride one day, said, "You know, Jack, if I had known I had all these abilities I would have gone into politics."

During this period, Sharon seemed a little disturbed by my having so many good-looking gals on the payroll. We had an unspoken agreement that we had an "open relationship," and, as far as I was concerned, we were lifetime partners, even though we were not legally married.

At this time, we were living high on the hog. I traded in my purple Porsche and purchased a Mercedes SL two-door sports coupe. Sharon and I were traveling to Mexico and spending time at Lake Tahoe learning how to ski. I was going full blast and beginning to realize that I was going to have to learn how to cut back on work and work-related pressures. One wintry Friday afternoon Sharon and I drove four hours up the mountain to Lake Tahoe, which is one of the Seven Wonders of the World, to spend the weekend. We got to our rented cabin miles from the hustle and bustle of the city. Everything was blanketed in snow and very quiet. Boy was it quiet. I was so high-strung from the pace of my life and my business activities that, having no stimulants in my system other than caffeine, I freaked out. We packed our bags and drove down the hill in the dead of night. Once back in the city I saw that if I couldn't deal with silence, it was time for a few changes.

One of the fiscal battles I was constantly dealing with was how to hold on to some of the money that was flowing through our business accounts. I paid cash for all expansion costs and we seemed to have enough money to purchase merchandise and publish our new graphics, mostly photomechanical reproductions. But dealing with government taxes on my corporate or personal income was a real headache. Imagine my chagrin when my accountant told me in his studied baritone voice that I couldn't pay myself more than the salary level at which I could hire someone to do my job. I also learned that my company could retain only a certain amount of profits; over that amount, I would have to pay more taxes. Even with write-offs and income-averaging it seemed that the more we sold the more we were building up a huge debt to local, state and federal taxing agencies. I brought in tax attorneys and accountants, but we weren't much of a match for the people who sit around government board rooms trying to squeeze out new taxes for their thirsty kingdoms.

I couldn't seem to keep my hands on the money that was streaming through. In frustration I hired an Armenian guy named Steve Jasmazian. Steve had just graduated from Stanford with a Ph.D. in math and this was his first business consulting job. We had fun trying to figure out various economic theories and all the hidden costs of doing business, especially all the taxes. Steve worked for me about a year. One of the ways I compensated him was to sponsor his Formula One race car; he put my corporate logo on his windflaps. Steve finally researched every aspect of my new art business and was able to help me get control of my finances. One thing we discovered was my mark-up was out of whack. I found that I was paying my artists too much and that I needed to make some changes. I showed my books to all of my artists and instituted a blanket change in our purchase and consignment dealings. From then on I stuck to that formula, and I credit it as the main reason I succeeded over such a long period of time.

When I proved to my artists that I needed a better mark-up because of my increasing costs, not one of them—fifty or more, at the time—left my gallery. Over the years some of my most successful artists would argue that they deserved more, more, more. I just held my ground and said no. I know that many felt I was unreasonable, but I knew that to do them any good I had to remain profitable in the business.

With all the galleries going full blast, we started generating enough capital to take to the airwaves with advertisements. Someone introduced me to Art Blum, owner of a PR firm, and I retained his company to get us television and media coverage. We started hosting auctions and giving all the proceeds to children's charities, we started a newsletter for our clientele, and we produced 30-second spots of our artists' works for Johnny Carson's "Tonight Show."

I was lucky to have found a graphic designer by the name of Steve Cardinelli who handled the brochures, the newsletter and the show invitations, and later, when I started publishing books of my artists' works, he handled the graphics and design. Steve had unfailing good taste and I relied on him for twenty years as an integral part of my team. Among his many talents, he always knew what hotel to stay in on the continent, what the "in" restaurant was, and who to call at the American Embassy in London.

He also introduced me to some great artists he had studied with. One was Mary Tift. Now in her eighties, she is still producing exquisite etchings. Once you're bit by the "Tift bug," as I have been, you're in trouble. I, for one, own about every etching she ever created.

Steve and I had our differences occasionally, but our friendship was so strong we always worked things out. Of all the business associates I dealt with over the years, Steve was the most enduring. Unfortunately, Steve was diagnosed HIV positive in the late '80s and passed away a few years later.

I was quite excited by my Mexican artists. Carlos Soriano of Mexico City was one; Francisco Zunica, the best known living sculptor in Mexico at the time, was another. I wanted to do a one-man show for Carlos, and so I sent Helga to Mexico City to pick up the paintings we were featuring in the gallery show. I still have some of his portraits of Orozco, Siqueiros and Diego Rivera. Carlos Soriano had an extraordinary zest for life! He was in his late sixties when I brought him to San Francisco and I couldn't keep up with him. He used to say that he would have plenty of rest when he met his maker.

The lavish show I had in mind for his work ran into a few glitches before we were able to carry it to completion. It turned out to be one more lesson in how to become a veteran in the world of retail art. A year or so before this event I moved out of my Sutter Street gallery and sublet it to my good friend and one of my star artists; I'll call him Jay. He was a fellow given to wearing Pierre Cardin suits on his diminutive frame. A genius when it came to his paintings, he was very abrasive and arrogant in his dealings with the public. I was selling his work in all my galleries and anticipated opening a gallery in Carmel, that exquisite seaside resort 150 miles south of San Francisco. I sublet the Sutter Street gallery to Jay for his use as a gallery and studio. In addition to its 3,000 square feet of street-level retail space, it had a 3,000-square-foot basement. Jay was to keep me supplied in art work and abide by the terms of the lease I had paid a commercial real estate firm to draw up. Right after we concluded this deal, there was an unexpected downturn in business. My star artist began to have money problems and he quit paying me rent. I complained; I cajoled; I explained that I was selling his work in my galleries and he could surely pay me from this income. He refused. I pointed out that I needed the money to open a new gallery in Carmel. He said, "That's too bad."

Exhausting all options, I brought him to court. My lawyer did only business tax work, so he got a novice lawyer to represent me in court, and thus we embarked on a long journey. First of all, it took six months to get on the court docket. When we finally got in front of a judge, the first thing the judge said was, "I view the law as compromise." Not what I wanted to hear. Then Jay's lawyer jumped up and down and started tearing into the judge, who appeared to be intimidated. I kept referring to the legal contract that very clearly said I was to be paid in legal tender on the first of each month. The judge took three days to finally decide to render a verdict sometime in the future. A few weeks later, he decided in my favor and told Jay to pay up or vacate.

Jay still didn't pay up and I had to hire a deputy sheriff to physically sit in his gallery and collect any monies Jay brought in. I think his wife's family finally lent him the money; at any rate, he paid me off finally, and moved out. Whew!

I decided to put Carmel off for a year or so and to move back into the Sutter Street gallery and remodel the space to house both a gallery and administrative offices. I hired the architect with whom I had been sharing an office in Sausalito to do the remodeling, giving him carte blanche permission to do whatever he wanted to do. Unfortunately, he ran over budget and he didn't complete the job on time. (I had planned a grand opening show for Carlos Soriano and had already printed four-color invitations. I had to throw them out and start over.)

It all worked out, though. We had a great show for Carlos; local politicians, TV personalities, and up-and-coming professionals donned their evening gowns and tuxedos for the event. Jake Wigand, my vice president in charge of personnel and "social director," arranged for the catering and live music, and it was his expertise that attracted just the right people.

The future looked bright. I now had offices on Beach and Sutter Streets, I hired consultants to computerize my inventory and profit and loss statements, and I investigated the feasibility of going public. It didn't take long for me to find out there were some drawbacks to that idea. Although you could raise a lot of money that way, you could sell only a small percentage of your stock and you had to be accountable to each and every stockholder. I backed out quickly from that plan.

One good thing came of my giving Victor fifteen percent of my stock: with him keeping a vigilant eye on my business practices, I had to maintain perfect books. The best thing I ever did, in fact, was, from day one, to separate my personal finances from my company finances. All money collected for the gallery, even cash transactions, went into the company account and I paid myself a salary and had taxes withdrawn. When I left Lou, I wanted to prove that a person could become successful in the art business through honest means. At the same time, it did help motivate me to have one minority stockholder looking over my shoulder.

As I picked my way through the minefields of operating my art business, something happened that I had not anticipated or planned for adequately. In my relatively easy climb to success, I gave no thought to the general economic climate. Thus far, it had had no adverse effect on me. In the winter of '75, however, there was a precipitous recession that popped up out of nowhere. I don't know what caused it; maybe it was just a market realignment in reaction to the Nixon Watergate mess, or maybe it was the gasoline shortage. Anyway, it was a quick but deep recession that flatlined my sales figures for months. I didn't have enough reserves to get by and, again, I had to turn to my banking friend and benefactor, Mr. Christiansen.

Unable to grasp the seriousness of the situation, I kept telling myself, as I always had, "We'll sell our way out of this." Defeat was not in my vocabulary, but, this time, neither was reality. I continued to spend as if nothing was wrong. Mr. Christiansen gave me numerous loans to keep me afloat but also tried to steer me on a safer course. Even when my books made it crystal clear that I was a bad risk, he threw caution to the wind and loaned me money under the table. Finally, however, when he saw that I was ignoring my plight and continuing to charge on my credit cards, he marched into my office on Sutter Street and, in front of Helga, demanded that I turn over my cards to him. I thought it was some sort of joke (that's how out of touch I was!) and complied. He grabbed a pair of scissors and proceeded to chop each card to pieces. I think I turned a few different shades of red. It took me a few seconds to recover from what I first saw as an unthinkable act, but when I settled down, it dawned on me that he was acting as a true friend. I knew it was time to acknowledge the recession and deal realistically with my business problems if I was to get the galleries back on track.

I recalibrated my business machine, cut back on expenditures, and got my artists to adjust their prices downward and be a little more flexible. I was duly chastised, but vowed never again to be so unprepared for such predictable downturns in the economy. As things started moving again, I opened additional galleries on the East Coast, but this time I kept my eye on the economy. I didn't want to go through "plastic surgery"—as Mr. Christiansen called it—ever again.

Early 1974 brought me into contact with a young lady who would become one of my most gifted artists, Jacquie Marie Vaux. Essentially self-taught, she specialized in doing the most extraordinary watercolors of wildlife; they were like portraiture. The first time I saw her work she was sitting in the waiting room at my Beach Street gallery. It was a rainy day and she was wet and bedraggled. She appeared to be in her late twenties, and, on a dryer day, a very attractive young woman with blond curly hair. She wasn't fully prepared to show her work, as it turned out. Her paintings revealed talent but seemed rather sketchy. I wasn't too impressed and told her that her work showed promise, but that I couldn't use it at this stage in her development.

A few months later I ran into her again while I was attending the Mill Valley Art Festival. There she was, standing amidst her paintings, hanging out with all the other pegboard revolutionaries. This time, when I looked at her striking paintings of all sorts of wildlife, I was stunned. She had improved amazingly (or else had not shown me her best work before). She worked mostly in watercolor and pen and ink sketches. I was especially drawn to a large painting she had done of a giraffe with a twig in its mouth. It was her "signature" to interject elements like that as a way of capturing the animal's uniqueness. I learned later that she painted only those animals she had had some chance to interact with.

That day, as I stood admiring her work, I noticed two little children hanging on to her long, flowing granny dress so popular at the time. They seemed to be about four and six years of age. They fit right in with the "hippie old world Renaissance" feeling of the festival itself. As I walked up to Jacquie to say hello, I overheard the children, still tugging on her, saying, "Mommy, mommy, we're hungry." I ran over to her, gave her a big hug, and said, "Now you're ready!"

"I am?" she said. "Ready for what?"

"To become a star, of course. What else?"

She laughed. "Oh man, I've heard that line before."

"What line?"

"Stick with me, baby, and I'll make you a star!" she mimicked.

"Yeah, but this time it's going to happen!" I whipped out my checkbook and bought a couple of her best paintings right on the spot, then told her to deliver the rest to my gallery posthaste.

I learned later that she had recently divorced her husband, who had a serious substance abuse problem. She and her two small daughters were living in a low-rent dump where the girls slept on the floor.

I signed her up exclusively for my galleries and offered to buy all her future work. Her paintings started to sell like crazy. No sooner would she bring them in and my framer put them into appropriate frames than we would sell them. Soon there was such demand for her paintings that I started selling them faster than she could produce. With that kind of demand, I was convinced that she was another artist for whom reproductions bearing her signature would do very well. I was right. I made 200 reproductions of one of her giraffe paintings and had her sign them. We priced them at around $150 to $200 each and the entire edition sold within thirty days. I followed the giraffe reproduction with reproductions of her male tigers, this time increasing the edition size to 300 and the price to $200. Again, they sold out in a month. It was a gold mine for Jacquie and for Swanson Art Galleries.

Of course, nothing is as easy as it seems. At some point, the gallery sold Jacquie's original tiger painting to a gas station attendant and his wife, a police dispatcher from the East Bay. As an inducement to make the sale, we promised to give them a few of the prints we had made of the original painting. They were amazed and, of course, pleased to see the prints sell so rapidly, which presumably made their original painting priced at $1,500 go up in value. When they multiplied $200 times 300, they started thinking that maybe they should share in the profits. Well, in our litigious society that means, hire a lawyer. I got a call from one of these legal seekers of truth and justice saying that he was bringing a lawsuit against me. Their lawyer reasoned that even though he didn't think his clients had a case, they were suing me in the event they just might have some rights in the artist's work.

After I went through a couple of depositions, hired my own lawyers to handle the case, and got copyright lawyers as expert witnesses, the couple offered to settle out of court for $10,000, knowing full well that it would cost two or three times that amount to take the matter to court. With some bitterness, I paid these extortionists off.

One year later, the U.S. Supreme Court ruled that artists and their estates were the sole owners of the copyright of their creations in perpetuity. This ruling was too late for me, but after the lawsuit I had a disclaimer printed on all my company sales slips stating that the customers were buying only the art work, not the copyright.

As with many of my other artists, success was coming to Jacquie very swiftly. I began introducing her to gallery people and taking her out to the theater and to some of the city's finest restaurants. She started dressing up like a rock star; it was fun to be around her childlike enthusiasm. From the start, I saw myself as her protector as well as her art dealer. One of my first moves was to open a special trust account for her. I would deposit ten percent of her earnings each time she sold a painting. She was doing great and in short order had a sizable nest egg. Everything was going swimmingly until Jacquie told me about a trip she and her current boyfriend were planning to take to Mexico. My alarms went off. I guessed rightly that they would not be streetwise, and would mistakenly assume that the Mexican police would not care what they did below the border. I warned her, but obviously she didn't listen.

Their careless behavior got them thrown in jail and, as everybody knows now, Mexican jails are the pits. Not only were the conditions poor but the prison sentence could be lengthy and indeterminate, especially for Americans. Naturally, I couldn't let one of my "stars" languish away in some rat-infested dungeon so I paid a young lawyer friend of mine to go down and negotiate their release. Her jailers let her go but kept her boyfriend hostage until she could return with a payoff. I was tempted to leave him to his fate. Instead, I made the now streetwise boyfriend vow to pay Jacquie back before we sprung him, because, just as I thought, the Mexican officials wanted the exact amount that Jacquie had put away in her trust account.

After that turbulence, Jacquie brought me at least one great painting a week for the next seven or eight years. Some of the most spectacular shows the gallery staged were in her honor. Her collectors were legion and fanatically loyal to her, many buying a number of her works. Her large cat paintings were now going for $5,000 to $10,000 and still her devoted collectors would eagerly await the announcement of a new graphic release and purchase one of each. Eventually we printed about forty editions of her different animal paintings.

One elaborate show we put on for her at our second Beach Street location involved creating almost a theme park. We built cages inside the gallery and through Jacquie's contacts at Marine World Africa USA and the San Francisco Zoo, we were able to bring in a 600-pound Bengal tiger for the occasion. We also had ocelots, birds of prey, cheetahs and other various and sundry animals.

I was addicted to sushi at the time so I hired a catering company owned by a Japanese woman, Sumi, to provide the fare. Sumi was personal chef to EST guru, Werner Erhard. Sumi spied an old row boat in Richardson Bay near Sausalito, plucked it out of the water, cleaned it up in the gallery and filled it with thousands of pieces of sushi. It was an unmitigated success and Jacquie was the center of adoration. Once again, I was struck with the great pleasure and privilege of doing what I most love to do and having the public be in sync with me.

Over the years I would have similar shows for Jacquie at my Sutter Street, Carmel, and Washington, D.C. galleries. She continued as one of my top-selling artists for nine years or so. I consistently paid her every two weeks during those nine years. We never had any problems. Jacquie produced through all kinds of family crises and weathered many personal growth challenges during those years. I promoted her by publishing her graphics, featuring her in a pictorial anthology of twenty-one California artists, and showing her off in one-woman shows and television commercials, at the same time, of course, displaying her work in my various galleries.

And so, naturally I was nonplussed when Jacquie started hinting that I wasn't doing enough for her and that perhaps she should take her career in hand and open her own gallery. After some harsh words—hers, not mine—she struck out on her own and opened a gallery in a shopping mall in Santa Rosa, a mid-size town in northern California, quite removed in distance and sophistication from the San Francisco art community. She spent a lot of money to develop her gallery but she showed only her own work. With limited offerings and a far more conservative buying public, it wasn't long until she was out of cash and out of business. Jacquie wound up losing a small fortune. She had to put up personal collateral to keep the bank from forcing her into bankruptcy. After this fiasco, she called to apologize for all the things she had said.

After Jacquie closed her gallery, she came back into the fold and repeated many times how she wanted me to take over all sales and marketing for her. I did, and we still maintain a friendship today. I'm "Uncle Jack" to her now grown daughters, and her daughter, Jennifer, even worked for me as a salesperson after she got out of college.

Another artist who deeply impressed me was a self-taught Italian-American named Silvio Giovenetti. But the raw talent that drew him into the art world and provided him with a substantial income did not prepare him for the price he would pay for his success. People were transfixed by his images and artistry. He was a natural—full of imagination and vision.

A handsome and charismatic young man with wife and kids, he had been raised in a small California town in the Sierras. His dad, to whom he bore a striking resemblance, even for a son, had been a goldminer who dabbled in sculpture. Silvio also enjoyed sculpting and took up his father's hobby, but he also experimented making steel bases for his heavy sculpture creations. He used different acids to give detail and add various patinas to his sculptures and bases. With practice he found he could control the effects of the acid-on-steel technique. He used dozens of different acids and varied the time he would allow each one to corrode, or etch, the steel. When the corrosion process was complete, he applied a clear polyurethane to protect and hold the colors.

Silvio's career skyrocketed from the first week his paintings hung in the gallery. As a gift to me for his rapid success, he offered me a painting of my choice. I still have it in my private collection—an abstract cityscape. He was so excited about the public's acceptance of his work that he brought me as many as thirty paintings a month. They all sold, some for thousands of dollars. I featured him in several art shows, to an enthusiastic buying crowd. I paid him a sizable amount of money every two weeks and, as was now my practice, asked for an exclusive arrangement. Although he agreed as far as gallery representation was concerned, he refused to give up selling his own work at outdoor shows. Two issues were at stake: He had a childhood friend, a drinking buddy, whom he kept employed selling his works around the country, and he simply didn't want to be controlled by one dealer.

Because Silvio was prolific in his output, I let this issue slide, but I was concerned that my other artists would follow Silvio's lead and continue selling at outdoor shows. Many of the artists who had meteoric success, such as Silvio did, feared it coming to an abrupt end and didn't seem worried about over-exposure or the possibility of burning themselves out.

In spite of this area of disagreement, however, Silvio and I have remained friends throughout his ups and downs—and he went through many. Silvio loved the good life. He spent more than one fortune over the ten or so years we worked together. He bought a fancy home with a pool, located right on a golf course, and a second home in the mountains. He drove the longest Lincoln I've ever seen. Despite my warnings, he continued to live it up.

One day we were having lunch in a fancy restaurant on Sutter Street, laughing and reminiscing about our respective histories. I said, "You know something, Silvio. You're the only well-adjusted, normal artist I know." The very next day, as if to prove me wrong, he announced that he was giving up painting because of personal problems and the pressures that led him down that destructive road. He equated the stress of creativity and monetary success with the pain and grief he later experienced.

Silvio kept his word. He went into partnership with some friends in the steel business and gave up painting. He is now a successful businessman.

13

The Sonoma Years

Sharon and I had been spending a lot of time checking out the wine growing regions of Northern California. I was having thoughts of owning a summer home in Sonoma, a historic town one hour north of San Francisco, and settling down to a pastoral life in the wine country—maybe even having a passel of children.

We had already made friends with many people in the Napa and Sonoma Valleys. We often hung out at a little house in the town plaza that served as the headquarters and meeting place of the Sonoma Historic League. Once belonging to General Joseph Hooker of Civil War fame, the house now had a cafe that served coffee and tea and pie. A group of feisty retired ladies manned the historic house with its display of memorabilia from early California settlers of the Sonoma Valley.

I struck up a friendship with a vivacious and personable "widow lady" who had moved to Sonoma to be closer to her grandchildren. One winter day when we were talking, I mentioned my idea of buying a house in Sonoma. She gave me her daughter Vicky's real estate card, and told me her daughter lived just outside of town in a hidden valley with only one entry road. The area was known as the Diamond "A" Ranch; it had recently been subdivided and there were now around eighty houses built on the old ranch site, each with a few acres of land.

Vicky turned out to be a cute young mother of two boys aged five and three. She had an all-American look and a beach bunny patina about her, which came from being brought up in a beach city in Los Angeles. She gave me a tour of Sonoma and showed me where she lived in Diamond "A".

She knew a couple who wanted to sell their house. Originally from Texas, he was being transferred back to their home state by the commercial airline company for which he was a pilot. Their house, hacienda style, was perched on top of the mountain. On a clear day you could see past the town of Sonoma all the way to the bay.

The price was steep but I took one look at this adobe and curved red tile five-bedroom house and said, "I'll take it." We were warmly received at all the newcomer parties given for us and found that parties were a constant thing at the Diamond "A" recreation center. Our neighbors were mostly airline people, pilots and flight attendants in their twenties and thirties who had it all—the house, family, ski cabin, and unlimited travel.

When I bought the house in Sonoma, I was filled with a sense of family and commitment. I wanted Sharon to feel secure in our relationship so I put the new house in both our names. And I saw nothing but blue sky ahead for Sharon and me. Although she seemed pleased enough, I found that when I started hinting at marriage—something I had assumed was in the offing—she kept putting me off. She was just as noncommittal when I talked about having children, although she did voice some fears about having children. Her mom had died at a young age of a brain tumor and she couldn't deal with the thought of her children experiencing what she and her brother lived through, should anything happen to her. In retrospect, I would come to realize that our major problem was total failure to communicate.

After remodeling our Sonoma house and furnishing it, I saw no reason to put off having a family. The first time it dawned on me that she and I were not in sync was when her parents came to visit from Hawaii. We wanted to show them the local sights in Sonoma. We started at the historical downtown plaza and visited a beautiful Victorian that had belonged to General Vallejo, one of the town's founders and a major historical personage. He had governed Northern California under the Spanish and Mexican governments.

As Sharon and I were walking around upstairs, we were standing at the iron grating that restricted visitors from entering the bedrooms. I remember that I had my hands on the iron grates designed to keep the hoards of tourists at bay. At some point, I mentioned filling our Spanish-style hacienda with little ones just as General Vallejo had filled his home with children and, eventually, grandchildren. We looked at each other and from the look in her face I knew she did not share that vision at all. A surge of adrenaline went through me and, without realizing it, my hand tightened convulsively on those iron bars until I bent the one I was hanging onto. Things were never the same for us after that.

In almost a decade we had never had a real disagreement or heated argument. Over the next few weeks we started coming to grips with our differences and talked openly about our hopes and plans. Sharon said, "I'm sorry, Jack. I don't want us to be married and I don't want to have children."

"Is that a fact?" I said. "When did you come to that conclusion?"

"I think I've always known it," she said calmly. "I can't tell you why, but I'm afraid to bear children."

"Come on, Sharon. If you need to go to a shrink, get past it. This is going to ruin our relationship if you don't get past it. Why didn't you say something before this? If this is really how you feel, how come you let me go on thinking you wanted the same kind of future I did?"

"Oh well. If you had ever sat down with me and asked my opinion I would have enlightened you a long time ago."

Of course, in her demeanor Sharon was still the soft-spoken young woman I had wanted at the start. But now I realized a quiet storm had been brewing all these years, lying dormant and just below the surface of her acquiescent smiles.

"Okay, then tell me something. If you've always known this, why the hell did you let me buy the new house with five bedrooms and put your name on the title?"

"Oh, well," she said with a girlish giggle, "a girl's got to cover her ass."

I had never heard her say anything crass like this the whole time I had known her.

I stared at her as if she were a stranger. "Are you saying that it's over?"

"Yes, that's exactly what I'm saying. But I'm sure you will do just fine without me and find someone who wants to have children."

I was devastated. Sharon found an apartment in Sausalito and moved out. We seesawed painfully for a few months, but it was clearly over.

I bought back the Sonoma house from her and made sure she got any possessions she wanted. She later invested her cash settlement in some valuable Sonoma real estate and ended up doing very well for herself. Sharon had never learned how to drive all the years we were together so you can imagine my surprise a few years later when she passed me on the freeway driving a Japanese car! I found out from friends that she eventually married a Japanese-American guy but never had any children.

Not long after I split up with Sharon around 1975-76, I hired a very enterprising young man. I'll call him Barry. Although Barry was about ten years younger than I, we looked enough alike to be brothers. Barry had come to San Francisco after graduating from an East Coast college where he and his wife, Kathy, had gone to the same New Hampshire school. Upon graduation they packed up their car and headed west. When he looked around for a job he spied my running advertisement in the local paper and noted that my Beach Street Gallery was right around the corner from his apartment. Impressed by his winning personality, I hired him on the spot.

Barry started as a salesman but he was sharp and he took responsibility and was always pushing for more authority. After a few years I made him my vice president and general manager. This meant he would manage all seven of the galleries I owned at the time.

I had to teach him a few things about style and wardrobe, but he was a fast learner. In fact, now, in addition to resembling me physically, Barry started dressing and talking just like me. And we had a lot of other things almost eerily in common. He, too, had come to San Francisco to make it, whatever "it" was. He, too, found himself drawn to the art business. His mother was from Texas originally, but he had been raised in Boston where my mother came from.

I knew I could completely trust Barry to represent the gallery: If you were talking to Barry, you were talking to me. In the back recesses of my brain, I knew that someday Barry would have to break away and find his own identity. Meanwhile, when we would discover we had both bought the same leather jacket with no prior discussion about it, I simply took it as some strange synchronicity—and a kind of tribute.

Barry's dedication to the business allowed me to take Wednesdays and weekends off. I had given him hands-on power, a company car and a pension/profit-sharing plan. Barry and his wife, Kathy, and I used to travel a lot together. They were great companions. I even got to know both sides of their respective families over the years.

At this point, we had a firm handle on our Bay Area galleries, including the latest in Carmel, and wanted to expand our operations to the other side of the country. My artists had pushed for the Carmel outlet and were now clamoring for East Coast exposure. Because Barry had been raised in the East and knew it well, I felt I would have few problems getting a new gallery started in New York City. The three of us hopped a plane to New York and we all got such a negative impression of the Big Apple—it was going through a bad economic downturn at the time—it was clear that Manhattan was out.

I wanted to look at Washington, D.C. and the surrounding area, including Alexandria, Virginia, a few miles over the Potomac River Bridge. The place was fabulous—there were monuments everywhere—the Lincoln Memorial, the Smithsonian, and the National Gallery museum, the brainchild of Lord Duveen, the world's greatest art dealer. Duveen had approached wealthy financier Andrew Mellon and persuaded him to pay for the National Gallery museum. He then proceeded to sell him and other mega-rich American businessmen most of the Renaissance masterpieces that inhabit the pink marble edifice Duveen's own architect had drawn up. At any rate, I fell in love with Washington, D.C. and Alexandria, finding many similarities between the Bay Area and this capital city with its very southern milieu. Everything was very laid-back in Washington, but it had an active tourist area in downtown Georgetown and Alexandria.

Being at the seat of power of our Pax Americana government was also very intoxicating. This place made news every day and its historical ambiance permeated the air. I ended up opening a gallery on "M" Street in the plush suburb of Georgetown, with Barry in charge as overall general manager. By now Barry had a hand in hiring most of the people who worked for me. Barry had hired my manager in Carmel, as well as the one for my new (fifth) Bay Area store on Union Street.

After we got the Georgetown gallery launched, we opened another one in Alexandria, Virginia right across the river. Alexandria, besides being a small historical town filled with brick buildings dating back to early colonial times, was a popular art colony. In some ways, it reminded me a bit of Sausalito. While poking around this riverside town, I found an old World War I naval warehouse named the "Torpedo Factory." The warehouse was now subdivided into artist studios and I saw there were hundreds of painters, sculptors, and printers who could certainly use my help with their "sales and administration" needs. I could see at a glance that the artists at the Torpedo Factory alone could fill my new galleries. My decision, however, was to include several of my California artists in my Georgetown and Alexandria galleries and my new East Coast artists in my California outlets. All my new East Coast artists had the same inventive energy I had found in California—which was fortunate because, with seven galleries, it was a never-ending battle to get enough merchandise.

Meanwhile, back in California I had my huge five-bedroom hacienda all to myself. For quite a long while, every time I visited my castle on the hill and put the key into the front door lock, my hand would shake. As much as I liked the house, it represented another failed relationship and a painful reminder that for all of my material success, it didn't mean much without loved ones to balance out my life.

My neighbors in Diamond "A" were supportive and made room for me at their dinner tables. I gravitated toward spending time with these wholesome families. Their concern with raising children intrigued me and got my mind off running the galleries and city life. I was drawn to country living. It reminded me of my upbringing in small southern towns and, now that I was an unattached bachelor, it helped ground me. I had never planned on being single at thirty-five and I wasn't about to hang out at "fern bars" that were all the rage in the city. I knew that it was going to take a couple of years for me to get over the Sharon thing. It was like having a clock that counted days in big green numbers on my forehead for everyone to see. Just 720 days to normalcy.

I had become close to three or four families in Sonoma and had billed myself as "Uncle Jack" to quite a few of my newfound neighbors' children. I spent the next few years getting to see up close what home life was really all about. It was quite an education watching these folks raise children and cope with life in the '70s and '80s.

I mentioned that there were about eighty houses in this hidden valley. Over the next few years I got to know about forty families in this area fairly well. A couple of them damned near adopted me, threatening to claim me on their income tax. I hoped that Sharon and I hadn't started a trend with our breakup, because over the next few years at least half of the people I knew in this little community filed for divorce. It was surprising to me that so many people were willing to break up their families and estates for what I saw as a game of musical chairs. Even with all the changes going on around me, it was great to be part of this Diamond "A" crowd and be privy to the innermost workings of these California families.

One family in particular really did take me in. This was the Schake family. I met Wayne, Celia and their three kids at the recreation center for our area. Their youngest girl, Kris, was around five years of age, their middle child, Kory, was twelve, and the oldest, Kurt, was thirteen.

I give a lot of credit to Wayne Schake for allowing me to be a participant in his family and watch his kids grow up. Wayne is from the East Coast originally and has a toothy resemblance to Teddy Roosevelt. He was a pilot for Pan American Airlines and his wife had a Ph.D. in Education but had decided to give up a professional academic career to be at home with her children.

Wayne was gone a lot of the time, as were many of the pilots that populated our Diamond "A" area. I don't know if I would have let someone like me hang around as much as Wayne and my other Sonoma friends let me. I would drop by many of these folks' houses at all hours. I was always welcomed and brought up-to-date on what was going on in everyone's lives. On my Wednesday midweek break, I would go with Wayne to watch Kurt and Kory run track or practice various sports. Kurt was on the baseball and football teams, and Kory was a champion cross-country runner. If Wayne wasn't home, I usually detoured to another house, quite often to Vicky's. (She was the realtor who introduced me to the area.) Vicky's husband was a pilot and was amazingly tolerant of having a single male around. Later, when Vicky and her husband divorced over his drinking problems, I seriously considered marrying her. I loved her two boys, aged five and seven at that time. But after some reflection on the true nature of our brother-sister relationship, I decided a long-term friendship was more advisable.

The Schake family was my focus for years. I had a wonderful time watching their children mature. I knew from the second I saw those kids that they would do special things. Kurt was very much like his father, and there was every indication that he would be a pilot someday. He had the look of a young man who should go to a military academy. Throughout his four years of high school, he excelled at all sports as well as academics, and was voted student body president. I tried to make it to all his football games on wintry Friday nights, even when it meant flying in from out of state. There's nothing like high school sports for great drama and entertainment. After all, it's a once-in-a-lifetime chance for the students to learn about life and their own capabilities.

Things had not changed much since I was in high school. The students still congregated under the bleachers and the mating dance was the same in small-town California as it was in small-town Texas.

Kurt was later accepted into the Air Force Academy and I joined the whole family to see him inducted into the military school in Colorado. I visited him quite a few times during his four-year stint at the academy, even going to his graduation and watching Wayne pin the gold Second Lieutenant's bars on him at a midnight ceremony. Kurt's younger sister, Kory, was also very bright. For a few summers in high school, she worked in my administrative department. She went on to Stanford and excelled there, too.

Wayne had been a fighter pilot in Vietnam at the very beginning of the war and had flown various missions and various aircraft. One of the planes he piloted was a prop plane; it had a specialized machine gun that earned it the nickname, "Puff, the Magic Dragon." This machine and its guns could spray an area the size of a football field with such a concentration of bullets that nothing remained unscathed when it stopped firing. Wayne served his tour of duty and got out. He loved flying so much he told me that he would do it for free. The guy would have made a great Marine platoon leader. Since he spent long hours in the cockpit of commercial airliners, he welcomed any opportunity to get some exercise. For the most part, he kept in shape by running, but we also played tennis a lot.

Everybody in the world seemed to have jumped on the running bandwagon at that time. Everywhere you went, you'd see people decked out in distinctive athletic shoes and sweat gear. Wayne decided he wanted to train to run in a marathon. Not one to go halfway, he had set his sights on running at the site of the original marathon in Athens, Greece. Seeing that he meant it, I told him that if he trained and felt up to it I would go with him to Athens, but as a spectator. (I liked running with him occasionally, but just around the neighborhood—none of this 26-mile stuff.)

We started planning our eventual trip to the "Plains of Marathon" where the "Western" Greeks defeated the Oriental

Persians hundreds of years before Christ. It was after this Plains of Marathon battle that a runner was sent from the scene to inform the Athenians, anxiously awaiting the news 26 miles from the battle scene, which way things had gone. This guy became the patron saint of runners; he set out over the steep hills on the 26-mile jog to town with the good news. Immediately upon telling the news, so the story goes, the winded hero expired.

Wayne practiced for months, slowly building up his time and distance. Finally he was ready. I bought tickets for myself and Barry, still my general manager at the time. At the last minute, Wayne almost backed out, but I pulled out my round-trip first class tickets right in front of his wife and kids. The dye was cast. He couldn't back out now. We headed for the airport a few weeks later. The Olympic Marathon was being held in Athens on the sixth of April.

We arrived at Athens Airport in the early morning, three or four days before the big event. Apparently, there had been a threat against some of the Israeli passengers aboard our plane, so the Greek authorities had us stop on the tarmac a mile or so away from the terminal, deplane, and walk single file to the airport between personnel carriers and lines of military police carrying machine guns. It was a rather unsettling welcome to Mediterranean Greece.

After clearing customs, we three musketeers hopped a cab and got the ride of our life to downtown Athens and the Hilton Hotel, where we were staying. Greek drivers know only one speed—fast. Gasoline was about four dollars a gallon at the time, and I couldn't help but wonder why they wasted so much of it screeching around.

Once ensconced in our hotel, we called around to find a car and driver for the duration of our stay in Athens. We hired a friendly old guy named Gus. He was a jocular and personable old-timer who assured us he was a first-rate tour guide. He loved his old car, a 1950 Mercedes with over a million miles on its diesel engine. The first thing we wanted to do was scope out the path the race was going to follow from the marathon "battlefield" to the Olympic Stadium in downtown Athens. We piled in Gus' Mercedes and away we went, up and down those steep hills for what felt like a hell of a lot more than 26 miles. We finally got to the starting place and Barry and I could tell that Wayne was wishing he had prepared himself better.

Over the next few days we toured Athens, a metropolis of three million people. We could see the Acropolis and Parthenon from our hotel window. What a rush it was to walk around the Parthenon, knowing that Alexander the Great had walked on these stones, as had millions of others, great and less great, over the centuries. Since I was a Middle Eastern History major, I couldn't have been more elated. Gus took us to some great little restaurants and drinking establishments around town, and introduced us to Greek folk dancing and, of course, their national drink, ouzo. We followed custom by breaking dishes and glasses in the fireplace. Barry and I lived it up, but Wayne would not break his training. Everywhere we went we were greeted warmly, especially when we introduced Wayne as our gladiator in the upcoming marathon. Quite a lot of the old men we talked to said they had participated in marathons in days gone by. They wished the American pilot well. More pressure was being heaped on Wayne's broad shoulders.

When we went to register Wayne with the Olympic Marathon Committee, we encountered a major snag. Wayne had never run in an Olympic event and, therefore, had no official sponsor, no country he was representing. They refused to give him an entrance number. After talking to some of the contestants who knew the ropes, we latched onto a tall young Greek who was the driver for the premier of Greece. Sympathetic to our problem, he wanted to help out. Not only did he manage to get Wayne an official entry number, he got our driver, Gus, an official pass for his vehicle so we could follow along the marathon route. For Gus, it was a dream come true. He had always wanted to be a part of this national event.

The day of the race was upon us. There were hundreds of runners from every country on the globe. Many countries, like Japan, Russia and Turkey, fielded professional teams trying to bring home the prize of finishing first. As it turned out, Wayne was the only one representing America. Considering all the TV coverage the event generates in Europe, it seemed that America should be more visible and involved. We motored over to the "Plains of Marathon" where Wayne started to limber up and psych himself up for the event. Barry and I walked around the statue used as a marker in the race. The statue commemorated the Greek heroes who had died defending their homeland, and all runners were obliged to make a small detour and pay their respects at this historical marker.

As the noontime sun started heating up, the race was about to begin. The runners congregated, each with the official numbers pinned on their shirts. In this wave of color, every nationality was in evidence. Gus, Barry and I watched from the sidelines ready to go the minute the starter pistol was fired. We heard the sound and jumped into our chariot. Sometimes we were in front, sometimes behind the long line of runners. We tried very hard to keep our man in sight.

As the race wore on and we went up and down the steep hills along the marathon route, we noticed a lot of contestants dropping out because of the difficulty of running against a stiff wind in the heat of the day. About halfway into the race our gladiator, Wayne, was holding his own. We could see he was a bit winded but he was still in the race. In the sharp wind, even Wayne's short, curly, reddish hair was blown straight back from his forehead. Wayne was more compact and stocky than a lot of the professional runners and, under these conditions, his build was a definite plus.

Barry, Gus and I took it upon ourselves to dispense water to runners at various checkpoints. Wayne was working hard and gave us some concern; we could see he was winded, and, as we learned later, he was having difficulty with blisters. As he hit the 20-mile mark he didn't look good at all. I was afraid that in his determination to finish he might go beyond his physical limitations. I was beginning to feel guilty for having put him in a "have to" situation.

As Wayne approached the home stretch, Barry and I got out of our comfortable car and started running alongside of him to keep him going. Three miles to go and throngs of people lined the streets of downtown Athens. The police cleared the way for the runners as they came into view. Barry and I were wearing running shoes but were otherwise dressed in street clothes. I even looked the tourist with my light leather jacket and a camera bag strapped across my chest.

We had intended to run along with Wayne for a few minutes and then jump back into Gus' Mercedes. But as we sprinted alongside our very tired buddy and were about to peel off back to our official staff car, Wayne said, "Don't leave me, guys, huh?" We hung in there, running past the assembled masses wildly waving the Greek flag. At first it was a lark, but after another mile, I began to sweat. With my camera bag flapping against my side, I had flashbacks to my Marine Corps days. I never fell out of a run back then, but I wasn't exactly in shape at this point.

We finally could see the Olympic Stadium in the distance; the finish line was at the far end of this horseshoe-shaped stadium. The three of us entered the Olympic arena going full tilt. The last two hundred yards continued under my feet for an eternity. My heart was pounding, shutting out all other noise, and I seriously wondered if I'd make it. Just a short distance to go but it seemed like a million miles off.

Wayne kept on grinding away, leaning into the wind as he ran across the finish line. I dropped back, whipped out my camera with its telephoto lens, and caught him going over the line. He made it! Wayne staggered around on the Olympic track and finally passed out in a state of exhaustion.

Barry, Gus and I picked Wayne up, put his arms over our shoulders, and hauled him to the stadium showers to revive him. No luck. He was out cold. As we carried him toward our car I made a mental note of the stela (a carved stone slab) at the finish line. It had an ancient Greek bust on top of the pillar and a pair of testicles midway up the stone column.

We decided to get our champion into Gus' car. With its official sign, we could get through the crowds and back to the Hilton Hotel, our marble palace. We literally dragged Wayne through the front lobby arm-in-arm. He looked like the victim of a shipwreck dressed in running shorts. We lifted him into the bathtub and turned on the shower. Not only was he dehydrated, but the knots in his leg muscles were dancing around in what was an unnerving sight to behold. When he came to, we fed him some beer and salty peanuts, and watched him begin to focus. I then grabbed the phone and called Sonoma, California. When his wife Celia answered I said, simply, "He made it!"

A few hours later Wayne was laughing and ready to hit town. I, on the other hand, was physically exhausted and emotionally drained. Just then, we got a call from the Olympic Committee saying that Wayne had come in 37th and was the last one of the runners being awarded a silver medal with the winged Venus of Samothrace stamped on the face of it. They apologized for giving him a hard time. To make it up to him, they wanted to take the three of us to dinner and formally award Wayne his medal and certificate. They also wanted to give Barry and me a bronze medal for jumping in to help a comrade. We were elated. The dinner was very festive and greatly appreciated.

Before catching a British airline to London and points home, we toured a couple of Greek islands. In London, I bought a coin with the bust of Alexander the Great on it and I wear it to this day. When we returned to San Francisco, I renamed my sailboat, a 32-foot Choy Lee ketch, "Marathon."

I was especially lucky to have my Sonoma friends at this time because it was about then that my mother had a debilitating stroke. She had to spend several months in the hospital. Being a nurse she was well cared for. She knew most of the doctors and nurses personally, and her long-time friends, Dr. and Mrs. Hawkins, made sure to see her daily. I flew in on a red-eye to see her, arriving in the morning after being up all night. I found her alert and aware of her surroundings, but she couldn't speak. Here was one of the smartest and most articulate people I had ever met, and she couldn't communicate. She was so frustrated she cried. All I could do was try and comfort her. When I got out into the hallway away from my mother and others, I felt the pain of the world strike me. We all know that we have to deal with the death of loved ones, but dealing with my mother's pain and frailty in this sterile hospital just about did me in.

A few years after her stroke, I got that dreaded phone call from my mother's best friend. At the funeral, I was pleasantly surprised to see that my mother's entire family on her brother's side, the Chicago contingency, showed up for her funeral, even if my father did not.

14

Courtroom Drama

As the fiscal pain caused by the mid-seventies' recession faded into the background, I began to notice certain disconcerting activities on the part of my Beach Street landlord, Gil Racine. I had signed a five-year lease with him with the stipulation that I could automatically extend it for another five years, although the exact rent for the continuation years had not been specified. Never having trusted this landlord, it occurred to me that I needed to start thinking ahead to when my lease would expire in 1976. My Beach Street gallery accounted for over half of my annual sales and I couldn't afford not to have it producing.

Whenever Racine and I saw one another, I would mention the extension, but he would clam up and walk away. Having seen him be overly friendly to the owners of Gallery X, the people he had rented to right next door to my business, I got the distinct feeling he was making long-term plans with them, even forming a partnership with these parvenus who were very successful selling what I considered to be bogus Dalí, Miró, Chagall, and Picasso graphics. Not only that, but Racine wasn't doing too well with his restaurant—every reason for him to try his hand at the art business.

Every time I saw Racine he seemed to be in secret meetings with the Gallery X people. It infuriated me that he treated me so cavalierly, since I knew he was deriving his living from the $10,000 or more a month I was paying him. It became apparent he was biding his time to take over my space, which I had spent years and more than a hundred thousand dollars to make into a viable business.

As I cast around for alternative locations, just in case what I feared came about, what did I see at the corner of

Beach and Larkin Streets but a "For Rent" sign on a wonderful two-story brick building, larger than my warehouse.
It was right across the street from Ghirardelli Square, smack
dab on the corner, and across the street from Victoria Park,
which ends at a sandy beach on the bay. No wonder people
are drawn to this scenic area. The Hyde Street Cable Car
line ends at Victoria Park; its turntable is in constant rotation.

Remembering that timing was everything and that I
couldn't wait around for Racine to make up his mind about
our deal, I went to the Italian lady who owned the brick
building that was for rent and quickly signed a ten-year lease
with her for a lot less than the $10,000-plus a month I was
paying Racine—and I didn't have to pay a percentage of my
sales to this new landlord. The building had started out
housing a horse and carriage stable and became an automobile
garage in the early 1900s; most recently, it had been a retail
outlet for Far Eastern imports. So I would have to remodel.

Without bothering to tell Gil Racine, I started to refurbish
my new place. I would have private offices upstairs, a state-
of-the-art frame shop, and a closed-off area with a pushbutton
garage door where I could just drive in and park. It even
had running water and modern conveniences such as bathrooms!
One day as I was supervising a crew of workmen inside my
new 16,000-square-foot, two-story gallery, I noticed Racine
driving by outside. For the split second when our eyes met,
I held up the keys to the new place, smiled, and shook them
in my hand. Racine nearly ran into a fire hydrant as he
grasped what I was indicating.

I had a year to go on my Racine lease and I simply ran
both these Beach Street locations simultaneously. Since I was
selling the same merchandise, my staff would run back and
forth between both galleries. although I found it hard to
run both places, the public's art fever was still high on the
graph. I was able to do equally well in both locations, and
that helped me pay for remodeling my new flagship gallery.
I was glad to see the year come to an end so I could make
plans to move out of my old warehouse. I was relieved that
I wouldn't have to deal with Racine anymore!

One of my managers at the time pointed out to me that McDonald's didn't leave its "golden arches" when it left a location. Following this line of reasoning, I decided to remove all the expensive improvements and trappings I had put into that drafty old warehouse to turn it into an attractive gallery. Legally I had every right to take whatever I had paid for that wasn't permanently affixed to the building. I hired a work crew and told them to dismantle the sliding redwood doors and keep them, if they wanted. The glass and wood was valuable. I also offered them the heating units, freestanding cases, and a gazebo I had built inside the space.

On one of the last days of our occupying this place that had meant so much to me, I was standing around with some of my troops, watching the transformation the construction workers were visiting on the old warehouse. Unfortunately, the men the foreman had hired got overzealous and were going a little far in their efforts. I saw a few of the workers crawling out on some beams and cutting down the outdoor space heaters, which dropped like giant rocks to the cement floor below. I would have preferred to donate those heaters to some charitable organization.

I was just about to complain to the foreman when in walked Gil Racine and a few of his buddies. He started jumping up and down, trying to articulate something through all the noise and dust created by the work crew. He flew into a sputtering tantrum right in front of me and my employees. Red-faced and snarling, he said, "You can't do this. I'll sue." I chuckled and did something I had always wanted to do. I leaned toward him, grabbed him by his tie, and with one hand on the front of his collar and one hand on his tie I said, "Watch me."

For my triumphantly playful gesture, Racine added a charge of "assault with intent to do great bodily harm" to the long list of things he was suing me for. I knew I was kissing my $20,000 security deposit good-bye, but I definitely thought it was worth it. Even though I hadn't removed anything that wasn't mine, Racine sued me. I knew he would. I was also sure that the process would wind its way circuitously through the legal system and take years to conclude. My gut feeling was that once everything was brought out into the open, and even if I was walking a fine line regarding the legality of my actions, I was morally in the right. I bet a million dollars on this intuition.

Racine brought suit on five or more charges, and asked for $500,000 here and $500,000 there and punitive damages of a million or so. It added up to more than this cowboy had. I was getting used to being sued, so I just filed it away in the back of my mind, deciding to deal with it when and if it actually got to court. Racine wasn't able to rent the building to his new partners from Gallery X for what he had been getting from me, having to give the guys from next door a break on the rent for darn near a year so they could remodel. I was right about Racine being in cahoots with his other art gallery tenants and wasn't too surprised when he made a career out of his lawsuit against me. The lawsuit took more than five years. The verdict was read aloud by the jury foreman just before my fortieth birthday.

These proceedings ran concurrently with other legal actions taken against me by ex-employees and artists. The climate was very litigious during the seventies, and got even worse during the eighties when the population of legal professionals mushroomed. To make a living, attorneys were, and still are, forced to contrive cases out of thin air. Each law school graduate has to sue someone just to prove that they are part of the fraternal order. Many competent lawyers who have represented me against bogus lawsuits have flat-out told me that if someone had asked them to sue me for what they, the attorneys, knew was an extortion attempt, they would take the case. Basically, what they are saying is that their financial needs outweigh moral considerations.

When I was first served by Racine, I checked to see whether my business insurance would cover me or provide legal counsel. The insurance company said, "?*%!@ #&^"—translated, "Screw you." I went out and found a lawyer for a mere $7,000 who specialized in suing recalcitrant insurance companies. I brought suit to force my carrier into defending me. I won. The insurance company agreed to pay for all my legal expenses and provide me with a hot-shot young lawyer named Jim Murphy. There was a catch though: The insurance company was bound to pay my attorney fees only if I was exonerated on all counts. Of course, opposing counsel wanted to see every bank statement, all tax returns, and receipts. I was lucky to have Helga, who kept every scrap of paper, receipt, and canceled check.

Jim Murphy told me that he believed Racine to be the low-life copycat miser I had told him he was. Of course, lawyers are paid to do your fighting and to get you, the client, to believe that they are on your side. It was clear that Jim Murphy was first and foremost working for the insurance company, but it was a comfort to know that he couldn't afford too many losses associated with his name and law firm. He told me that court cases quite often were beauty contests between the defendant and plaintiff, and since Racine *looked* like the kind of guy who would evict a destitute unwed mother in a snowstorm, I would probably win.

The day of the trial finally came. Murphy had done his best to get jurors who would be anti-landlord. The judge thought it would be a two- or three-day trial. It turned out to be two weeks. When the trial began I was anxious but pleased at the same time that I had finally lured my enemy into an arena from which he couldn't escape.

The judge brought the court to order and asked if the defendant was present. I was sitting at a desk next to my lawyer and didn't understand the question or didn't see myself as the defendant, since I thought of myself as the aggrieved party. There was a hush as the judge and jury looked around for the perhaps tardy miscreant defendant. Before Murphy could nudge me, it dawned on me that I should rise and make myself known to the actors in this melodrama. Everyone was taken aback when I stood up. I guess the three-piece suit with pinstripes had thrown everyone off. They had thought I was one of the lawyers. I took it as a serendipitous omen.

Racine had a whole legion of witnesses. He had charts showing his losses in terms of rent and pictures taken by some tough-looking guys Racine had hired to take possession of the warehouse the last day of my lease. The tough guys were called on the stand to testify and show pictures of the mess we left behind. Racine's lawyer had a crowbar that he said had been left behind at the scene and that suggested my intent to do damage. He left the crowbar on the desk throughout the trial. Every once in a while he would pick up the heavy piece of metal and tap his hand with it.

As far as I was concerned, these people were trying to ruin me. If they prevailed and were awarded court costs and even part of the several million they were asking for, it was over for me. Racine took the stand to testify and quickly revealed what a petty and vindictive miser he was. My lawyer, Murphy, had a good time with the stacks of correspondence Helga had saved regarding a $10 a month charge for water that we'd argued about for years, since the warehouse he was renting to me had no running water.

Our side brought in witness after witness, including the head man of the work crew I had hired to work on the warehouse. He made a good impression and explained away how certain things had happened. Knowing how important the outcome of this trial was to me, I imposed a very strict regimen on myself all during it, trying to eat right, exercise, and not touch one drop of alcohol, not even a glass of wine. I focused on the jury and did my best to maintain a sense of composure. When I finally took the stand, I was able to talk directly to the jurors and explain the penurious and malevolent actions of Mr. Racine. This courtroom experience helped me understand why we need a legal system: It serves as a pressure valve, giving litigants a way of dealing with problems in a civilized manner rather than turning to frontier justice, as I might well have done, left to my own devices.

The trial was a high stakes drama that took on a life of its own. It was more like a murder trial than a civil suit. When the two opposing counsel finished their impassioned closing arguments, the jury went out to deliberate. They didn't reach a verdict that first day. We came back the next day and after eight hours, still no verdict. We all assembled on the third day. By now I was getting to know the courthouse and many of its denizens quite well. This was the big day, also the day before my fortieth birthday. Finally the jury sent word they had reached a decision. They marched into the courtroom while I was reflecting on the fact that my business insurance would pay my legal expenses only if I was exonerated on all five counts that made up this lawsuit, not to mention the fact that if I lost I would have to pay any award that might be levied against me, and Racine's legal bill.

I held my breath when the lady juror who had been picked as foreman stood up and read very solemnly: "We, the jury, find the defendant on the first count, not guilty; on the second count, not guilty; on the third count, not guilty; on the fourth count, not guilty; and on the fifth count, not guilty." Racine's lawyer collapsed and fainted dead away on the spot. Racine and his supporters didn't look too good either. I had dodged a bullet and my lawyer was ecstatic, racking up another victory in the win column.

As for Gil Racine, he collapsed in his chair. The iron crowbar on the desk in front of them was suddenly stripped of meaning. His face was a ghastly shade of white. He had bet the bank on this litigation, letting other areas of his life and business suffer while he played this legal lottery game. He was also, of course, heavily in debt to his law firm. As it says in the Bible, "As ye sow, so shall ye reap," and Gil was about to reap. His restaurant went belly-up within weeks of the court ruling. It certainly was a pleasant surprise a short time after the trial to walk by my old landlord's place and see that it was closed for good. A few months later I ran into Jim Murphy and found out that Racine's lawyer had to fold his law firm because of nonpayment by Racine and losing the case. I found it hard to suppress a smile.

My insurance company was obliged to pay my lawyer and his support team. Just the cost of the trial alone was staggering. Naturally I was overjoyed with this triumph, but, at this stage of my life, I made a personal vow never again to risk everything I owned on one roll of the dice. The trial was a defining moment in my life. It toughened me up and made me able to deal with the psychological games people play in general, and with future lawsuits in my life.

15

The Wai Ming Saga

Following my success with Jacquie Vaux came another once-in-a-lifetime discovery—a young Chinese artist by the name of Wai Ming. I had just remodeled my Sutter Street gallery and installed Helga in her new administrative offices, replete with new furnishings that reflected our newfound status. I was in my office doing administrative work when I was summoned to the front reception area. There stood a young Chinese artist with a couple of canvasses rolled up inside a tube; he had asked to talk to me. I usually didn't view a prospective artist's work myself, or on the spot, because it put me in an awkward position of rejecting them. My policy was to have them leave things and let the "art committee" get back to them.

As I approached this young man of slight build with a burr haircut wearing various and sundry pieces of western clothing, none of which matched, he nodded and smiled a greeting. He introduced himself as Wai Ming. I could tell he couldn't speak English. He proceeded to unroll his paintings. I smiled, introduced myself and took a look. I was impressed. One of the two paintings Wai Ming showed me was a realist painting done in a western style of a young mother with a child on her back. The other painting was an abstract depicting an undersea world. Both were exquisite. I was overwhelmed by this man's awesome talent. Here was a person who was such a virtuoso with oils and paintbrush that, in my mind, he compared favorably to many Renaissance masters.

I threw my arms around him and said, "Son, I'm going to make you a star." He looked at me a little nonplussed and rattled off something in Cantonese. I later learned that he thought I was touched in the head and wondered why I was making such a big deal over him, especially since he had been turned away from other galleries on Sutter Street (who would later regret their actions). Since he spoke no English and I couldn't speak Chinese, we managed through awkward sign language to set up a time to meet the next day. He was to bring an interpreter.

The next day he came back with an attractive young Chinese girl to be our go-between. She was not really proficient in English, and we were getting nowhere fast. Then one of those fortunate and unpredictable things happened. An assistant bookkeeper we had just hired came out of the administrative office and started talking to Wai Ming in Chinese. I asked her to explain that I wanted to deal with him, and to tell him how happy I was to have him with the gallery. I wanted to display his "signature pieces" but not sell them until we had built up a following for him, and she managed to convey all that easily. He told my bookkeeper that he had just arrived in America and that he didn't have proper papers. He was here on a visitor's visa. Wai Ming was actually destitute at this point; he was sleeping on the floor of a friend's apartment in Chinatown and spending his days taking his paintings around to San Francisco's galleries. He had only these two representative examples of his work with him. His wife and two young boys had remained in Hong Kong, along with his debts, so that he could strike out for the "Golden Mountain," the Chinese name for California.

Then I gave him $500 so he could buy some canvas and paints and start his career with Swanson Galleries. He was back in a week or so with some paintings of the Aberdeen fisher folk of Hong Kong harbor. They were somewhat sketchy, not anywhere close to the others, but these wet canvases sold quickly. He would stop by each week with new works, mainly of Chinese children and the Chinese fisher folk who were being slowly squeezed out of their harbor in Hong Kong. Wai Ming had gone to live amongst these people on their junks and floating homes and captured their way of life.

Wai Ming couldn't paint fast enough. We set the retail price at less than a thousand dollars for his first rather sketchy paintings, but as he started producing better and better paintings, we raised the price to $1,500, then $2,000 and up as his popularity rose. I made a print of his masterpiece painting, the first painting he had shown me, the "Mother and Child," which now had a $20,000 price tag on it. One of my ace saleswomen, Margarette DeMelo, sold it to a collector who owned a town, or at least had it named after himself, in Alaska.

This newcomer from Hong Kong became phenomenally successful in a short time: during that first year, he made over $60,000. I assigned my Filipino/Chinese bookkeeper, Manuella, to work for him one day a week to keep his finances in order. We got him a green card and a Master Charge card and helped him find and buy a house and pay off his creditors in Hong Kong, thereby clearing the way for his wife and kids to come to San Francisco. Not bad for a guy who walked into my gallery half-starved, bedraggled, and in mismatched clothes a few short months earlier. When Wai Ming's income doubled the second year, he sent for his wife and two sons to join him in his newfound paradise.

When Wai Ming came to America, he had no legal documents giving him citizenship anywhere, not even in Hong Kong, because he had entered that British Colony illegally. He had spent his life as a man without a country. I became his official sponsor and, when he applied for U.S. citizenship a few years later, I went with him to his official hearing before the immigration authorities. His citizenship was granted and he was given a U.S. passport. Wai Ming told me that it was the first time in his life he had what he called "face." By that time he was earning a great deal of money and the gallery had published his art work in two different books. One of the books was devoted to his life and paintings.

When I first met Wai Ming's children they were around ten and twelve years of age. Wai Ming and his wife asked me about American names for their children. They decided to call their oldest boy Jack! I was Uncle Jack to these boys, and over the next nine years I kept tabs on them. Several years later, I was instrumental in getting my namesake to go to UC Santa Barbara.

My instincts about the high caliber of Wai Ming's talents proved to be right, as was brought home to me during the first months I showed his work. We had four of his paintings depicting young Chinese children on junks or *sampans* in Hong Kong harbor. The paintings were in the front section of my original Beach Street gallery. I had became aware that a lot of people thought the children were Vietnamese. With this thought in mind, I asked the gallery manager to move Wai Ming's paintings to the back of the gallery; U.S. forces were evacuating Saigon that very day and I thought the images of these fisher folk might upset people walking by. I was wrong. We sold all four of his paintings on that fateful day that marked the end of a long drawn-out war that had so divided us here at home. In fact, a lot of Wai Ming's appeal, as it turned out, came from the subconscious switch people made with his paintings of boat people. It was amazing how many people thought his paintings were of Vietnamese children. But the legacy of Vietnam aside, his genius was undeniable.

Wai Ming and I never put any of our dealings in writing. I did try to get him to sign an exclusive contract, but he had such a bad feeling about what a Chinese art dealer had done to him once that he broke down and wept when I pressed him to sign anything, despite having Manuella write up the contract in Cantonese. I dropped it, and we continued our relationship on a handshake. I produced dozens of graphics for him and always gave him an accounting of his sales, paintings, or graphics, and a check every two weeks. He got into a routine of showing up every Friday afternoon with a new painting or two. This went on for nine years.

When I met his wife I realized that she might resent how successful her husband had become, how well Wai Ming and I got along, and that she hadn't had a hand in our dealings. I didn't know it but she also was an artist. She was good, but she had fallen into the trap of painting in the same style as her husband. Unfortunately, she didn't have his spark of genius.

I was right. From the first, she regarded me as a rival and an enemy. She spoke fluent English so she quickly replaced Manuella, my bookkeeper, especially since Wai Ming had become quite fond of this self-effacing young woman. Mrs. Wai Ming was the new interpreter, but I kept Manuella in the wings to make sure there were no misunderstandings.

Mrs. Wai Ming asked me to sell her paintings. I didn't want to do it, not only because she copied her husband's style but also because I had had some bad experiences with other couples where both husband and wife were painters. If I did well with one and poorly with the other, I had to deal with at least one disgruntled person. In some cases, both parties would get upset about the disparity in their sales.

I held my ground for a couple of years against taking in Mrs. Wai Ming's work, but then I foolishly dropped my guard and gave in to Wai Ming, telling him I would give his wife's work a try. He had made a plea to help him out when he came down with an intestinal problem that was going to require surgery. Knowing he would be incapacitated, for a time, he wanted me to attempt to sell her work to help his cash flow. I knew it wouldn't work, but try telling that to a distraught person about to go under the knife. I took some of her work and displayed it. It was not well received by either my sales help or my customers.

Wai Ming and I had become close enough at that time that he revealed his fears of not making it through this serious rendezvous with the scalpel. He assured me that if he lived through the operation I would be the first person he would call. The day of the surgery I was at my Sutter Street gallery when I got a phone call from Wai Ming. By this time he had learned a few words of English. As I put the receiver to my ear I heard his barely audible and heavily sedated voice. He muttered in his broken English, "Hey boss, okay. Thank you." Click; he hung up.

A few months later he made a complete recovery and was back on his regular schedule, dropping off one painting a week. (Like most of my painters, he worked on many canvasses at once.) Since we were not selling Mrs. Wai Ming's work, I delicately told her I was returning her art work. From her tight little smile of acknowledgment, I had the distinct feeling that her former resentment of me had shifted into a fierce kind of hatred. And sure enough, from then on, Mrs. Wai Ming seemed bound and determined to rescue her victimized husband from my "clutches."

Making a mental note to keep a weathered eye out for Mrs. Wai Ming, my plan was to promote the prolific Wai Ming even more than before. We now had a public relations firm that put together some great, if expensive, television ads. Each time we ran a 30-second spot on a local channel it cost me $1,000. I spent $70,000 one year on TV commercials which, fortunately, had the desired impact. Wai Ming was now famous in the Bay Area. We published a new print of one of his paintings almost every month during this time, and watched them sell like proverbial hotcakes.

Wai Ming's success had a lot to do with the American public's sensibilities and conflicts about the far-off Asian war. His paintings of Asian children evoked a pathos that hit the heartstrings of the general public. But his skill and artistic talent was in a league all its own and people from all corners of the globe started buying up his work. Considering the short time he had been on the scene, the prices we charged, and got, were astronomical. We started selling his best paintings for $20,000, then $30,000, and soon there seemed to be no ceiling. For those who wanted a Wai Ming, money was no object.

Mrs. Wai Ming, meanwhile, was lurking in the background. She was continually bringing up little things that I call "clunks in the transmission"—bad noises you know you will have to deal with someday. Mrs. Wai Ming questioned our bookkeeping and, specifically, the royalty payments for Wai Ming's paintings. I would try to laugh off her paranoia, and explain that we paid every two weeks and kept complete records. Wai Ming himself wanted representation in other areas, such as Carmel, and I assured him that we would expand not only to Carmel but also to the East Coast. It would take six or seven years for Mrs. Ming to drive a wedge between Wai Ming and me, as I will explain later. Eventually it seems, adversarial situations arise between dealer and artist.

16

Bicentennial and Beyond

The bicentennial celebration marking America's 200th year was a high watermark economically for our country. San Francisco was one of the major tourist destinations for domestic and foreign travelers at this time and, to my good fortune, San Francisco not only attracted a sophisticated tourist crowd, it was a magnet for artists from every country in the world. What a great time to be alive, I thought. Even though I was still trying to get over my breakup with Sharon, I was kept busy opening my second Beach Street gallery and my long-awaited Carmel gallery. Many artists, and especially Wai Ming, had been lobbying me to open a gallery in Carmel. I liked the idea of having a gallery outside the immediate San Francisco area but still close enough to drive to in a day. Barry and his wife, Kathy, and I went down to Carmel often looking for the perfect space for our new gallery. We finally found a suitable location.

Carmel is a quaint beach town, a few hours south of San Francisco. It is known as one of the places to go if you are interested in browsing around art galleries. There were probably thirty galleries around town at that time; years later, the number proliferated to more than a hundred and the town council voted to impose a moratorium on opening new galleries.

When we had the Carmel space ready for occupancy, I rented a huge truck, helped load it in San Francisco, and personally drove it down to this art mecca. Driving that truck brought back a lot of memories. After grinding a lot of gears on the winding cliff-laden highway south, I decided that we would hire professional movers in the future.

I remember walking around Carmel when we first opened up the gallery. It was magical. Everything—all types of flowers and vegetation—seemed to grow in this foggy, artsy, California paradise. I was tempted to buy a house on the beach, but decided not to since I already had a second home in Sonoma. (When I see now what they are asking for real estate in the Monterey-Carmel area, I wince, of course.) I had thought about selling my Sonoma house, but I couldn't bear to give up my role as Uncle Jack to the neighboring children, especially Wayne and Celia's kids and Vicky's two young boys.

By 1976 my business had settled down nicely. I had signed a long-term lease on my new mainstay gallery, the one on the corner of Beach Street. Best of all, business was booming. I was publishing two or three graphic editions a month for my various artists, and my company invested over one million dollars publishing about two hundred different editions of etchings, serigraphs, and photomechanical reproductions.

I had also built up a persona. I had taken to wearing leather blazers and rose-colored sunglasses to go with my 1970s' sideburns and mustache. I didn't fully appreciate it at the time, but because of my single status, I was able to travel without worrying about the cost of limousines or restaurant and hotel prices.

I would drop by all my local galleries almost every day, leaving much of the management and other administrative matters to Barry and Helga. Most of my time at work was spent talking to my twenty or more star artists. (Representing so many artists offered protection: no one artist could fatally blackmail my business. Furthermore, if one stopped producing, or lost public favor, others were available to provide needed revenue.) Frequently, when I visited the galleries, I would move around the art work, rehang walls, deliver impromptu motivational sales talks, set goals and reward the faithful. Naturally, I hoped that my management team would be with me forever, but things rarely work out the way you hope they will.

One of my biggest disappointments happened at this juncture: Helga decided that she had proven her point and fulfilled her business destiny, and no longer wanted to deal with the day-to-day grind. She quit. I broke out in tiny little red welts all over my body. My vision had been that Helga would stay with the company forever; I envisioned her at age seventy-seven as a venerable gray-haired grande dame, dropping in only for board meetings. After I got over the shock of her announcement, I tried to be supportive. I've kept in touch with her over the last twenty years. A few years ago, I was in Sonoma and noticed a gray-haired lady in an old 1964 Mustang driving around town. I honked my horn and pulled over to see if it was Helga. It was. She looked great. She was looking for a retirement condo in Sonoma.

After Helga left, I hired a new controller, a young lady by the name of Dell. She was right out of college and, though very attractive and well-meaning, she just didn't have Helga's maturity and sophistication. With Helga gone, I was the oldest person in the organization at thirty-five. Most of the forty people on the payroll were in their early twenties. I threw a party on the Fourth of July for all company employees at my Sausalito gallery, and as I looked around I decided I'd never seen a better looking group of men and women. I've noticed that people always seem to date those with whom they are in close proximity, such as next door neighbors, school chums, fellow employees. For that reason, I asked that I be kept informed about living situations: it was nice to know when I was talking to one of my people whether I was also talking to their live-in partner.

I dated a lot of the women working for me. I was no Lothario, however. Usually I would wait to see how someone I was interested in fit into the scheme of things and whether my dating her would disrupt her working life or the gallery's organizational chart. Actually, I wanted a wife and family at this stage, and most of the girls I went out with were those I felt might be "the one." It wasn't as easy as I thought to find a significant other, a person I could trust to raise my kids and fit into my busy life. American men are famous worldwide for their "Hello, I love you, won't you tell me your name?" line and, although I was also guilty of this approach more than once, I was no playboy. Unlike some of my drinking and sailing buddies who went to bed with a different woman almost every night and who obviously were not too discerning in a lot of areas, I wanted a real relationship and life-enhancing experiences.

I walked into my first Beach Street gallery one day and was greeted by an apparition of loveliness. I introduced myself. My vice president in charge of hiring people, Jake Wigand, had hired her. She had just moved to San Francisco from Wisconsin with a degree in hand. Her face was as beautiful and fresh as her cheeks were rosy. My heart started to pound in my chest. Those people who downplay physical beauty don't know what they are talking about. Real beauty in a woman is an almost tangible power. Although she worked for me for a couple of years, and every time I talked to her, my heart started hopping around in my chest, nothing came of my infatuation. She already had a boyfriend. Shortly after we met, in fact, she showed some bad judgment by giving in to some abusive demands her fiancé made: he threatened to kill her if she didn't marry him, and so she did. She soon got pregnant and I moved her from selling to an administrative job so that she could work right up until the baby was due. (Her husband was unemployed at the time.) After she had the baby, she left for another job.

One of the reasons I was spending so much time in Sonoma was that I vaguely thought I might find my future wife in the country. I thought a country girl might be more stable, and have more down-to-earth values. Of course, I was invited to a lot of parties by my country neighbors and quite often I was the token bachelor. They were trying to fix me up with someone. None of these blind dates every panned out. Most of the ladies I met that way were not yet over their divorces and already had children, with no desire for more.

I started giving elaborate parties for my Sonoma friends, and as one of the only bachelor hosts in town I gained local celebrity status. The bad news was that I would hear some of my neighbors' wives, many of whom were former flight attendants and were downright beautiful, tell their husbands that they should be more like me. I feared that one night I would see these husbands winding up the hill toward my house with torches and a rope to hang me from the big oak tree in the center of my driveway!

Hanging around Sonoma and fulfilling my role as Uncle Jack, particularly at the Schake household, led to my first trip to Europe. The two oldest Schake kids were signed up for a student tour of England and various other countries and it sounded like a great chance for me to take some vacation time with these kids. Wayne, one of the tour leaders, urged me to come along. As a white-knuckle flyer I was a little leery of flying nonstop from San Francisco to London, but since I had always wanted to see England and France I said, "Let's do it."

I flew over by myself and met up with the tour. Wayne and I took some of the kids to different museums and attractions. After a week I left my fancy Savoy Hotel and the kids behind and flew to Paris. Paris was the most exciting city I had ever seen. I hit all the museums and legendary sights, from Napoleon's tomb to the Eiffel Tower. Always on the lookout for art work, I started checking out the gallery scene. The French galleries were more reserved than our American galleries and even the London galleries. If you asked the price of a work of art in a Parisian gallery you would have to go through a ritual with the proprietor or salesperson. You had to sit down, have coffee or tea, let them get to know you, and only then would they deign to give you the price—maybe. What a far cry from the way we did business back home. I wondered what my customers in San Francisco would do if I used that approach to retail sales in my galleries!

One gallery I visited had some artists who I felt would be wonderful additions to my own stable, enough so that I was willing to go through the time-consuming process required to build a working relationship with the gallery salesgirl. She spoke English rather well and helped me negotiate a favorable deal. While I enjoyed sightseeing in Paris, I was getting lonely and, since I couldn't remember much of my college French, I was beginning to know what people mean when they say that the French are not fond of Americans.

To remedy my sense of isolation, I asked Nicole, the salesgirl I had met at the gallery, to dinner. She accepted.

That night we wound up spending the night in her apartment. We walked hand-in-hand in the Tuileries Gardens enjoying the glorious autumn weather. Nicole moved into my hotel, George V, a venerable establishment. We shocked the conservative sensibilities of the staff by our undisguised affection for each other. I felt socially out of sync here: It was the '70s, but in Paris it could as easily have been the immediate postwar years. Even the nightclubs we went to had '40s' furnishings and '40s' entertainment. I hung around for a week longer than I had intended but finally the time came for our good-byes. Not wanting this liaison to end, I impulsively asked Nicole to visit me in San Francisco, promising to send a round-trip ticket so that she could spend a month here.

Once home in San Francisco, I couldn't believe I had extended the offer, but, gentleman to the last, I sent the ticket, hoping she wouldn't read too much into it. A few weeks later I drove to the San Francisco Airport to pick up my French lover. Her plane arrived on schedule. Every one deplaned, but there was no Nicole in sight. Just as I was about to leave, I saw her emerge, quite distraught. She ran over to me crying. She was glad to see me but she acted like a war bride, unsure of her decision to emigrate. On the drive to Sausalito, she settled down.

Once she got some sleep and was somewhat acclimated, things were better. However, being in a strange country and out of her environment was obviously a huge pressure on her. The way she dealt with this pressure was to talk. She never stopped. Not even during sex.

Being the dutiful tour guide, I showed her around the city and my galleries. It didn't take long for me to realize that we were not suited for a long-term relationship. Typical of the French, it seemed that anything not French was inferior in her view. One afternoon around sunset we were driving across the Golden Gate Bridge. She actually refused to look at the panoramic view. It was as if she acknowledged the beauty of the San Francisco skyline, she would be betraying her country. When she reacted negatively to the George Lucas movie, *Star Wars*, I knew it was over. She hated it because it was so American.

I took her to Sonoma and introduced her around. She loved the country and wanted to spend much of her time there. I started finding excuses to leave her alone, saying I was called away on business. A girlfriend of Nicole showed up out of nowhere and moved in with us. I think her arrival was less happenstance than part of a preconceived plan.

As I was furtively looking around for a way to put distance between me and my garrulous houseguest and her uninvited friend, Vicky came to the rescue. She was taking her two boys to Disneyland and wanted to know if Nicole and I would like to join them. I begged off but offered to pay for Vicky and her children's entire trip if she would take Nicole with her, leaving me in blessed solitude. Vicky accepted and took Nicole and kids off to the Magic Kingdom. By the time they got back I had arranged for Nicole's return passage to France. While we were saying our tearful good-byes at the airport, I was promising myself to be more careful with invitations in the future.

A few of my buddies and more than one of my lady friends (including Vicky) ribbed me mercilessly about my French affair. My friend, Wayne, even went so far as to bring back a cocktail napkin from the George V Hotel and leave it at the gallery as a little reminder of my amorous European trip and the consequences of my impulsive behavior.

Realizing I probably couldn't import a future spouse from a far-off land, I decided to stick closer to home. Most of my energy was now going into day-to-day administration of the galleries and my weekly meetings with my "star" artists. Almost every artist who was making it big would bring me a painting every week. To accommodate them, I arranged for validated parking a block up from my Sutter Street gallery. My really exceptional artists always wanted to speak to me directly. Occasionally, two "big" stars would run into each other that way, and it was always a ticklish situation. Even if they were friends, they weren't comfortable sharing the limelight.

Time just rocketed by. I loved my various roles as art dealer, father figure, banker, advisor, and benefactor. It's probably just as well that I didn't find Miss Right at this time because I was fully employed trying to help my artists reach their fullest potential. My top artists, who accounted for a great deal of our sales and whom I could not afford to lose, required more time and attention than the others. Now that I had built this retail gallery machine, it had to be fueled. I likened it to a little black box where a lot of paintings, sculpture, and prints were put in the front opening and would mysteriously all get sorted out, sold and transmuted into enough money to pay all the bills and keep everyone employed.

I took my job seriously and tried to be there for all my artists. I would even help them find housing. Some, for example, were always being evicted from their living accommodations; if I felt that it wasn't too much of a risk, I would rent them places in my name. Many artists were such free-spirits they did not pay taxes or make allowances for such bourgeois necessities of life. They usually didn't have checking accounts let alone a working relationship with bank personnel. I would step in and give them loans and take care of many of their mundane responsibilities. Some of my artists abused the privilege, charging me more than I was willing to pay, both in coin and personal hide.

One of the most outrageous examples of someone who took too much "out of my hide" is an artist named Debo. Debo has a childlike quality, probably what allowed him to tap into "cosmic" forces as he painted. I've watched him paint and he often appeared to be in a trance-like state. Completely self-taught, Debo decided one day to check out some library books on painting technique. He focused in on how medieval Renaissance masters applied oil to canvas. He practiced and finally mastered these age-old practices, even priming his linen canvases with a white gesso material used in the late sixteenth century. Debo's treatment of light and dark, *chiaroscuro* (I knew I would someday find use for this word I learned from my art history classes) in his oil-on-canvas portraits is remarkable. I first saw his work at a gallery in

Sausalito in 1968. I had just moved to San Francisco and hadn't started my gallery career. I didn't know who the artist was but I was floored by his sensitive portraits of African Americans. The Civil Rights movement was strong and the recent assassination of Martin Luther King Jr. was on everyone's mind.

It was a few years later that I took over the gallery in Sausalito that had been exhibiting his work. Regarding him as a modern-day Rembrandt, I really wanted to have his art work in my gallery. Like the others after him, this self-taught artist brought me at least one good size canvas each week. We usually sold them while still wet for thousands of dollars. Although I paid him every two weeks, in a few days he would be broke. He seemed to have one crisis after another: His refrigerator stopped working; I bought him a new one. He moved to an inland city and found it too hot; I sent a stockperson to Sears to buy him an air conditioner. He was evicted from his house; I rented him a place or stood as a reference. He would go through bouts of depression and quit painting, then borrow money from me. He once got into debt to me for a considerable sum. Nevertheless, putting up with his peculiarities still seemed worth the trouble.

He decided to live in Mexico. With his wife and three children in tow, Debo left and rented a mansion in Cuernavaca, a beautiful area right outside Mexico City where the Aztec emperors chose to live. Soon his children were speaking Spanish and Debo was happily living it up in his mansion with its tennis courts, pool and servants. Every few months he would fly to San Francisco to bring me a few rolled-up canvases.

I had a premonition that he was flirting with some unsavory people. I hoped not, especially since he had a family that could be in harm's way if there was trouble.

All of a sudden my fears were realized. There was the anguished phone call for help. Seems that he had been involved in some questionable activity and suffered a blow to the head. He was now in trouble with the Mexican police. I called the lawyer who had bailed out another one of my artists and sent him down to Mexico. We managed to get Debo and the whole family back to California.

Over the years Debo and I have stayed in touch. His production has slowed down and he does more portrait commissions than he used to. He makes his living mostly doing portraits of well-to-do winery owners in the Napa Valley. His family has remained close and supportive. His children are grown and married, and all live near him.

Every time one of my star artists disappeared or withdrew from the gallery, another would magically appear. With success and the free time that came with it, I traveled extensively, always on the lookout for new and exciting work. I went to Chicago to see what was happening in the art scene there. There were two gallery chains in the windy city that impressed me. One was the Finlay Gallery. The Chicago branch was one of five or six galleries owned by Finlay and members of his family. I had met Wally Finlay in San Francisco. He was a wily old guy up in years. Wally had tried to open a gallery in San Francisco near my gallery on Sutter Street, but it opened and closed quickly; he had probably overextended himself trying to run his other galleries as well. I was impressed with his personal style and felt compelled to travel and personally view each of his galleries, hoping to emulate some of his success. He carried primarily European artists and did a good job of promoting them. Wally Finlay's family had started in the framing (gold gilt) business and, over a hundred years or so, the business evolved into a well-respected gallery chain with branches in New York City, West Palm Beach and Beverly Hills. I went to see Wally Finlay at his Beverly Hills gallery, taking Barry with me. Eighty years old at the time, Finlay was a savvy businessman and had some wonderful stories about his life and times, particularly his real estate deals. In fact he was so absorbed in those that he didn't mention art even once in the time Barry and I spent with him.

There was another gallery chain (not Finlay's) that I liked to visit in Chicago. They had started out selling mass-produced factory paintings bought at merchandise marts, but over the years had upgraded and established a reputation as being a top-flight art gallery. Again, most of the art was by European artists, but I was surprised to see paintings by some of the same Mexican artists I was showing. Over the years I watched one of the family members take over this established family business and introduce Salvador Dalí prints manufactured by publishers of questionable repute. I couldn't believe it. Why supposedly reputable gallery owners sold this stuff was beyond me.

I went into one of their galleries located in downtown Chicago and noticed that they were displaying watercolor paintings that were purported to be by Salvador Dalí. The paintings may have been by Dalí, but what struck me as being wrong was that they were selling photomechanical reproductions of these Dalí paintings and calling them etchings. A young lady (who appeared to be fresh out of college) approached me and started extolling the virtues of these so-called etchings. I asked her how it could be an etching when the prints were clearly reproductions of the watercolors on display right in front of us. She was momentarily taken aback but felt compelled to spout what she had been told. I surmised that these prints had been done on presigned paper and that an etching plate had been pressed against the photomechanical reproductions so the publishers could claim that an etching plate was used.

It sure chafed my hide that so-called legitimate galleries were selling these concoctions. It even pushed me out of shape more when I realized that tens of thousands of these prints were being sold to the public and that perpetrators of this deceit were doing irreparable harm to our industry. As I traveled the world I began seeing these bogus prints surfacing everywhere. No matter how I tried to explain how questionable these prints were, most of my fellow dealers just kept on selling them and racking up huge profits. I've already pointed out that the cost of these prints to the dealers were about 10% (sometimes all the way up to 30%) of the selling price.

17

High Watermark

Now, with seven galleries going simultaneously, many of my best-selling artists couldn't keep up. The continuing demand necessitated publishing more and more reproductions of their art work in addition to raising prices on their original paintings. In this business atmosphere, many of my artists began to lose their desire or need for money and that, of course, affected their need to produce. There is something surreal about artists who were "starving" a short time earlier and now made a couple of hundred thousand dollars a year. I watched success do its damage and concluded that fame was more devastating to them than obscurity or failure had ever been.

By 1978 we needed quite an administrative infrastructure for our seven galleries. We had two main offices, one at my large gallery on Beach Street and one at my fancy Sutter Street gallery. I sent all invoices and sales receipts to Sutter Street and all merchandise came through the Sutter gallery and then was transferred. There was very little theft or damage but the paperwork and storage for 60,000 or more prints and paintings was a nightmare.

After Helga left we went through a few controllers before we found someone up to the job. As fate would have it, we hired another lady who had a German background. Barely five feet tall and Jewish, she and her family had fled Nazi Germany for Central America during the Second World War. She finally emigrated to America. Master of German, Spanish, and Yiddish, she spoke very little English. I hired her anyway.

Henny was around sixty when she came to work for me and stayed on until she retired five years later. We always got along, although I was occasionally thrown by her aversion to being the bearer of bad news. It would have been a lot easier on my nerves if this reticence to discuss money problems with me hadn't been so ingrained.

Henny came up to me one day, looking grave; her hands were shaking. She asked if I could look at some financial papers and give her a few minutes of my time. I asked her what was up. She looked down and said, "We have some financial problems; we need money." Unaware that we had any financial problems, I asked, almost playfully, how much we needed. Voice faltering, Henny mumbled, "$200,000!" Taken aback by this pronouncement, I managed to smile as I asked her how soon we needed this magnificent sum. Henny answered, "Today."

I took the computer printouts from Henny and headed for the door. I walked outside to a waiting limousine driver cheerfully opening the car door and saying he had been called to drive me to Carmel, round trip. Inside the limo, I perused the data Henny had just laid on me and wondered where I was going to get $200,000, quick. I called my new banker, Larry, the replacement for Cliff Christiansen who had been squeezed out of the bank for making unauthorized loans. Cliff had been my staunch supporter and one of the few professional business types who never let me down. I phoned Larry from the limo and told him I was in a bind and needed a loan. Before Cliff left, he had told Larry to give me anything I wanted, so Larry simply asked how much I needed. I said that $200,000 would be perfect. Larry said, "No problem; would that be in 10s or 20s?" Whew. Larry transferred the cash to my business account that very day. I didn't even have to sign papers.

Years later during a recession, Larry called in a $300,000 business loan by saying that if I didn't pay off the full amount he would lose his job. He told me that the bank felt he shouldn't have given out that size loan. Thank God they didn't authorize more because this was during the Carter presidency and the interest rates charged by the banks shot up to 24%, the highest in American history, except during the Civil War. Luckily, I was able to pay the loan off. It saved Larry's job and reduced my monthly payments, which had gone from

$3,000 to $9,000 a month. (I now make sure that I see a cap or limit on how much interest a bank charges.)

Yet another story involving Henny and our communication gap happened when one of my artists came into the Sutter Street gallery and asked Henny for all of his paintings back— forty or fifty oils. I was away on a trip at the time. The standing gallery policy was never to give things back to an artist unless I approved the transaction. In this case, Henny knew that the gallery had received a subpoena from the artist's ex-wife, instructing our gallery, as part of the divorce settlement, to give her an accounting of all her husband's artwork that we had on consignment. We had received a court order telling us to give *half* of the art work to his wife and to pay her directly when and if any of his remaining paintings sold while in our possession. I should have given back all the paintings to the warring parties right then and there, but, until then, I had figured we would just comply with the court order. Since I was not present the day the artist himself confronted Henny, he was able to talk her into giving him all of his paintings, including, of course, those legally belonging to his ex-wife.

Henny forgot about my "no return" policy and about the court order, with the end result that I was sued by the ex-wife. Apparently, she had remarried someone who was a lawyer. She sued me for $27,000, the value of the paintings, adding $500,000 for mental cruelty or some such crazy thing, and another $500,000 for conspiring with her ex-husband to defraud her.

I quickly called my artist and told him to bring back the paintings that legally belonged to her. He said that "we" would fight to the last ditch. I said, "What do you mean 'we'? Just give me back the paintings." He told me then that he'd sold them. Back to court I went. The fast-talking artist who was going to fight to the last ditch quickly declared bankruptcy and refused to even show up to meet with my lawyers. I settled out of court for $27,000, but it was an expensive lesson. In the future, any court orders demanding splitting up consigned merchandise were handled by immediately returning all art work to the proper parties and not dealing with the litigants until everything had been straightened out.

Henny was a lot more leery of smooth-talking artists after that affair, although we did get involved in one more expensive imbroglio before she retired. While Barry and I were in Greece with Wayne, Henny was preparing our corporate year-end taxes for the IRS. She noticed that we had overpaid our taxes the year before by $5,000. Delighted at this wind-fall, she sent in for a refund. Upon my return from Greece, Henny told me about the overpayment and her contact with the IRS. My heart sank. My hunch that it was a mistake for Henny to ask for a refund, even a small refund, was correct: in less than two weeks from her letter, we were audited by the IRS. They took over my bookkeeping offices and went through every scrap of paper that Helga and Henny had carefully filed. They agreed that I had overpaid $5,000 for that year but found that I owed them $20,000 for previous years. They applied the $5,000 to my new bill. I grimaced and added this amount to what I figured my Greek adventure had cost me.

Around the time I opened up the East Coast galleries in '78, I had been representing PoPo and Ruby Lee, a husband-and-wife team, for a few years. PoPo and Ruby Lee worked on their oil-on-canvas creations together, although I always suspected that PoPo's participation was minimal. Their paintings were primarily of beautiful young women who had a flavor of Native American Indian and Oriental mix. Ruby Lee is a strikingly beautiful Eurasian (Chinese and European) woman. These two artists had started showing their sensual paintings of buckskin-clad maidens in outdoor shows and were immediately big sellers. After a few years of loading up their van and driving to outdoor shows, they sought a more stable situation and appeared at my Sutter Street gallery in the mid-seventies. I was impressed by their beautiful and exotic paintings. Ruby Lee was in her early twenties and every bit as beautiful as the women she painted. She actually used herself as a model for many of her paintings.

Ruby Lee had a way about her that was ethereal and earthy at the same time. She was so mellow that she floated. I think

PoPo found her in a bad state and became her Svengali. He told everyone he was part Apache and that Ruby Lee had spent time on a Native American reservation near Taos, New Mexico. As they prospered, they moved from their mountain home in Lodi, California to Sausalito. This dynamic couple produced prolifically and were featured artists of the gallery for many years.

PoPo was a strange guy of medium height. He reminded me of certain cult leaders, and it was evident that he really enjoyed himself during the hippie revolution. He had his spiel down pat regarding Eastern philosophies and how he thought they worked. Even though he was "way out there," he was certainly fun to talk to about art and what was going on in the various art communities. Though not handsome and always clad in hippie threads, he had a magnetic personality when it came to women, ensuring a ready supply of new models for this husband-and-wife team to paint. I got to know a few of these models, usually Eurasian and exotic types who worked on the cocktail waitress circuit. They refrained from telling me all that went on in modeling sessions with PoPo, but they gave me a glimpse into some bizarre happenings aided and abetted by booze and dope. The thing that surprised me was that quite a few of these young women went back for additional shoots—something about getting close to the flame. I was a little miffed at PoPo for not sharing the videos of these encounters, but he always claimed client confidentiality.

PoPo would visit me quite often and we would talk about art in general, other gallery artists, and how to promote the gallery and its artists. Even though PoPo didn't have a degree conferred on him by an academic institution, he was well-educated in the arts and loved to hold forth on religious mythology. He had been part of the Beat generation as a youngster and had many stories of his days in Greenwich Village in the late '50s. He was there in '59 and witnessed the coming of Abstract Expressionism and its representative artists, such as Jackson Pollock and Willem deKooning. He used to visit Leo Castelli's gallery on East 77th Street and watched in amazement as pop art became the vogue of New York's art world. He was taken by Jasper Johns, Roy Lichtenstein,

Andy Warhol and Robert Rauschenberg, all of whom were featured artists of the Castelli Gallery.

PoPo was the only one of my artists who ever wanted to discuss various aspects of the art world. For him "real art" emanated from New York. The east was where it was at. I was not convinced. So one day I surprised him with a round-trip ticket to New York. I told him I was going to take him to the Big Apple and he could show me all the great art and culture in this place he loved and which I regarded as rather unholy, and bombed-out to boot.

We boarded the plane and saw an in-flight movie called *Fame* about a school for the performing arts in New York. It helped to set the mood for our search for art and creativity. We stayed in downtown New York at the United Nations Plaza Hotel. From our hotel window we could hear the teeming city 36 floors below and gaze out on a seemingly limitless forest of skyscrapers.

PoPo and I didn't agree on much except that we both appreciated figurative paintings, the beauty of composition, and artists who weren't afraid of innovation. We talked about the New York publishers churning out the Dalí prints. He felt that it was no big deal. At that point, neither of us could know that, eventually, dealers and publishers would sell hundreds of millions of dollars worth of these prints and shake the belief systems of a large portion of the art-buying public.

When we started our odyssey to rediscover the New York art scene PoPo fondly remembered, we did the obligatory museum circuit—the MOMA, the Whitney, and the Met. PoPo took me to the Village and we poked around his old haunts. All the galleries and coffee shops he remembered were gone. We went to Central Park on a Sunday morning to eat at one of his favorite restaurants. It was boarded up and covered with graffiti. At least we didn't get mugged. This was the late '70s and if we thought of it as a bit dangerous then, still, it was before crack cocaine and drive-by shootings. We headed for Soho to hit the galleries. Few featured any paintings on canvas; most were showing the latest trend, "installations." The artists doing installations didn't want to be constrained by canvas or even hanging things on walls. I remember one gallery we visited where someone had filled the whole gallery with dirt and set up a miniature chair with a spotlight backlighting it and throwing a large shadow of the chair upon the gallery wall. We found no galleries where regular folk could go and view the abstract expressionists that PoPo remembered.

PoPo and I had some great discussions about Modernism. He thought that you had to shock the bourgeoisie, but grudgingly admitted that the exciting and innovative era he had witnessed in the '50s had given way to art theory. I brought up Tom Wolfe's book, *The Painted Word*, where he debunks the American modern art movement. I agreed with Wolfe that with the advent of the abstract expressionism and pop art based on "art theory" formulated by New York art critics (masters of double-talk), one had to be well-versed on whatever new theory they were pushing to be able to "see" a painting, sculpture or installation by these so-called modern artists.

Tom said, "Call the cops. Modernism is finished." That's exactly how I felt. My gut feeling was that America's elite, whether from wealth, business position, or academic achievement, were using art theory and modern art as a way to distinguish themselves from the hoi-polloi. The small population that made up this beau monde art world felt that those who couldn't understand Jackson Pollock's drip paintings or Roy Lichtenstein's blowups of panels from the comics, just weren't at their level. Wise ones say that, if a person is smart, he or she will not discuss religion or politics at a cocktail party. I would add modern art to that list.

After a disappointing but instructive week in New York, PoPo and I flew to see my new galleries in Washington, D.C. While we were in Washington, we went to the east wing of the National Gallery museum which houses the modern art collection. We walked up some stairs into this angular building, incongruously placed next to the neoclassical National Gallery building, and what do we see but a long, white canvas about ten feet high and forty feet long. Along the length of the painting, right down the middle of the canvas, was a long, thin, black line. There was a rather rotund armed security guard standing vigilantly next to this huge canvas and many other similar creations. I looked at the painting, then at the protective guard. The guard looked at me and we both broke out laughing at the same time.

After a couple of days in the capital sightseeing and saying hello to my gallery staff, PoPo and I winged our way back to California. Somewhere along the line PoPo told me he didn't know if I knew it or not but he really wasn't an Apache Indian. I acted surprised, even though I had been told by a friend of PoPo that his real name was Bernie Schwartz and he originally hailed from Detroit. PoPo went on to tell me he was of Russian Jewish descent. There wasn't much I could say but, silently, I worried about the negative effect on his psyche if he continued carrying on this charade.

Years later, he and Ruby Lee dissolved their personal and professional relationship and it became painfully evident that Ruby was the artist and not PoPo. Ruby was devastated by the breakup, and shared with me some disturbing statements PoPo made repeatedly about ending his life. Shortly thereafter, PoPo made good on these statements with a .45-caliber pistol.

Over the years that I dealt with PoPo I knew he smoked marijuana regularly and liked a drink of gin, but I never realized the extent of his addiction to these substances or his precarious mental health. I was shocked to learn of his death, but couldn't help reflecting on his denial of who he was, his drug use, and his flirtation with seductive but double-edged forces in the universe.

These years, for the most part, were a blur of traveling and staging art shows. During one of these shows we sold $80,000 worth of Wai Ming's paintings to a woman in her thirties who told me she wanted to amass an art collection to rival that of Armand Hammer of Occidental Petroleum fame. The Swanson Gallery staff now numbered about sixty people, primarily women. Barry oversaw the seven gallery managers, six women and one man, who headed up the Carmel store.

My Sutter Street manager at this time was a beautiful young blonde who had worked for me for quite a few years. I'll call her Allison. There was something about her that made me wonder from the start if she could be trusted. Allison worked for me through the crescendo years of '78 and '79. Sometimes I would see her interact with other employees at company parties and I would wonder at her choice of friends. Allison was one of my employees in good standing, so I brushed off any conspiratorial ideas, but I picked up on something that I couldn't quite figure out. She was extremely chummy with one of my troops, a young man I'll call Dean. He was as handsome as she was pretty. When I saw them together I would always tell them they should get married. They probably would have, but Dean, with his perfectly coifed hair, was gay. About this time Dean committed some horrific faux pas at one of the galleries he had been charged with managing. I can't remember what he did but it necessitated my calling him into my office and asking him to hand over the keys. He hesitated and said something to the effect of, "Could you just wait until tomorrow to fire me?" Even if I had known what he was referring to, it was my unpleasant duty to maintain conventional business practices. There was no choice but to collect the keys. I fired very few managers over the years. It had a terrible effect on morale. When a higher-management type could be fired, it made everyone feel threatened.

Not too long after Dean's departure, Allison went through some personal changes and solemnly gave her notice. She sat in a chair in my office, my desk between us, and tried to answer my questions about why she was leaving. She hesitated, started to blurt out something but checked herself, and then left the gallery.

A few years later I found out what Allison and Dean were involved in just before they left Swanson Galleries. I was having lunch at a San Francisco landmark called Sear's, a restaurant specializing in breakfast. (Their pancakes and eggs are such a draw that you usually have to stand in line to get a seat.) On this occasion I had to share a table with someone, and as I polished off my 18 silver-dollar-sized pancakes I introduced myself to the guy across from me. He said hello, introduced himself and pulled out his business card, telling me that he was a retail union organizer. He then went on to reminisce about how he and some of my employees had almost unionized my company back in '79 and asked if I remembered Dean and a good-looking blonde named Allison. It turned out that Dean's leaving a day early had foiled their plan.

By 1979, Swanson Art Galleries, Ltd. had been around for eight or nine years, building up an exhilarating momentum. Each part of the gallery entity was at full throttle, and the artists were producing and being exceedingly loyal. The economy was soaring and the collectors were filling up their available wall space. The sales staff was fully employed and self-satisfied. It was like fishing at a trout farm. The galleries had a fabulous stable of talented living artists.

I decided that what was needed was an art book celebrating my best painters and sculptors. It was a tremendous undertaking. First we had to determine how many artists we could comfortably include. Each artist had to be interviewed, photos of their work taken, and a contract signed granting permission to put their work in the publication. Out of about fifty possibilities, we narrowed the field down to twenty-one. I vowed never to try to get that many talented artists, egos and all, to cooperate in a spirit of harmony—ever again. We entitled our first publication, *21 California Artists*. Many artists were not incorporated in the book, a few because we no longer had a business relationship and others because they were just too hard to deal with. I couldn't believe the number of people who made unreasonable demands, from asking for excessive royalties to wanting absolute editorial control.

The *21 California Artists* book was a unique design accomplishment. My friend and graphic designer, Steve Cardinelli, put together a great format and worked closely with the printers. Although he started dragging his feet toward the end of the job, through sheer force of will and a lot of screaming we finally came up with a great book. Of course, we were over budget and months past our original deadline, but the book was an overwhelming success. Over the years we have sold almost the entire printing of 5,000 books. I had personally invested a lot and the gamble paid off. I've made a lot of money on my investment and gained the respect and long-term business associations with all of the artists featured.

With the book prominently displayed on the shelves of my galleries, I decided to take some time away from work and meet my good friend Wai Ming in Hong Kong. Wai Ming had gone back to Hong Kong to visit family and friends and to gather material for future paintings. It was right before the Christmas holidays in 1979. He was staying with family so I arranged to stay at the Peninsula Hotel, famous for its lobby. It is said that if you sit there long enough, everybody will eventually walk through.

My reasons for going during this time of year were numerous. I was planning to do an art book featuring just Wai Ming, so this would give me more material and insight regarding him, and I had never been to Hong Kong. And traveling over the holiday season would allow me to avoid the schmaltzy commercialization of the Yule season, or so I thought. Once I got to Hong Kong, I was amazed that even though this was a non-Christian society, the people were probably the world's most dynamic capitalists. I never saw so many Christmas lights and gung ho merchandising in my life.

I didn't like being parted from my new love interest over the Christmas holidays, but I thought this trip would give me time to think over the direction my life was taking. I had just begun a semi-serious affair with my secretary, Barbara, who worked at my Sutter Street gallery. Barbara was in her early twenties. She had been raised in Los Angeles and graduated from an expensive private school—the type of college where everyone joins a sorority or fraternity and can count on graduating eventually, no matter what. She wore her shoulder-length brown hair in a conservative bob style.

Barbara made no demands on me. When I went off to Greece with Wayne and Barry, or to the East Coast to check out the galleries, or, now, to Hong Kong to see Wai Ming, she sweetly bid me bon voyage and continued to do her job at my main office.

A week or so before Christmas, Barry drove me to the San Francisco Airport and waved good-bye to me as I boarded a huge 747 Pan Am plane bound for Hong Kong. This "bird" had special fuel tanks that allowed it to fly nonstop the 7,000 miles from California to Hong Kong. The trip took thirteen hours. These Pan Am jets offered an upper-level private lounge in first class; given the length of the journey, I was glad I had opted for it. The gorgeous woman seated next to me lightened my mood quite a bit. She was on her way to meet a boyfriend for a weekend in Hong Kong. I was really impressed when she showed me a current *Playboy* magazine in which she was prominently featured. As we discussed the pros and cons of various poses, the time in the air just seemed to evaporate and I kept thinking, there is a God.

I bid this playmate fond adieu when we landed at the Hong Kong airport. To my surprise there was a Rolls Royce limousine provided by the hotel to pick me up and take me to the Peninsula Hotel. After giving me time to catch up on my sleep, Wai Ming picked me up and we started our two-week odyssey. I got to see Kowloon and the New Territories through Wai Ming's eyes. We took *sampans* all over Hong Kong harbor and were rowed around, sometimes by little old ladies and sometimes by young kids, in these water taxis that ferried us to gigantic floating restaurants where we ate all kinds of exotic fare.

Wai Ming had a special mirrored periscope-type attachment on his camera that permitted him to aim at his intended subject without appearing to. This was important because the rather simple fish folk he wanted to capture did not like having their pictures taken, fearing loss of privacy, even loss of soul. We took side trips to remote fishing villages in the New Territories next to the Communist Chinese border, all the while Wai Ming taking his clandestine photographs.

In Aberdeen harbor, Wai Ming introduced me to some of his godchildren from various families with whom he had lived. This fishing village was rapidly disappearing as Hong

Kong aggressively made room for modern expansion. The *tanka*, or fish folk, were being relocated to high-rise buildings and losing their way of life as a result. In other words, Wai Ming was capturing a quickly vanishing culture. The more I saw of these people and their dwindling freedoms, the more I understood why Wai Ming invested so much of himself and his time painting these people who, for him, personified the true Chinese.

When not sightseeing with Wai Ming, I visited antique shops and galleries hoping to find artists whose work was at Wai Ming's level. Although I did meet a few great artists, none matched Wai Ming.

As our trip drew to a close, I accompanied Wai Ming to a famous alley filled with birds for sale. The Chinese revere birds. We had tea at an outdoor stand and gawked at thousands of birds of endless variety. This "bird alley" is a must-see. Wai Ming bought a couple of rare birds for which I had to lend him some money. We then spent a good deal of time getting travel permits for his feathered icons. I kept telling Wai Ming they would be quarantined once they reached the U.S.—and they were. When he was finally permitted to pick them up, the poor birds had expired. He was devastated, to say the least, and even more so when his wife made him pay me back the two thousand dollars I had loaned him for their purchase.

Wai Ming did a substantial number of drawings, many of which we used in his book. He had kept 4 x 5 negatives of many of his earlier paintings so we were able to put together a pictorial retrospective of his paintings. It took the better part of a year and a small fortune to bring his book to the public, which we did in 1980. The Wai Ming book was another unqualified success and, as I had hoped, it propelled Wai Ming to new heights of popularity and financial success. Wai Ming regarded my having published this book as a sign of my great power. I enjoyed his elemental appraisal of my efforts on his behalf.

Upon returning home from my Asian vacation, I was picked up at the airport by my trusted lieutenant, Barry. It was nice to see his smiling face. He brought me up to date on gallery happenings, even what was happening with some of our mutual friends in Sonoma. Since the Greek trip, Barry and his wife had been frequent guests at the home of the Schake family. I would have been pleased if this friendship had encouraged Barry and his wife to start a family, perhaps even move to Sonoma.

The 1979 business year had been our best yet and 1980 was on track to at least match it. We were on a roll. And the comfortable relationship I had with Barbara continued. Even though I occasionally took Barbara up to my Sonoma house, I usually went to see my friends and their children by myself, not wanting to change these established relationships.

18

Love of My Life

One night when I was visiting Sonoma, I walked into a newly opened and very popular Italian restaurant, already the watering hole for the locals. I walked up to the hostess, looked at her, and stood there, transfixed. I knew that I was going to marry this girl. She was nineteen, I later learned, and her name was Eileen. Angelically beautiful, Eileen had soft blond hair of various hues. After she seated me, unbeknownst to me, she went over to one of her coworkers and asked him who I was. Before he could tell her that his father and mother were good friends of mine through the Schake family, she blurted out, "You know, that's the kind of guy I want to marry."

From then on I made a point of dropping into Marioni's restaurant alone so I could chat with Eileen. I found out that she was raised locally, that she'd been in Kurt and Kory Schake's 4-H Club, that she was attending junior college in Santa Rosa, and that she did modeling when the opportunity presented itself. One could clearly see why she qualified as a model. She had delicate wrists and hands, tiny feet, and the long legs of a dancer. I've always been attracted to dancers, so I was really glad to hear she had been in local ballet productions for the last ten years; she had even taught dance to some children of my friends in Diamond "A". She also exuded a kind of natural goodness, a quality I felt I sorely needed in my life. That she was physically desirable, for once, was not the compelling factor. What I wanted was a chance to get to know her.

The next time I stopped in at Marioni's, it was late. Their dinnertime was over and I took a seat at the bar. I noticed that Eileen was sitting and chatting at the other end of the bar with a girlfriend, who turned out to be a young girl I was acquainted with. I went over to say hello and start a conversation. By her warm greeting I could see Eileen considered me one of the good guys. Just then the bartender and co-owner of the restaurant called out to Eileen from behind the bar and, with a twinkle in his eye, asked Eileen if she knew Jack Swanson. I was surprised by his indirect introduction and the stamp of approval it conveyed. Eileen and I talked for awhile, giving and getting some particulars about our lives.

I told Eileen that I lived up in Diamond "A" and asked her to come over for a drink. (I can't remember if I said anything about my redwood hot tub.) She demurely explained that she had a date. I offered to buy her a drink before she had to leave, but it was then she said that she was nineteen and couldn't be served. I told her I hoped to talk to her again. Then I realized why the bartender/co-owner had introduced me. Eileen left the restaurant with the bartender's brother, the other co-owner and her date for the evening. I surmised, correctly I think, that the bartender had wanted to throw a monkey wrench in his brother's relationship with their hostess.

I called Eileen later that week and tried to arrange a date, but she was busy juggling a couple of beaus, school, and work. We finally set up some sort of get-together, but she had to call it off. Determined, I kept calling. I even talked to her mom. (It never hurts to have the parents on your side.) Finally, after a few weeks, we set up a daytime date and I picked her up in my two-seater Mercedes sports car, definitely the "in" car of the late '70s and early '80s. I drove her to Sausalito, where a friend of mine was getting my sailboat ready for a race that afternoon. I had talked my buddy, Eric, a shipwright and master sailor, into sailing this race with me. At the start of the race, I made sure that the boat's rail was in the water, heeled over as much as possible. The rush of the water as we sailed along was exciting and worked according to plan: Eileen had to hang on to me for dear life. Eric knew all about currents and racing strategies but, still, we surprised everybody when we came in second.

I got Eric to partner with me in many future races when Eileen was with us, but we never did better than that first race.

Eileen and I began dating steadily from then on. She had no exposure to the art world and, of course, had never heard of Swanson Art Galleries. I had great fun taking her to the city and introducing her to my artists and galleries. She gradually cut back on dating some of the eligible guys she had been going out with and saw only me. Eileen was even-tempered and easy to be with; it was clear she hadn't let her beauty go to her head. Although I was never conscious of our age difference or the generation gap between us, I still didn't want to tell my Sonoma neighbors and friends, particularly the Schakes, that I was going out with a contemporary of their oldest son. I'd confess that when I had to.

As I got to know Eileen better, I marveled at her gift for sharing her world with me. This girl gave me a rare insight into how it felt to be her, how her mind worked. It opened my eyes and helped to expand my own understanding of people. Of course, she had many other qualities that swept me away, but this was the one facet of her personality that delighted me most, that and her irrepressible sense of humor. For her upcoming twentieth birthday, I took her to Carmel for the weekend.

I drove up to her house in Sonoma. When I rang the doorbell I was met by Eileen who looked irresistibly cute in jeans, a white blouse and navy blue blazer. One of her sisters was in the backyard sunbathing—Eileen was the youngest of four girls—and her father, a builder, was out by the vineyard finishing a carpentry project from his shop. Eileen asked me to come with her while she told her dad we were leaving. Great! There I was, a thirty-eight-year-old art dealer taking a nineteen-year-old student to Carmel for the weekend. Eileen bid her father good-bye, telling him that she was off to Carmel with Jack for the weekend.

Her dad was in his late fifties and was hard of hearing, so he put his hand to his ear and yelled, "What?" She yelled back, "I'm going to Carmel for the weekend with Jack." He still couldn't hear or grasp what was happening. We finally got it across that we were going to some art shows in Carmel and would be back in a few days.

We had a great trip to Carmel. Eileen regaled me with stories about her family. We stayed at a lodge in Carmel Valley. Eileen enjoyed my gallery and the quaint town of Carmel. One night we went to Highlands Inn, a well-known restaurant and hideaway overlooking the cliffs of Big Sur. She wore a black silk dress with a slit up the side that showed off her shapely long legs. I was having a hard time dealing with what, until then, had been a platonic relationship.

That night, even though we were sharing a king-size bed, Eileen sweetly insisted we wait until a future date. She tamed my passions with her wit, at the same time making sure I knew she cared for me. I remember she made light of my being so much older than she and teased me about my thinning hair. Although difficult, delaying our intimacy suited me as well. I didn't want to rush our mating dance because I was so sure we were destined for a long and lasting relationship. One of my favorite sayings at the time was Henry Thoreau's: "If you are related, you will meet!"

A few weeks later, we made plans for her to spend the weekend with me at my home in Sausalito. We were going to a newly opened country western dance hall nearby that was having an "urban cowboy" night. Country music was all the rage. We both liked this type of music and dancing and even donned western outfits for the occasion. After the dance, Eileen and I were flying so high that when we got back to my place it was clear to both of us that our love affair had reached the "moment of truth." We fell into a passionate embrace.

Eileen spent more and more time with me. We were definitely in love. When we were together, neither of us could think of practical matters like the future, for instance, or what other people might be saying about us, or the difference in our ages. I couldn't believe my amazing good luck in finding her. What if I had never walked into that restaurant in Sonoma on that particular night?

After awhile I induced her to quit her job at the restaurant and work in sales at my Sausalito gallery. This way we could see a lot of each other, and it also prevented Eileen and my secretary, Barbara, from running into one another at the Sutter Street gallery. Hard as it may be to believe, I hadn't told either one about the other.

Eileen represented wild passionate romance but, at the same time, solid, country, all-American values. Barbara represented a more sedate, comfortable, big city sophistication. It was quite a contrast. Eileen loved the new experience of working in a gallery and I enjoyed teaching her what I could about art and art sales. She commuted an hour each way from Sonoma to Sausalito. We still hadn't told all of our friends about the growing seriousness of our love affair.

Even though I didn't have a biological clock ticking away in terms of being able to have children, I did start having some nagging doubts. I knew that I wanted to marry and start a family in the next couple of years, but I had heard horror stories about younger girls having children before they had a chance to experience life. Even though Eileen was doing everything right regarding our relationship, I started wondering if I shouldn't give her the chance to go out with guys closer to her own age.

My feelings for Eileen hadn't changed one iota since the moment I first saw her, but somehow I felt compelled to place barriers between us, which I would later recognize as being totally artificial. Deep down, I still wanted her more intensely than any other woman I knew, but I rationalized that she wasn't really ready for marriage, that she wasn't mature enough, that she wasn't giving off the signals that would encourage me to propose.

I found myself allowing my relationship with Barbara to become more serious. When I thought of settling down and fathering my own lively brood of children, it was someone of Barbara's maturity, age twenty-four, who seemed more ready to play the role of wife. In any case, that was how I rationalized my decision at that crisis point in my life.

I gradually stopped calling Eileen and I began seeing Barbara more steadily. I even took Barbara to Hawaii. Eileen retaliated by starting to date some of her old boyfriends, and, as upset as that made me, I was determined to do the noble thing and bow out of her life. Barbara started talking about our future together and how much she wanted to have children. I convinced myself that she was ready for the kind of marriage and stability I wanted in life and finally, believing I was deeply in love with her, I asked her the fatal question. She said yes so quickly, I was reminded of how beautifully we got along together and, even more incredibly, how we never once had a serious disagreement. Perhaps that alone should have forewarned me that something was seriously lacking in our chemistry.

Everything appeared to be going along great. The last two years had been phenomenal in terms of gallery sales. People just seemed to be throwing money at us. As far as I could foretell, it was clear sailing ahead. This is where the Japanese saying comes in: "In the moment of victory, tighten your helmet strap."

Just before my wedding to Barbara, I started getting some strange vibrations from my general manager and VP, Barry. I began to feel a few "clunks in the transmission." Barry had been spending a lot of time back east overseeing our two galleries, and, it appeared, reestablishing friendships with some of his college chums who had moved to the Washington, D.C. area. One of his friends was in the cable TV business. He would buy time on the new satellite transponders and sell "air time," such as pay-per-view events and evangelical ministries, to individuals and groups. When Barry told me about hanging out with his friend in Washington, I didn't think much about it, even though I did have the feeling that his wife, Kathy, was pushing him to strike out on his own. One spring day, sunny but cold, I got a call from Barry. He had just come back from Washington having spent time with his friends in the telecommunications industry. Barry said that we had to get together and talk—clunk. I canceled an appointment and met him at a downtown restaurant. He was somber as he explained he had a great opportunity and was quitting.

I felt as if one of my close family members had died. Barry was adamant about leaving. I knew that it was going to have an enormous impact on every person who worked for the gallery, and our artists. Over the last few years he had taken over Jake's personnel responsibilities and basically did all the hiring or had a hand in hiring just about everyone who worked in our seven galleries. There was shock and disbelief among my troops, especially my other managers. Barry was absolutely crucial to the organization as we had set it up. When he left, I had to transfer my manager in Carmel to oversee my Beach Street flagship gallery, leaving Carmel without strong leadership. I wasn't surprised that my managers in Washington, D.C. quit. Barry had hired them and been their main contact with the company. I also got the feeling from our staff and many of my artists that I must have done something to my VP. All I could do was run around and try to plug up the holes in the dike.

The East Coast galleries became a hassle from then on. I had to rob Peter to pay Paul—transferring good managers or freshly promoted assistant managers clear across the country to run my galleries in the Washington area. Every time I sent one of my troops from San Francisco, they found out either that they hated the East Coast and the Washington area, or they were offered such enticements by other retailers that they promptly quit. My Georgetown and Alexandria galleries were a drain, but I had no choice but to keep them afloat because of my long-term leases. I sent some of my best producers and managers to this black hole, and it ate them. I lost hundreds of thousands of dollars before I was able to close down those galleries, and even then, I had to keep paying on the leases long after we packed up and left.

Barry took his pension and profit-sharing money from the gallery and went on with his life, starting a successful teleconferencing company, which eventually gained some sort of virtual monopoly selling time on satellite transmission to cable channels.

As 1981 was coming to a close, I was glad that our company had downsized, even though I had not seen another hard-hitting recession coming. If I had held onto our East

Coast galleries, it might have done irreparable harm to our company. The 1981 recession was bad, not as bad as in 1975, but this one was a nasty jolt from left field. I felt lucky to have enough financial reserves and momentum to carry the company forward.

I noticed that some of my competitors who were still selling the questionable Dalí, Picasso, Miró and Chagall prints were doing a brisk business, probably because buyers, even in lean times, swallowed their spiel—that these presigned or facsimile-signature-stamped prints were a great investment. These gallery owners had made up fancy brochures with graphs showing how these prints were supposedly climbing up in value.

During business downturns, I would be struggling along selling original paintings for my artists, sometimes sweating bullets about how to keep everyone afloat financially, and then what do I see but galleries selling these bogus prints. As far as I was concerned, those gallery owners were no better than drug dealers.

Barbara and I announced our wedding plans over the winter holidays. We planned a summer wedding. Neither Barry's leaving nor periodic blips on our economic roller coaster derailed me. It was my second church wedding but I regarded Barbara as my third wife, considering the more or less common-law arrangement I had with Sharon. After a properly festive wedding, with one of my artists, George Sumner, as my best man, Barbara and I flew to Hawaii for a three-week honeymoon. Marriage didn't seem to add or detract from our intimacy, and I hoped that the ensuing months would bring a child into our lives. However, I couldn't help but compare the affectionate but "adequate" sex life I had with Barbara to the passionate relationship I had experienced with Eileen. I began to wonder whether I had made the right decision.

The three-week honeymoon we spent at the Hyatt Regency in Maui should have been idyllic. The weather was predictably glorious. We sunbathed every day by the largest pool I had ever seen. We got the obligatory tan and generally lived the high life. But it wasn't very long after we returned from the honeymoon that I started asking myself, is this all there is? Just Barbara and I, joined at the hip for all eternity?

Oh, it was true enough that Barbara and I were comfortable with each other. She continued to work for me down at the gallery and she was really good at her job. She also got along famously with most of my artists. However, we just seemed to co-exist; we had all the material things but no spark. I could tell that Barbara had lost interest in "pillow talk," as the Japanese call it. I certainly didn't want to admit to myself or anyone else that I had screwed up again, so I set my sights on having a family, figuring at least we could have kids to show for our mistake. It was, after all, the one commitment we still shared: we both wanted to raise a family.

Intent on getting Barbara pregnant, we undertook a seven- or eight-week sexual marathon. As I kept repeating my performance night after night, it began to seem more like some voodoo ritual then any kind of lovemaking. I was wondering whether one of us had a fertility problem but decided to give it a year or two before we made a trip to a specialist. It wasn't until much later that I discovered her guilty secret.

I had this feeling of loss in my life when Eileen's picture flashed across my mind. She, quite naturally, had quit working for my Sausalito gallery when I announced my engagement to Barbara. And here I was, months later, feeling myself relentlessly pulled toward Eileen. When I was in Sonoma I started driving past her parents' house, flitting close to the flame. I hoped I would get a glimpse of her. One day around dusk I saw her in the front window. I stopped, turned around, and drove past again. I knew she had seen me and I was sure both of our hearts stopped. I went to a favorite Mexican restaurant, La Casa, and telephoned her with an invitation for dinner. When I got her on the line I could tell she was miffed, but she did talk to me.

"Oh Jack, I don't believe this. You've got to be crazy."

"Is that a yes?" I ventured.

"Here you drop me for no reason at all and you walk out of my life, you bastard! Then you marry another woman and out of the blue you call and expect me to drop everything and be at your beck and call."

"But listen," I said, "you don't have to tell me what a clumsy idiot I have been. The thing is, I think I've made a really serious mistake."

"That's tough," she said. "But it so happens I don't go out with married men."

"Let's just have dinner. That's all I ask."

"I've already had my dinner."

"Okay, then how about a drink? I'm at La Casa."

She said nothing for a moment but I could hear her breathing.

I said, "I need to talk to you."

"Okay, see you in an hour," she said and hung up.

As she walked into the living room, her mother said, "Did I hear you talking to someone on the phone?" "Oh, just a friend. I'm going downtown. See you in a bit."

When she got to La Casa I was finishing off dinner. She looked like a sailor's dream, dressed in light faded jeans and a country style blouse. We said our awkward hellos and looked around at a lot of familiar faces, which included those of the parents of one of Eileen's girlfriends. I cautiously suggested we go to an old-time saloon and hotel down the block so that we could talk privately. She agreed. As she got up and left the dining area I could see the admiring glances. She was in real good shape with a fighting weight of 113 pounds.

We got a room in the turn-of-the-century hotel reputed to house General Vallejo's bed. I got the room key and led Eileen up the stairs. I wanted to get caught up on her life and to try to convince her to date me again. I also couldn't help myself from trying to remove her clothes. I hoped we could pick up from where we had left off. Eileen allowed a few kisses only; she took umbrage to the direction in which things were quite obviously headed. Some painful memories must have escaped her subconscious mind and reminded her conscious mind of how I had stomped on her heart. She called a halt to our little reunion. She was still hurt and angry—infuriated—although she didn't cut off all communication. As we left the room I asked, "Can I see you again soon?"

"Okay, maybe," she said.

We left the old hotel and I walked her to her car parked close to Marioni's where she was working again, the same place where we had met a year and a half earlier. It now seemed a million years ago. I stood there as she drove off in her little black car, a Japanese compact. These little foreign imports were now a part of the single girls' dress code.

Seeing her alone again convinced me of what a fool I had been. It took a lot of phone calls and a few months to get her to somewhat forgive past transgressions and agree to see me for a harmless rendezvous. We had to plan carefully so that we wouldn't be seen by anyone we knew. We began to meet on the sly from time to time, and, of course, the need for secrecy added a touch of intrigue to our encounters. Periodically, Eileen tried to get me out of her life. She'd move, change her phone number, and get a new job. I'd have to sweet-talk her mother into divulging her whereabouts.

Eileen left her restaurant job and took a position in a woman's clothing store in suburban San Rafael where she worked for about six months. The pay was minimal so she and her then roommate applied and were hired as waitresses at a popular restaurant in Sausalito, formerly the Trident and recently renamed Horizons. It was right across the street from my Sausalito gallery. Eileen's motivation for waitressing at this tourist hangout was to earn more money, but I flatter myself in thinking she wanted to be closer to me as well.

With Eileen so close by, opportunities to see one another just seemed to multiply. I still had my house in Sausalito and my sailboat was docked a few minutes from Horizons. This made it easy to arrange liaisons, mostly at my boat. I was still taking off one day mid-week, and now I spent it with the beautiful Eileen. No description I can offer would do her justice. Suffice it to say, I couldn't be near her or think about her or talk to her without every cell in my body exploding. It was a sensation I had never felt for any other woman.

At this point in my double life I didn't want to face my marital blunder. I told Eileen that Barbara and I were trying to have a family. Meanwhile, our Wednesday afternoon meetings at my boat had become a part of my life I wasn't about to give up. Just about every Wednesday I would stroll down the Sausalito waterfront where I berthed the *Marathon* and I would find Eileen waiting for me.

After renewing my friendship with Eileen, I was even more convinced that Barbara and I had some serious problems. But because I still wanted children, I continued to try to have a family with my wife, still completely unaware that Barbara had always suffered from a powerful phobia about childbirth. Years later, I learned that she never intended to have children. I think she hoped that I would change my mind about wanting children and things would somehow work out. Instead of revealing this cogent fact, she remained silent, and just let me keep on keeping on.

Even in these idyllic days with Eileen, the country was in an economic downturn, and I was forced to concentrate on the company. Losing Barry had been a blow, but I did manage to find a replacement for him. Given the severity of this '81 recession, my forced withdrawal from East Coast expansion serendipitously happened in the nick of time. Now I was back to five places of business. I could drive to all of them in a day. There is a military saying, "You only control the ground you are standing on." I also discovered that it was easier to find four or five capable managers than six or seven. As '81 drew to a close, I had rebuilt my staff and I continued to have shows for our main artists, and I was publishing more and more graphics. The latter was a godsend during recessionary times and helped support the artists with royalty payments.

Five years had passed since I had moved out of my original Beach Street gallery to the larger brick building on the corner of Beach and Larkin Streets. There was an alarming rise in real estate prices and the rents property owners were charging. Every time I went to renew a lease on one of my galleries, I'd find the rent hiked astronomically, sometimes to double the old fee.

Eileen and I continued to see each other, occasionally spending a weekend together. She dated other people from time to time. As much as I didn't want to share her with anyone else, I knew she had to move on with her life. After many games and angry good-byes that would last only a few minutes before we called each other back, it dawned on both of us that we loved each other deeply. If we split up it was going to leave scars and wounds that might heal in time but would never be completely resolved.

Still not knowing where our liaison would lead us, Eileen rented a cute apartment in nearby Larkspur so we could have a place to ourselves without concern for roommates or weather. Now Wednesdays were split between the boat and the apartment. We never tired of one another. Even though I'm quick to point out Eileen's beauty and youth, there was much more to our relationship. I found that she was as smart a woman as I had ever met. I was pleased when she started taking art history courses at the nearby junior college, but even without that, we never ran out of things to discuss.

Before I knew it, Barbara and I had been married for two years and Barbara hadn't become pregnant. I didn't want to undergo a medical exam, but it was disconcerting to think that there might be a problem with one of us. Actually, if I had been in my right mind at the time, I should have been relieved that we were still childless.

My affair with Eileen was relatively hassle-free, but as I got increasingly jealous about her seeing others, we both realized that it was destructive for us to continue to play this game. She was spending too many weekends and holidays alone and she wasn't able to tell her parents or sisters what was really going on in her life. The subterfuge and secrecy began to take its toll; she signed up to go to college in England. The plan was to work as a nanny, attend school, and see the world. Eileen saved up the money for the airline ticket and set a date for departure. She and I both knew that this was a crossroads for us. What to do?

I had a serious discussion with Eileen and asked her to put her trip to England on hold—indefinitely. I knew that I wanted her in my life. Without making any promises to

Eileen I explained that I wanted to take Barbara on a trip to Hawaii to see if the marriage could be saved. Barbara and I revisited romantic vacation spots on Maui and in Honolulu. The vacation was fine but the romance was over. I hadn't made any promises to Eileen but I had intimated to her that if I saw no opportunity to patch things up with Barbara that I would ask her for a divorce. Eileen couldn't tell any of her friends or family; she had to wait rather stoically to see what decision I would come up with.

After spending two weeks in Hawaii with Barbara, it was painfully apparent that I needed to tell her our marriage was over. Late one afternoon just before we were to head home, I initiated the conversation. I told Barbara that I didn't want to be married to her anymore. It was the most painful thing I had ever done. I never mentioned Eileen's name or even the fact that there was another woman.

Barbara was hurt, but accepted the finality of my decision. She felt that it would be best for her to fly to Los Angeles and live with her mom for a while and have me ship all her belongings there. Although this was a very tough situation, it was a relief to have at last made a real decision instead of allowing things to drift on and on. It was distressing to realize that Barbara was going to be uprooted from the people she knew in the Bay Area—her friends at work, the artists she had come to know. Her whole life was turned topsy turvey, but in her characteristic equanimity, she seemed to resign herself to the situation.

I assured Barbara that I would help her get established wherever she decided to live. I offered to ship her car, pay for new furnishings, and to let her keep her credit cards. I wanted to make this split as amicable as possible.

She requested some paintings that we had chosen together and some art work done by artists who had also been her friends. Divorce is hard on art collections. Even though Barbara said she wouldn't contest our divorce, her lawyers managed to drag out the divorce proceedings a year past the normal six-month period.

It was while I was going through her belongings at the house in Sausalito that I came across her supply of birth control pills—a whole drawer full, perhaps a five-year supply. It dawned on me then that Barbara and I had been deceiving each other in our different ways: I hadn't known she was lying to me about the contraceptives and she didn't know about my love for another woman. Most significant of all, Barbara did not know about Eileen.

After I got back from Hawaii I asked Eileen to move in with me. I knew that it would be at least six months until we could make anything official. Summer was approaching and I made plans to go to Kurt Schake's graduation from the Air Force Academy. I didn't want to spring Eileen on my neighbors during this special event so I planned for Eileen to skip the graduation and meet me in Dallas for an art auction.

I attended the graduation bursting with pride. Kurt's dad pinned the gold Second Lieutenant's bars on his son at a midnight ceremony. The Air Force F-16 jets roared overhead just as the graduating cadets threw their hats in the air, marking the end of four tough years. Kurt's sister, Kory, was already attending Stanford University so I felt that I could now sell my house on the hill in Diamond "A" Ranch. I had fulfilled my obligation as Uncle Jack. I told the Schakes about my impending divorce and my involvement with Eileen. Although taken aback, they remained steadfast friends.

Eileen and I flew into Dallas from different cities, and when we met at Loew's Anatole Hotel it seemed to mark the beginning of our new life together. The auction we went to in Dallas was awesome. It was a formal dinner affair at the Adolphus Hotel where we watched as wealthy oil people and the mayor of Dallas bought up two million dollars worth of Western Americana paintings in one hour. I was so inspired that I decided to organize my own black tie dinner auction as soon as I got back to San Francisco. San Francisco may not have had the oil wealth of Dallas but it was beginning to catch up with its aerospace, defense, and Silicon Valley industries. The auction would prove to be a good way for me to get rid of some excess merchandise from my East Coast galleries, and boost my financial reserves.

Right after Eileen and I started living together, I decided to take her to see my old alma mater, UC Santa Barbara. I had traded in my two-seater Mercedes for a black Jaguar. This turned out to be a big mistake, but I had been told that Jaguar's were now more trouble-free mechanically. As we drove the shiny new car down Highway 101 headed south, I popped the question. "Will you marry me, Eileen?" She said, "Yes."

The conversation turned to our plans and hopes for the future. We were absolutely in agreement about wanting children. At forty-one years of age I hoped we would have a child or two fairly soon because I wanted to be around when they graduated from college and got married. We started talking about religion and whether or not we should have a church wedding. When Eileen mentioned that she had always assumed she would get married in the Catholic church in Sonoma, I almost ran the car off the road. We had never discussed religion in all the years we had known each other. My Episcopalian grandmother probably would have rolled over a couple of times in her grave at the thought of my marrying a Papist. I figured that religion shouldn't have any bearing on our marriage and asked Eileen if we couldn't marry in a nondenominational church and raise our children as Protestants. She acquiesced, but knew her family would not take kindly to this news.

After we settled this religious matter, we decided to buy Eileen's wedding ring as soon as we returned to Sausalito. We thought that my divorce would be final in six months so we weren't very diligent about contraception. We both agreed that we wanted a family as soon as possible. A few weeks later Eileen started having typical symptoms and had a pregnancy test. The rabbit died; she was pregnant.

Eileen's folks knew that we were planning to get married and that we had the ring and a date in mind. The baby news meant she might be quite far along when the divorce was final and so we had to clear the way for our wedding. I approached her folks saying: "There's some good news and there's some bad news." The good news was that they were going to have another grandchild and the bad news was that

I had just learned my soon-to-be ex-wife was holding up the divorce and we were going to have to trash the engraved wedding invitations we had just had printed. I was glad that Eileen's father and his two sons-in-law, both six-foot-two and over 220 pounds, didn't go ballistic. Her family certainly looked at me with jaundiced eyes, but I could tell that Eileen's mother was still my friend even in this trying moment.

It never occurred to us that anything could go wrong with the pregnancy. We traveled, worked, and maintained our regular pace and lifestyle, the only concession being that Eileen gave up alcohol and watched her diet. We threw a black tie auction at the Beach Street gallery, staying up late with friends after the event. I had more than my share of martinis, not giving much thought to the fact that we planned to drive a rented motor home to Texas the next morning to participate in an art expo. We were going to feature the paintings of our best-selling artists, including Wai Ming, at the Dallas Art Exposition.

The morning after this smashingly successful auction, we drove to San Rafael to pick up the motor home. We were told that the regular size model we had selected was not available and that we would have to navigate a 60-foot long monstrosity. It was going to be a long trip. As we drove across the Golden Gate Bridge to the Beach Street gallery to pick up the selected prints and paintings, I managed to smash the side mirror on the bridge toll booth. (Coincidentally, I did the same thing two weeks later to the other mirror when I was returning north.)

We drove east to Fresno and spent our first night with my mother's niece and her husband, Ellen and Frosty Sloan. The next morning we headed for Bakersfield and across the desert to Arizona and New Mexico. Just as I mentioned to Eileen what surprisingly good mileage we were getting, the engine died. We were out of gas although the fuel gauge had hardly moved. We had to leave the RV right at that spot and hitchhike back to Bakersfield to a gas station. The station owner was a good old boy and offered to drive us back to our "rig." This was definitely farm country: while we were at the station we heard his wife proclaim that "junior" had just taken a prize for his heifer at the 4-H county fair.

The station owner dominated the conversation as he took us back to our RV, praising Bakersfield and reciting all the opportunities it offered. When he heard I was an art dealer he said, "Why, if you were to get up a bunch of those oil paintings on velvet, I bet you could set up on the highway here and earn yourself a good living." Eileen and I stole glances, promising to give it serious consideration.

When we finally pulled into Loew's Anatole Hotel, we were more than ready for the high life of Dallas. Eileen contacted her friend Surette, whom she had met in a beauty pageant. I had flown in one of my lady managers to help us at the expo, and the four of us partied together. I hired a mile long Texas-size limousine with a gorgeous blonde as the driver, and she whisked us from disco to disco the whole night long.

Dallas was at its peak with the price of oil at $40 a barrel and no hint it was ever going back down. It was a different Dallas a year or so later when oil prices sunk to $15 a barrel and the city was plunged into a horrible depression. Although they weathered the storm, it took years for Texas to diversify its economic base and to regain its footing. My father was still living in Houston at the time. He had just retired from dentistry at seventy-eight years of age and was in failing health. He lived in a retirement home for awhile, but, irascible codger that he was, he got kicked out for hitting someone with his cane. He wanted to go back to his boyhood home in Minnesota for his final days and opted to move to a retirement home in Buffalo, Minnesota (population 5,000) overlooking one of the state's 20,000 lakes. He also had brothers and sisters still living in the vicinity.

The art expo in Dallas was turning out to be a great success, especially since our gallery was just about the only exhibitor and wholesaler not trying to sell Dalí, Miró and Chagall prints. The nightlife was great. We weren't as rowdy as we could have been because of Eileen's pregnancy. Often Eileen looked on soberly as the others took part in celebrating the last days of the great Texas boom. A few days into our

Dallas experience, Eileen began having cramps. As cautious as she had been in taking care of herself, the drive across country may have been too much. We called her obstetrician in California who immediately advised her to hop a plane home. Taking a week to drive back was out.

When Eileen returned to California her condition improved. I drove the motor home back across the mountains of New Mexico by myself. Armed with a .45-Colt automatic, I wasn't too worried about someone stealing my cargo of Wai Ming paintings. I drove through Santa Fe, New Mexico to check out the gallery scene and was pleasantly surprised when a young woman tapped me on the shoulder and I turned to see Ruby Lee and PoPo. They were staying at a Native American Indian reservation outside of town.

My drive back home was not without incident. I almost got myself killed coming down the mountain from Santa Fe when a rear right wheel tire blew out (one of two, thank God). The brakes didn't respond well and I went careening down steep mountain curves. When I gratefully pulled into Grant, New Mexico to fix the flat, I found out why the brakes almost failed. There was a leak from the axle which soaked the right rear brakes with oil. When the RV company was contacted, they authorized the repair and then told me that they never inspect their vehicles, preferring to let the customers fix things on the road. I made a mental note that if I ever bought or rented another motor home, I would make sure that the fuel gauge, brakes and steering mechanism were checked by a qualified mechanic. This was not an experience I cared to repeat.

The gallery got along fine while I was gone, and a week or so after I returned from Dallas we had a show at my Sutter Street gallery for Mark Inge Saastad, a seascape artist from Norway. Mark had been a merchant seaman and combined his knowledge of the sea and his Nordic heritage to create unique paintings of the Oregon and California coast. The show was on a Friday night. Eileen and I drove there in separate cars. She had been feeling a little peaked and was just going to put in a cameo appearance. During the show we had a few local glitterati drop by. Eileen wasn't feeling well at all and said an early farewell to the honoree, also asking me to come home as soon as the show was over.

I left the gallery around eleven that evening and drove straight home to Sausalito. I walked into the house and could tell something was wrong. Our bedroom was dark. When I turned on the light, there was Eileen in a pool of blood. I scooped her up, carried her to the car and drove her to the hospital emergency room. She had had a miscarriage. We were devastated and wholly unprepared for this turn of events, having blithely thought any past problems had healed. We regretted the Dallas trip, thinking that may have been to blame. Besides that, my ex-wife was still holding up the divorce and there was the added pressure, especially on Eileen, of having the baby out of wedlock. It was harder than we thought to go against established societal norms.

The miscarriage was quite a blow. I had already started telling people about the baby on the way. I nursed Eileen back to health; it took months before she regained her mental and physical well-being. We decided to move ahead and planned our wedding for spring of the coming year, 1984. My attorney assured me that I could count on receiving the final decree by that time. We picked a wedding date in May and ordered a new set of engraved invitations.

Two months prior to our wedding we sold my house in Sausalito and bought a new home under construction in Sonoma. Eileen didn't like the thought of living in a house previously inhabited by two of my ex-wives, so we pledged to start over. We moved into our new ranch style home in Sonoma in April, a month before the wedding. Things seemed stable again in my business and I looked forward to reducing the time I spent in the office. I had inklings that there were some problems with a few of my artists, but I didn't feel overly concerned.

Eileen would meet me at my Sutter Street office on a regular basis. It was she who noticed how uptight I would get every Friday when Wai Ming brought in his paintings. He had started making demands that seemed innocuous on the surface, but led to tension between us. I began to fear that it could lead to a parting of the ways.

In addition to rumblings I was getting from Wai Ming, I was completely surprised when the new guy I had promoted as my general manager requested a meeting a few weeks before the wedding and insisted on having a raise in salary. Ron complained that some of his salespeople made more than he did; I had to explain the obvious—that their earnings were more volatile and when they made exceptional sales they should be compensated accordingly. I was perturbed at his demands but gave him a raise and, to make sure he realized how much I thought of him, I also sent him to a local car dealership to pick out a new BMW with all the bells and whistles to use as his company car. I was hoping that in the future when I cut back on my work schedule, my new general manager would be there to pick up any slack. We were doing exceptionally well financially so I also traded in my problem-infested Jaguar for a gold four-door Mercedes and bought a white Mercedes diesel station wagon for Eileen.

Three or four weeks before the wedding I went to the Marin County courthouse and was granted the final divorce decree. Eileen and I immediately mailed out the wedding invitations. Although I felt a little silly inviting friends and relatives to another wedding in the space of three years, I was determined to throw one heck of a party.

Eileen and I were married at the Sonoma Mission Inn the third weekend in May, 1984. The Episcopal Church refused to perform the ceremony unless I applied for special dispensation from an archbishop in Boston. I had to eat a little crow because I had told Eileen how nondogmatic and enlightened the Anglican Episcopal Church was compared to the Catholic diocese. We found a wonderful minister from a nondenominational church, Dr. Moffet Dennis, who married us with no questions asked, other than if we loved each other. We invited Eileen's family and friends, which comprised a substantial part of the old Sonoma population. Her Italian grandparents on her father's side were pioneers of this northern California wine region. The wedding went off without a hitch. No one jumped up with a reason why we shouldn't be joined in holy matrimony. The bar bill was enormous, the dinner turned out splendidly, and I felt sorry for anyone who wasn't me.

We sped off to the airport to start our honeymoon. We flew nonstop to New York on our way to Europe. Our itinerary was to spend a week in London, take the Orient Express from Victoria Station across the English countryside to the white cliffs of Dover, and then take a ferry across the English Channel to Calais, continuing on the Venice Simplon Orient-Express through France and Switzerland, finally disembarking in Venice. We would spend a week in Venice, a week in Florence, and a week in Rome.

London was a great place to begin our grand tour. We had gone to the Met and Frick museums in New York, which only whetted our appetites for the British Museum, the Tate Gallery with its collection of Turners, the National Gallery, and the Victoria and Albert Museum. So much to see, so little time. I'm not going to write a travel log or give a blow-by-blow account of our trip, but the trip had its high points that bear recounting. We discovered, for example, that the Orient-Express is definitely the way to travel. We boarded the pullman cars from Victoria Station (British Rail) to Paris (Continental Rail) and steamed through the night, passing castles in Switzerland before coming to the end of the line in Venice. The overnight compartments were far more comfortable than I would have thought. Every compartment had an attendant hovering nearby. They never let you run out of Evian.

The best meals I had the whole trip were in the dining cars, which are magnificently decorated with lacquer panels and Lalique glass, and are most distinctly Art Deco. This train, its cars and its route, had only recently been saved from extinction; it was reinaugurated in 1982. Everyone dressed for dinner. The men were in black tie and dinner jacket, the women in '20s' style dresses, with headbands and jewels. After dinner Eileen and I went to the bar car and drank martinis until 3 A.M., listening to a talented young man in a tuxedo play the baby grand piano. The next morning we awoke to the train whizzing by alpine peaks and fairytale castles. What a sight. A few hours later, around noon, the Orient-Express pulled into Venice.

After gathering our luggage at the train depot we found a water taxi to take us to our hotel. What a strange city. There are no cars; these water taxis are the only mode of transportation other than walking. We got into this passenger boat and, within minutes, we were in the middle of a huge waterway, a channel, with ocean-going steamers and large boats going in different directions. Our boat zigzagged in and out between heavy vessels as if it were a taxicab in a large American city.

Venice is certainly the most picturesque city in the world. It's filled with great public plazas, churches, antiquities and artifacts that the once politically powerful rulers of this port city amassed from their foes. I never took so many photographs in my life. Eileen and I finally began to unwind from the buildup to the nuptial party and the long-awaited wedding. We did all the guided tours, took the gondolier rides, rolling up our pant legs at high tide, and walked around the flooded St. Mark's Square. Our only disappointment was that the famed Harry's Bar was closed the day we tried to drop by.

We traveled from Venice to Florence by a regular run-of-the-mill train, quite a comedown from the Orient-Express. When we arrived in Florence we checked into the small marble-encrusted Hotel DiMedici. We stared out at the surrounding hills and scenery and were transported back in time. The landscape, with its cypress trees and Italian architecture, looked just the same as the Renaissance masters had depicted them so long ago. Eileen and I could hardly believe our eyes when we stood in front of Michelangelo's David. You could imagine David coming alive and his eyes drawing a bead on Goliath's head. Photographs do not convey the beauty or the impact of this work of art that once stood in front of the Medici Palace. We went to the Uffizi Gallery (once the Medici Palace) and I would have to say it is the most impressive museum in the world.

We lucked into hearing someone talking about the Pitti Palace, another palace the powerful Medici family had owned after vanquishing the original owners. Now a state-owned

museum, the Pitti Palace is the second most beautiful museum
I have ever seen. It was full of Titians and Raphaels and
many of the earthly treasures that had once belonged to the
mega-rich Medicis.

After a trip to the Ponte Vecchio Bridge to buy a gold
bauble or two, we headed for the train and a long day's ride
to the eternal city, Rome. When we got to the Florence train
station we found that the first-class passenger train we were
scheduled to take to Rome had been canceled due to bad
weather and mudslides. Whatever the last-class train was,
it was the only option. Loaded down with luggage, we
boarded the train and found out there weren't any available
seats; we sat on our luggage in the drafty hallway for the
entire 400-mile trip. It was still an exhilarating adventure.
When we got to Rome we stayed at the ultra modern Hilton
Hotel high on a hilltop overlooking the city. We toured the
Vatican, St. Peter's Basilica, and all the obligatory sightseeing
attractions. It was a sobering experience to drive on the
Appian Way where the Roman legions had marched out into
their widespread empire. After a week in Rome we decided
that our plan to spend an additional week in Italy, mainly
to visit Milan and say hello to some of Eileen's paternal
relatives, was overly ambitious. We had been gone long
enough. It was time to return home.

A few months after we got back to our new home in
Sonoma, Eileen got pregnant. This time we cut back on our
social life and travel, and a few days before our one-year
anniversary, our daughter, Christina, was born. The nurses
at the Sonoma Hospital told us that Christina, with her short
reddish blonde hair, was one of the most beautiful infants
they had ever seen. We told them they probably said that
to all the new parents, but they assured us, "No, this little
girl was special." Of course, we had to agree!

At last, at the tender age of forty-three, I had become
a family man. Starting a family was every bit as rewarding
as I had hoped. Of course, being awakened every night at
all hours damned near did me in. My mother-in-law lived
about one-half mile from us and was a godsend. She laughed
at our efforts to cope with our newborn, and, thankfully,

took on the role of the consummate professional. It wasn't too long before I was urging Eileen to have another baby, but with the proviso that we would wait until Christina quit waking up every night at 3 A.M. It was three long, sleepless years before that happened.

When Eileen and I returned from our honeymoon in June 1984, we were pleased to find out that the galleries had just had one of their best months in retail sales. My intention to cut down on the time I would spend at work might even turn out as planned. I was hoping to spend only a few days a week in the office and the other days at home in Sonoma. As Murphy's Law would have it, however, things didn't go that way.

When I returned to work, my controller, Paula, told me about a phone conversation she had heard between my general manager, Ron, and Wai Ming. From what she could discern, they were plotting to open their own gallery, taking my mailing list, some of my artists, and a number of my sales staff. Not only that, they were considering moving into a retail gallery space next door to me on Beach Street, or possibly in Chinatown. Although I had picked up some disquieting vibrations from Wai Ming, I couldn't believe that he would destroy the momentum we had built up over a decade. We had just sold one of his paintings for over $40,000. Ron had gone against some company policies to conclude this large sale of Wai Ming's painting entitled *The Gamblers*. He lied to me and, as far as I was concerned, he had been insubordinate. As soon as I returned from our honeymoon I met with Ron and asked him if it was true. He answered that it was, and I asked him to resign and hand over the keys to the galleries and the company car I had just given him. He seemed nonplussed that I hadn't waited until he and Wai Ming were ready to open their own gallery before firing him.

Wai Ming stopped supplying my gallery with paintings from then on, saying I had cheated him out of royalties on his print sales and that I hadn't paid him commission on some sales of his paintings. I think he even went so far as to accuse the galleries of reporting a lower sales figure to him than his paintings actually sold for, as a way of reducing his share of the commission. He did not come up with one customer to corroborate this fabrication, even though he had been dropping in on many of my galleries once a week for nine years. He had also met most of his collectors at the one-man shows we held for him at the various galleries. If his accusations were true, Ron would certainly have been able to check the books any time to see whether such chicanery was going on.

It took Wai Ming, his wife, and Ron a few months to open a gallery in Chinatown. Wai Ming and his wife bankrolled the venture and were the legal owners. Wai Ming had always wanted me to open a gallery in Chinatown but I repeatedly explained to him that the general public associated Chinatown with cheap goods, and that he would not be furthering his career by displaying his art there. He didn't listen.

They had some success with the gallery, but even with many of my former artists and salespeople, his own paintings, his self-published prints, and the Swanson Gallery format, he wound up having to close shop after four years.

After Wai Ming opened his own gallery there was a definite chill in the air between us. To me, all of his accusations were manufactured. He could not come up with any documented instances where I had failed to compensate him, but he was sure I or my bookkeepers had "cooked the books." You can imagine how I felt about Wai Ming's false accusations after I had befriended and sponsored him in his successful bid for citizenship, and had paid him over $1 million over the last few years.

I called Wai Ming repeatedly and explained that I didn't owe him anything. I told him that my bookkeepers were above reproach (none of them were family) and they would not allow me to not pay or cheat any artist, even if I had been so inclined. I pointed out that when Jacquie Vaux left to open her own gallery claiming we owed her money, the exhaustive records' review that ensued revealed that she owed us $7,000 for some paintings we had inadvertently paid for twice.

But Wai Ming wouldn't budge. He demanded that my bookkeeper go back through our records and research every Wai Ming sale ever made. After she completed this task, which showed we owed Wai Ming nothing, he still refused to believe it. I then invited Wai Ming to send over his own accountant. He went through the books and had to admit that he found no proof of misappropriation of monies. Wai Ming then demanded another audit of the gallery. By this time, my bookkeeper was fed up and refused to go along with the request. She quit.

Wrangling over the bookkeeping for Wai Ming continued from 1984 to 1989. He seemed determined to prove I was the bad guy. During this period of fits and starts, I hired a professional accounting firm (one of the Big Six) to audit all of Wai Ming's sales and payment records to answer, once and for all, Wai Ming's allegations. Two young accountants showed up at my office and started going through all our accounting records and retail sales slips from 1974, when we first began to represent Wai Ming, through 1989. They typed all the information into their laptops. It took almost one year of full-time employment to finish the job. Their company sent me a bill for $77,000. This audit confirmed that I didn't owe Wai Ming a dime. Finally, Wai Ming had to agree to drop his demands.

To make sure I would not have any accounting problems with him in the future, I traded Wai Ming a mailing list and some of his graphics for outright ownership of the remaining 6,000 prints I had published of his work. Years later, in 1994 to be exact, Wai Ming told my Taiwanese bookkeeper, in Chinese, that he was sorry he had left my gallery. He said he regretted it and had lamented his mistake. He was sorry he had listened to those around him, and he now knew that I was the only one who truly believed in his talent and would promote him in the way that I did. He lost a lot of money in his Chinatown effort and had to sell off personal assets to extricate himself from his failed venture. He and Ron had a falling-out after a year or two and Ron left to work at another gallery. The strain of running his own gallery, even with his wife doing most of the administrative work, proved to be such an ordeal that after a couple of years Wai Ming was producing fewer and fewer paintings. Quite often there would be almost no Wai Ming paintings in his own gallery—a far cry from the halcyon days of old when he brought me a painting a week and kept all my galleries well supplied.

19

End of an Era

I was so busy with Eileen and baby Christina that my dealings with the artists no longer carried the same weight. Once I got plugged into the responsibilities of real fatherhood, I lost interest in playing the role of daddy to my artists. I also noticed that my artists were getting older and, through normal business attrition, were leaving the gallery. Recessions were coming closer and closer together, and there were strong indications that '85 was going to be a down year economically. This seesaw economic situation was having a destabilizing effect on the workforce and society in general, making people wonder about the value of anything.

I still hired mostly young college graduates. My galleries were a good place to start in the business world, a "clean well-lighted place" that surrounded employees with art work. Many of the young people we hired did not, or chose not, to fit into the corporate mode.

I can't enumerate all the things going on in the economy, but halfway through the '80s there were a lot of people, even higher-echelon white-collar management, being displaced because of corporate downsizing, merger mania and global competition. The United States had produced 40% of the world's products in the '50s and '60s and now, in the '80s, Europe and Asia were gaining parity in the world markets; the U.S. was producing only 20% of the world's products. All this change and uncertainty in the economy seemed to affect everyone, even my artists.

My plans for being a country squire, spending more time with my new family in Sonoma, was no longer realistic. If anything, I would need to spend more time managing the galleries. And so I found myself commuting from Sonoma to San Francisco almost every day, quite often getting stuck in traffic for an hour or more each way. We soon realized that living so far from work was no longer feasible. We decided to move closer to the city and found a house in Tiburon, a much-loved waterfront community in Marin County, a ferry ride from San Francisco. We found the house on Christina's first birthday, which seemed like a good omen, and we moved right in. It was a relief to be so much closer to the galleries, and it had the added benefit of being an area code away from Eileen's family. Now when we dropped in, we were treated as out-of-town guests. But, again, thank God for grandparents. I don't know that we would have made it through Christina's early years without their help.

Our lives started to be defined as "before Christina" and "after Christina." I had no idea what all my friends with children had been dealing with all those years. I had always sworn I wouldn't change to accommodate a baby, but I was wrong. I think the loss of sleep was the hardest thing we had to contend with; being awakened night after night over a long period of time was excruciating. When Christina was first born, I would sometimes come crawling into work in the morning only to have my bookkeeper laugh at my obvious exhaustion and instruct me to turn around and go right back home.

Six months after we moved to Tiburon I got a flurry of calls and letters from my Minnesota relatives, especially from my cousin, Kathy Varner, who worked at the nursing home where my dad lived. Kathy told me that "Uncle John" was in failing health and required around-the-clock nursing care. She also pointed out the expense—something in the range of $7,000 a month. His resources were dwindling and I would have to be ready to bear the burden.

My father passed away a few months later at age eighty-three, a fairly long life considering the excess weight he carried for so many years. Eileen's parents took Christina, and Eileen and I boarded a plane for Minnesota to attend his funeral. My dad's surviving three sisters and one brother also were present.

Although my father's passing didn't sever my ties with the Swanson family, I did notice subtle changes toward the adopted member of the family (me) right after Pop was no longer around. For example, a short while after my father passed away, my Uncle Red died. He had been a well-known football coach in Minnesota and was married to my dad's sister. Uncle Red was one of only two uncles, so I always remembered him and his wife, Aunt Mary, on Christmas and dutifully sent a card to them every year. I was surprised and hurt that no one had thought to notify me when he died or to invite me to his funeral.

Later I was reminded of my "adoptive status" again when my sister, Sally, had one of the Minnesota Swanson clan call me to say "Mama Anne" was near death. My long out-of-the-picture biological mother had become very ill and was given only a short time to live. I had had no legal or formal attachments to this lady for forty years and here was my adopted extended family requesting that I call home. I yelled at my cousin Kathy about how I perceived this act downright insensitive. A few years later, I got a letter from my ninety-six-year-old Aunt Rose, one of the finest persons I have ever met, and in her scrawled and barely legible handwriting she said that she wanted to "keep me in the family." That act of kindness went a long way in smoothing over my hurt feelings.

Right after my father's funeral I got into a conversation with a woman who worked at the retirement home where he had been living. She did hospice work with the elderly, helping people to make the transition they faced. She sought me out after the funeral service and told me that she had known "Doc Swanson" for the last few years and had helped him come to terms with his mortality. She went on to say that she had a message from him. "He asked me to tell you that he loved you." He had never spoken those words to me, and he had never shown up for any important event or milestone in my life. But upon hearing those words, his silence didn't matter any longer. I forgave him in that instant.

After Eileen and I had moved to Tiburon (which means *shark* in Spanish), I began to notice a rather monotonous pattern emerging in the way I felt towards my business. I couldn't differentiate one year from another anymore. I felt I was falling into a rut. I started pondering the idea of selling my business. It wasn't a firm decision, but the seed was planted. By this time I had built up another management team headed by a very young woman by the name of Kyle Garcia. She was a natural leader and excellent salesperson. I had also been fortunate to find another extremely smart and well-educated person to take care of my bookkeeping and administrative needs, Heide Walsh. And, as luck would have it, about the same time Wai Ming walked out of the gallery, his replacement walked in.

This new find, Dave Archer, did paintings of outer space on glass. If "reverse glass" paintings of outer space sound a little strange, I thought so, too, the first time I laid eyes on them. Dave explained that he and another artist had been painting on glass panels for the last few years, first doing landscapes and then graduating to the cosmos. He knew a guy who made Tesla coils that could be used to guide electricity through a wand of some sort that gave Dave the idea of experimenting with how electricity would affect freshly applied paint on glass. After he discovered that the arcs of electricity left pleasing patterns in the paint on the glass panels, his imagination was stimulated; he knew he was onto something. Dave took his paintings to outdoor shows and was an instant success. But it was apparent that traveling around the country selling his own paintings had its downside. As he said, he had recently done well at an art show but it meant he had not been free to paint for three weeks. Now he wanted to be represented by a gallery and have time to do his art work.

Even though his paintings were impressive, and I liked the uniqueness of his ideas, my first reaction was, no, not now. Dave was persistent and after a few weeks left me some paintings to view at my leisure. I gave them back—not interested, so sorry. He left another grouping of his universe paintings a few weeks after that, saying that I had represented scores of artists he knew personally who had started in the outdoor shows. I finally weakened and, the way I have come to dramatize his story is by saying that Dave used his last dime to call me from a pay phone near the Golden Gate Bridge and threatened to jump if I didn't give him a try. Even though it didn't actually happen this way, his persistence was impressive and won out. I finally told him to bring in a grouping of his reverse-glass paintings.

Dave's first paintings didn't do very well. But most first paintings an artist brings me don't sell well in the beginning. I asked Dave to bring in a new set of paintings and requested his permission to put them in the silent auction area at a marked-down price, just to generate some interest. As soon as I put auction tags on them something magical occurred. They started flying out the door. It was interesting to note that the segment of the population who were the most avid buyers of Dave's space creations were primarily the young, high-tech, computer generation from Silicon Valley. The NASA and aerospace people also couldn't get enough of these colorful and exciting renditions of outer space.

Soon we were selling at least one of his paintings a day for substantial sums. Dave became a celebrity. Every television station in the Bay Area did a story on his work, which was then followed by national TV exposure. He even received extensive coverage on Japanese TV. We published prints of his paintings and had a serigraph printed on glass. Dave Archer's one-man shows, held once a year for four years, were spectacularly successful. His shows brought me back to the excitement of when I first started out in the '70s.

It was satisfying to note that I was selling the work of live artists and doing business on the up-and-up, unlike many other gallery owners at that time. I still wondered if it was time to get out of the retail gallery business, especially after the dip in the economy in '85. I decided to hold off on a decision and perhaps cut back on the number of stores I was trying to maintain. The rents on commercial property were rising faster than my annual sales and/or profits. Even though I had weathered the '85 downturn, I wondered why I had signed up for yearly rent increases in a few of my locations. I worked on remodeling my two-story Beach Street gallery adding new artists like Dave Archer and re-signing past artists like Jacquie Marie Vaux.

I was more than a little perturbed about the six or seven galleries within a few blocks of my Beach Street gallery that were still racking up astronomical sales with falsely signed prints of Dalí, Miró, Chagall and Picasso. Questionable prints of such illustrators as Erté and Rockwell were also beginning to emerge. Interestingly, at some point Dalí admitted signing blank printing paper and that it had led to abuses; in 1980 he signed an affidavit stating that he had stopped this practice. Although infirm and bedridden, the flow of his prints on watermarked paper made after 1980 did not cease, not even after his death in 1989!

Some of the proliferating boutique style galleries were doing astronomical sales figures with these questionable prints. I've always said that major artists such as Chagall and Miró certainly would not have signed these huge editions. I wondered what Picasso would think about unscrupulous people getting their hands on an old etching plate of his (something that should have been destroyed but wasn't), having it nickel-plated so additional etchings could be printed out ad infinitum, then having someone stamp his name on it posthumously, and, finally, daring to sell it as an original, signed etching.

When the last of the "Big Four" (Dalí, Miró, Chagall and Picasso) passed from the scene in 1989, the profiteers were cranking out more and more editions, claiming that they had been signed by these eighty- or ninety-year-old artists prior to their demise. The general public finally started to balk at this merchandising frenzy. In fact, it was the publishers' zest for marketing that helped set off investigations into the probity of these prints. Certain dealers-turned-publishers were beginning to reprint some of the best-sellers, such as Dalí's *Lincoln Vision* print, in different sizes. So much for "limited" editions. When consumers began to contact various governmental agencies about these suspicious practices, and the Federal Trade Commission and U.S. Postal Service became involved, lawsuits began to fly.

The Wall Street Journal had published a front-page story on this scandal a few years earlier. The article focused on how the U.S. market was being flooded by Dalí forgeries and fake prints. How I smiled when I saw this spread. Even though the jig was up, it still took a few years for the authorities to close down this huge scam. Publishers in New York, Paris, Los Angeles and Hawaii had been plying these fake prints for so long they had begun to believe their own lies. A whole industry had been built on their production, from printing presses to retail distribution. Some of the gallery retailers saw the handwriting on the wall and started backing out of selling these easy money prints, but many just couldn't give it up.

The biggest Dalí marketing frenzy was not in Europe or the Continental U.S., but in Hawaii. Bill Mett, the owner of Center Art in Hawaii, boasted of being the nation's largest retailer of Dalí's art, grossing tens of millions of dollars a year. I've heard that the combined sales of his gallery chain went up to $40 or $50 million annually. One Japanese investor bought $2.1 million worth of questionable Dalí art work from Center Art. There were many other major buyers such as this, but the bulk of the purchasers were just regular folks who happened into a Center Art location and thought they were buying something of value.

Center Art Gallery published many of its own Dalí editions, both prints and sculpture, and bought huge quantities of graphics from other stateside publishers. One such publisher, Leon Amiel, had a printing press in New Jersey and offices in New York and Paris. In 1987 the federal authorities swooped down on Center Art Gallery en masse, and, simultaneously, a huge team of officers invaded other Center Art locations. They stretched yellow crime-scene stickers marked "Do Not Cross" across each site, and packed up art work, advertising materials, price lists and customer sales receipts. Three days after Salvador Dalí's death in January 1989, a federal grand jury issued a 93-count indictment against Center Art, its owner Bill Mett, and his right-hand man, Marvin Wiseman. The charges included mail fraud and wire and securities fraud. Many of the prints sold by Center Art had been manufactured on watermarked paper that bore a date after 1980, the year Dalí signed the affidavit that he had stopped signing editions or his name to blank paper.

After a long and expensive trial, Judge Fong, the presiding judge of that Honolulu District Court, announced a "guilty" decision on all but six counts. Of 79 counts, Bill Mett was pronounced guilty of 73, Marvin Wiseman of 63, and the corporation of 72. The guilty verdict applied not only to the Dalí prints, but to other celebrity art that had been misrepresented as well. Center Art had been selling Dalí prints for more than fifteen years; it's possible that they sold over $100 million worth of the questionable signed prints and sculptures. But Center Art was just one of hundreds of galleries and frame shops that sold these graphics, and Dalí was just one of many artists misrepresented in this money-making scheme.

Judge Fong sentenced Bill Mett to three years in federal prison, with no opportunity for early release. Marvin Wiseman was sentenced to two and a half years. They both were allowed to remain free, pending appeal. The judge levied fines totaling more than $1.8 million and ordered restitution for the victims named in the indictment. A class-action lawsuit filed by a Honolulu lawyer recovered $6 million for his clients in an out-of-court settlement. A few years later Bill Mett closed all but one of his galleries and appeared in court with Wiseman to explain that he couldn't pay the $1.8 million fine to the government. Since then, the government seized his last remaining gallery and he has started to serve his prison sentence.

One of Center Art's many suppliers was, as I mentioned, Leon Amiel. Leon had many family members involved in this enterprise, some of whom were even helping him sign tens of thousands of the fake prints. The raid on the Amiel publishing outfit was impressive. The postal agents who busted his operation in July 1991 found tens of thousands of fraudulent Dalí prints spread over a few hundred titles, thousands of Picassos over ten titles, and over five hundred Chagall prints bearing sixty titles. The government proceeded to seize almost a million dollars in four of Amiel's bank accounts, as well as cash and New York property valued at a million or more for a total of around three million in assets. Amiel's prints were being sold in the U.S., Japan, Sweden,

Belgium, Germany, France and Switzerland. In 1992, the U.S. government announced that it had halted one of the biggest source of counterfeit prints and had filed 20 counts of mail fraud against various Amiel family members. They also shot down many other publishers and dealers at the same time, and more or less brought to an end the biggest distribution ring of fake art in history.

Although I had long predicted the collapse of this presigned paper house of cards, I still can't believe that it became a billion-dollar fraud scheme lasting over twenty years. It hurt tens of thousands of people, did inestimable damage to the art market, and led to justifiable mistrust among the art-buying public.

In the latter half of the '80s, most if not all of my competitors on Beach Street were selling these fake "name-brand prints" and the gallery business was changing into something resembling the way the fashion industry sells designer colors—"pinks and pastels are big this year." The idea of semi-retiring kept coming to mind, although I would have laughed at the idea, or been offended, had someone else broached the subject. But by 1986 I began to feel that small business was an endangered species. Congress passed the Tax Reform Act that year, and it raised my taxes from 20% to 40% of my income and wiped out all write-offs and income averaging. With California state income taxes and state sales taxes, I began to wonder if it was really worth it to be in business and deal with the constant headaches of employees, pension plans, lawsuits, high rents and the personal problems of my artists.

With all the changes going on around me, I held a conference with myself and said: "Jack, my boy, why don't you set a retail sales goal for one year, from September '86 to September '87, and see if you can make it. If you make it, decide at that time whether you want to continue business as usual." I set the one-year goal high so that if I made it, I could make decisions about my future from a position of strength.

A friend of mine who owned a jewelry store kept telling me it was an "over-retailed world." I began to believe him.

When I started my pegboard revolution art gallery in 1970, I was the only gallery on Beach Street and in the Ghirardelli Square area. By 1986 there were six art galleries within two blocks of each other on Beach Street alone.

As I started my one-year all-out sales effort, I went to New York on my annual pilgrimage to the retail art expo. I called up my old friend and former right-hand man, Barry, for a visit. Barry had contacted me a few months earlier to tell me he was doing well in the telecommunications market. He wanted me to give him a call whenever I was in town. Enough time had passed that I was able to put our past problems behind me. I met Barry at the Oak Room bar at the Plaza Hotel where the bartender greeted Barry by name. We talked about his business and the fleet of trucks he was using to beam all kinds of news events, prize fights, even the 1984 L.A. Olympics to the satellite transponders on which he had a virtual monopoly. We then hit a few hot nightspots. Barry was known by the bartenders everywhere. Then he took me to his newly purchased penthouse apartment. We looked over his art collection, many of which were from Swanson Art Galleries' artists. His wife Kathy was in San Francisco at their other home. They had decided against children, which fit with Barry's jet-setter lifestyle. He regaled me with stories of dealing with heads of state, and setting up a European version of his American enterprise.

Barry told me he and Kathy were having some problems and asked if I could keep a secret. I nodded, but hoped he didn't have anything weird to divulge. He said he had an Oriental lady friend, someone he worked with, and she was the reason he was spending so much time away from home. Barry said, "I don't know if the one day a month I spend with my wife is too much or too little." What could I say?

Barry brought up the possibility of our going into business together. He was on the verge of launching a sports network, hoping to be the next Ted Turner, and mentioned the possibility of our making movies together in L.A. Even though I wasn't ready to sell my art business, it sounded good to me. I was certainly open to new ventures. We said our good-byes and planned to get in touch soon. A few months went by with no communication from Barry. I called him in New York but couldn't reach him, I never heard from him again. I guess we weren't as close as I had thought.

During my one-year "trial" period, I threw quite a few art shows and exhibits. The economy seemed to be heating up so my investments in these promotions really paid off. My new manager, Kyle, did a great job in bringing in sales. Anything her troops didn't do, she would do herself. We ended up hitting my September-to-September goal, but each and every month was hard fought. Even though we had met our year-to-year goal, my sixth sense told me it was time to do something new, perhaps write a book, have another child, or pick something from innumerable possibilities. The thrill of retail art was gone: I decided to sell out.

My business plan was to divest myself of my four smaller galleries first, consolidate and move everything to the large gallery on Beach Street near Ghirardelli Square and eventually sell my gallery on Beach Street and take a mid-life break. I was too young to retire.

The Carmel gallery had become a bit of a burden because my lease allowed the landlord to escalate the rent each year and it was no longer a profitable location for me. I was able to negotiate a deal with the landlord that would let me terminate the lease. We moved out.

My Sutter Street gallery, which occupied half of the first floor of a hotel, had a lease that was about to expire in six months. The hotel had recently been sold and was undergoing major reconstruction. Because of the inconvenience caused by the construction noise and dust, the new owners reluctantly offered to let me out of the lease early. I called Bekins Moving Company and they moved over 80,000 prints and paintings to my Beach Street stock rooms. The moving bill was astronomical.

I put the word out to some local merchants in Sausalito that I wanted to close my gallery and sell the building. Within days I got a couple of offers and ended up making a very large profit. At close of escrow, I moved out.

Left with my profitable gallery on Beach Street, which was one of the best retail locations in San Francisco, I set

a dollar amount and a date for when I wanted to conclude
the sale of this gallery. I wanted to hold a giant "going-out-
of-business" sale by the end of 1988 and then close by
January 1, 1989. There were only four months to go in 1988
so I had to move fast. I called the owners of three major
gallery chains and informed them of my plan. All three
organizations became active bidders to take over my gallery
even though they weren't going to use the Swanson Gallery
name. This was in September. In October, I opened serious
negotiations with prospective buyers. After in-depth talks
with representatives of each business, I decided that a New
York-based gallery chain by the name of Dyansen Galleries
was my best bet.

Dyansen featured primarily Erté's Art Deco sculpture.
The company, which had just gone public on the N.Y. Stock
Exchange, was building a foundry for its bronzes in L.A.
and wanted to expand its retail operations. The owner and
major stockholder of this corporation was a former stockbroker
from New York named Harris Shapiro. Harris was a charming,
smooth-talking, Wall Street type of guy who, when he helped
the original owner go public, saw a lot of potential in the
Dyansen Company. Harris thought so highly of the company
that he became the new president and owner. I had an instant
rapport with Harris, even though New Yorkers, I suspect,
think West Coast people or Southerners with accents are not
too bright. I knew Harris was negotiating with one or two
other galleries on Beach Street to buy them out or establish
some other sort of business arrangement, and it was just a
matter of which location he would choose.

I called my travel agent and arranged a trip to Paris leaving
November 10. Eileen and I had been to Spain in May and
were fast becoming seasoned travelers—as I said, thank God
for grandparents. Right after I firmed up our travel schedule,
I called Harris in New York and told him I was leaving for
Paris and our deal, if we had a deal, had to be paid in full,
signed, sealed, and delivered by November 9, or the whole
thing was off. He said, "I'm leaning toward your deal. I've
just gotten a large cash infusion and I think we can work
it out. I'll meet you at your San Francisco gallery before

you leave on your trip." I called my lawyer and made sure he would be available on the 8th or 9th of November.

Harris, good to his word, showed up on the 8th. He and my lawyer worked around the clock to hammer out a deal. Harris then handed over a cashier's check and that was it. The place was his on January 1, 1989. He agreed to take on my star artist and some salespeople, and I made arrangements to rent an office and showroom gallery to store my twenty-year accumulation of prints, paintings and sculpture.

Eileen and I flew off to Paris and stayed at a quaint little hotel some friends had recommended. It was unseasonably sunny for the month of November. We attended the Salon d'Automne art show at the Grand Palais. Although I had just sold my last remaining retail gallery to Harris, I couldn't stop scouting out talent. I found some very gifted artists but didn't make any business deals. I did, however, take down the name and address of a Japanese artist who lived in Tokyo, and ended up coincidentally meeting him six months later in his native city.

Paris has got to be the most romantic city in the world—great art, gourmet food, fashionable clothing stores and a great transit system. We loved it. Eileen and I had finally gotten over the shock of having our first child, had more or less forgotten about the years of sleepless nights, and decided to have another baby. Surprisingly, no progeny came from the Paris trip, but a few months later Eileen got pregnant and, in January 1990, delivered a healthy baby boy we named John Howard Swanson III; he would later take on the nickname of Jack Jr. The baby was conceived on Cinco de Mayo on my new 46-foot yacht bought with some of the proceeds from the Dyansen deal. When Jack Jr. was born we called him "Juan" in smiling reference to the Mexican holiday.

After I sold out to Harris I decided to buy a motor yacht and a Harley-Davidson (big eighty-cubic-inch engine), and to travel. I set up an office and showroom in downtown San Francisco on Maiden Lane to keep my hand in the art business. I was lucky to have capable people helping me so I could devote most of my time to writing and raising my family. A few months after I sold the Beach Street gallery,

I flew to Japan. The journey was part business and part nostalgia. A friend of mine, Greg Sankovich, had some art business connections in Tokyo and offered to give me a guided tour of this huge city. I hoped to find some outlets or galleries in Japan that might purchase some of the large number of prints I was now storing. Greg had a last-minute problem and couldn't go with me but I went anyway. I looked forward to seeing firsthand the changes that had taken place in Japan since I was stationed there in the 1960s. I couldn't believe that almost thirty years had passed—I still can't believe it. At least this time I could book myself into the Imperial Hotel, a far cry from my Marine Corps days.

I spent a week sightseeing in Tokyo. I hired an interpreter and went to visit some museums and art galleries. I wasn't able to conclude any print sales but did get to drop in on Greg's gallery in downtown Tokyo. While I found Tokyo exciting, and on an economic upswing, for me it lacked the vibrancy of the early '60s. By the time of my visit in 1989, the capital city had been completely rebuilt and seemed too westernized. There were no kimonos in evidence, western music (usually '50s rock and roll) blasted in the department stores and malls, and American baseball games could be heard on car radios. The taxi drivers were no longer the kamikaze drivers I had remembered. A new law in Tokyo mandated that if any car with a dent or beat-up fender could not be driven on the street, it must be taken in to be repaired. It was eerie to drive around Japan and not see any dinged fenders or old cars. The taxis still sped around, but I didn't witness one accident during my entire visit.

I took a bullet train to Kyoto and stayed for a week. It was wonderful to visit Kyoto's historic shrines and think back to the good old days when I had come to this beautiful city as a young Marine. It helped put me in the mood to write about my experiences when I was stationed at Atsugi Air Base next to Tokyo, but it was also a reminder that things change and you can't go home again.

The next time I spoke to Greg he had just returned from a trip to Tokyo where he spent some time working at his main gallery. I thanked Greg for the hospitality his Tokyo gallery personnel had shown me. We talked about Japan and business and Greg said, "You'll never guess who walked into the Tokyo gallery when I was there; talk about small world department! It was Harris Shapiro of Dyansen Galleries." Greg told me that Harris had supplied his Japanese outlets with Erté sculptures and wanted to connect on a personal basis. Upon walking into the Tokyo gallery and, by happenstance, running into Greg, Harris started laughing. Knowing Greg was a friend of mine, he blurted out, "Hey, Greg, you know what my claim to fame is? I'm the guy who retired Jack Swanson." Greg and I had a good belly laugh over Harris' remark and I told Greg, 'Yeah, I almost named my new 46-foot yacht, "Shapiro One".'

For me, it was the end of an era.

ORDER FORM

CONFESSIONS OF AN ART DEALER

FAX ORDERS: (415) 433-1030

TELEPHONE ORDERS (415) 433-9091

Please have your AMEX, VISA or MASTERCARD number ready.

POSTAL ORDERS:

Vitality Publications

111 Maiden Lane, Suite 400

San Francisco, CA 94108

Please send _____ copies of **CONFESSIONS OF AN ART DEALER** @ $29.95 per copy to:

NAME_____

ADDRESS_____

CITY_____STATE_____ZIP_____

PHONE_____FAX_____

SALES TAX:
If shipped within California please add 7.5% (or $2.25 per book) sales tax.

SHIPPING & HANDLING:
Book rate: $2.50 for the first book and $1.00 for each additional book.
Allow 3-4 weeks for delivery.
Air Mail: $4.50 per book.

PAYMENT:

❏ CHECK

❏ CREDIT CARD   ❏ AMEX   ❏ VISA   ❏ MASTERCARD

CARD NUMBER_____

NAME ON CARD_____

EXPIRATION DATE_____

SIGNATURE_____